P7-DZP-969

CASS SERIES: STUDIES IN INTELLIGENCE
(Series Editors: Christopher Andrew and Michael I. Handel)

CONTROLLING INTELLIGENCE

CONTROLLING INTELLIGENCE

Edited by
GLENN P. HASTEDT

FRANK CASS

First published 1991 in Great Britain by
FRANK CASS & CO. LTD.
Gainsborough House, Gainsborough Road,
London E11 1RS, England

and in the United States of America by
FRANK CASS
c/o International Specialized Book Services, Inc.,
5602 N.E. Hassalo Street,
Portland, Oregon 97213

Copyright © 1991 Frank Cass & Co. Ltd.

British Library Cataloguing in Publication Data

Controlling intelligence. – (Cass series, studies in intelligence).
1. American intelligence services
I. Hastedt, Glenn P.
327.1273

ISBN 0–7146–3394–1

Library of Congress Cataloguing-in-Publication Data

Controlling intelligence / edited by Glenn P. Hastedt.
p. cm. — (Cass series—studies in intelligence)

ISBN 0–7146–3394–1:
1. Intelligence service—United States. 2. United States.
Central Intelligence Agency. 3. Intelligence service—Canada.
I. Hastedt, Glenn, 1950– . II. Series.
JK468.I6C655 1990
353.0089—dc20   90–36572
                                                         CIP

*All rights reserved. No part of this publication may be reproduced in any form
or by any means, electronic, mechanical, photocopying, recording or otherwise,
without the prior permission of Frank Cass and Company Limited.*

UNIVERSITY LIBRARY
Lethbridge, Alberta

Typeset by Selectmove Ltd, London
Printed in Great Britain by
Antony Rowe Ltd, Chippenham

CONTENTS

PART ONE

PLACING THE PROBLEM IN CONTEXT

1

Controlling Intelligence: Defining the Problem

GLENN HASTEDT

FRAMING THE PROBLEM

The qualities that characterize an effective foreign policy are not difficult to identify. They do, however, constitute an imposing list. Even a partial cataloging of requirements would include the following traits: it should be flexible yet consistent; capable of bold and imaginative undertakings; pragmatic yet guided by a sense of vision, internally coherent; have public support; and not abuse its power base. Our concern in this volume is with one ingredient in the formulation and execution of a successful foreign policy – intelligence – and one aspect of intelligence policy – control. The time is long gone when policy-makers could function as their own intelligence analysts. The complexity of military technology, the speed of events, and the lengthy foreign policy agendas spread out before the world's leaders require that they enlist the services of intelligence professionals housed in bureaucratic structures.[1]

While the need for intelligence is well established, the place of intelligence in the policy process remains controversial and poorly understood. At the center of the riddle lies the need for secrecy. The very nature of the intelligence function requires a protective cloak of secrecy. Yet, at the very same time that secrecy is serving the needs of intelligence, it also works against the establishment of the atmosphere of trust that must exist between the intelligence professional and policy-makers.[2] Secrecy makes it difficult for policy-makers to gain an appreciation of both the ways in which intelligence can contribute to policy and its inherent limitations. All too often, policy-makers have shown an inclination to treat intelligence as a free good, see intelligence organizations as capable of herculean tasks, and to equate intelligence analysis with fortune telling. As a result intelligence failures,

3

which students of strategic surprise stress are inevitable and which critics of covert action constantly warn against, bring forward charges of betrayal, incompetence, and rogue elephants on the loose.

Disagreement over the proper place of intelligence in the policy process is especially evident in the area of control. Consider the following efforts to frame the problem of controlling intelligence:

Christopher Andrew argues that intelligence systems in democratic societies have grown more by a process of creeping growth than by the conscious will of governments. Controlling intelligence thus is a game of catch-up to overcome a history of neglect, ignorance and apathy on the part of policy-makers.[3]

After reviewing testimony and evidence on the Iran–Contra affair, the Tower Commission concluded that no substantive changes needed to be made in the operation of the National Security Council system. Control mechanisms were adequate and in place. What was needed was for the people operating inside the system to respect its rule and procedures.[4]

Kenneth Sharpe argues that the Iran–Contra affair was not an aberration but inevitable given the nature of US foreign policy. A tension exists between the nondemocratic nature of the national security system, of which intelligence is an integral part, and the democratic domestic system. Control only becomes possible when the national security system is democraticized, something which requires changing the basic nature of US foreign policy.[5]

Harry Ransom argues that control over intelligence moves along a permissive-restrictive pendulum as the President and Congress attempt to dominate intelligence policy. Controlling intelligence thus might take different forms depending upon the nature of presidential-congressional relations or it might be impossible under certain conditions.[6]

Angelo Codevilla asserts that in the aftermath of the reform drive of the 1970s it is now recognized that intelligence agencies are not 'rogue elephants' but normal lethargic creatures. The challenge is to make them useful for their intended purpose. He concludes that this is no easy task given the challenges facing American intelligence in an increasingly hostile world. A prerequisite for lessening the incongruence between these challenges and the capabilities of US intelligence may be to undo some of the reforms instituted in the 1970s.[7]

Clearly, disagreement exists over how to approach the problem of controlling intelligence. A moment's reflection, however, leads to the insight that while each of these statements either makes use of the terms 'intelligence' and 'control', or holds obvious implications for controlling intelligence, the authors give these terms different meanings. The lack of conceptual clarity and agreement in these statements is all too commonplace in the literature on intelligence.

AN OVERVIEW OF THE LITERATURE ON INTELLIGENCE

Writing in 1980, Harry Ransom argued that 'the functions of intelligence constitute the single largest gap in our understanding of how foreign policy decisions are made'.[8] Ransom penned these words in the midst of a virtual outpouring of writings on the Central Intelligence Agency (CIA) and the US intelligence community as a whole. He divided these works into four categories:

1. memoirs defending the intelligence system;
2. whistle-blowing exposés of the intelligence system;
3. scholarly analyses of intelligence;
4. government reports.

While raising the visibility of intelligence in the public's eye, these works did not immediately contribute to our understanding of intelligence for several reasons. First, they tended to be written in order to further a political agenda. The 'whistle-blowing' exposés of intelligence abuses, excess, or failures wanted restrictions placed on the activities of the intelligence community (or, in the extreme, to have certain of its activities – covert action – eliminated) Memoirs written by retired intelligence professionals sought to undermine the case being made by the whistle-blowers by stressing the contributions made by intelligence to US security and the challenges facing the intelligence professional. Second, although they contained more detailed information about intelligence than did earlier writings, much of it remained largely unverifiable and was often contradicted by other authors pushing the opposite political agenda.

In a follow-up review essay six years later, Ransom concluded that in spite of a continued stream of publications, theory on the relationship between information and action 'remains weak and tentative, and secrecy of evidence remains a formidable problem'.[9] Ransom's observations were echoed by other reviewers of the field of intelligence. Roger Hilsman, who like Ransom was almost alone within the academic community to produce insightful accounts of intelligence in the 1950s, surveyed eleven works written between 1977 and 1979. He concluded that if one used as a criterion for judgement the ability of a work to make a serious contribution

5

to our knowledge about intelligence, then 'the books under review, with few exceptions, are disappointing'.[10] The strengths and weaknesses of the literature on intelligence as they relate to the problem of control come into sharper focus as we turn to a more detailed examination of how four key questions are dealt with in the literature on intelligence:

1. What is intelligence?
2. Why is intelligence needed?
3. What is the relationship between intelligence and policy?
4. What is control and how should it be realized?

WHAT IS INTELLIGENCE?

One of the most difficult tasks facing anyone venturing into a new field of study is becoming comfortable with its language. A hurdle that must often be overcome is the realization that no clear-cut definition exists for many of its most basic terms – power, war, international system. Intelligence is such a term. Not only does it not have a precise and agreed definition, but those who attempt precision give it multiple meanings.

Four definitions constructed by scholars are particularly revealing of the range of opinion that exists. Sherman Kent identifies three distinct meanings of intelligence: knowledge (what we need to know), activity (broken down into seven functional stages progressing from problem recognition to presenting ones findings), and organization (administrative problems and organizational forms).[11] Decrying what he sees as the unwarranted tendency to use the terms intelligence, spying, and secret foreign interventions interchangeably, Harry Ransom's definition of intelligence focuses on its role in providing policy-makers with the information they need to make decisions.[12] He identifies three categories of intelligence – strategic, tactical and counter-intelligence – and like Kent, Ransom sees the intelligence process as encompassing a series of functional steps which culminate in the dissemination of intelligence to policy-makers. While agreeing with Kent that intelligence is knowledge, process and organization, Roy Godson takes exception to definitions of intelligence which focus only on its informational aspects.[13] He argues that intelligence is made up of four different elements which cannot be separated out from one another. Intelligence must do all four – and do them well – if it is to meet the informational needs of the government. The four elements of intelligence are clandestine collection, analysis and estimates, covert action, and counter-intelligence. Complicating matters further is the fact that government documents do not provide us with a consistent or enlightening definition of intelligence. Jeffrey Richelson uses

6

the definition of intelligence found in the *Dictionary of United States Military Terms for Joint Usage*: 'the product resulting from the collection, evaluation, analysis, integration, and interpretation of all available information . . .'.[14] Yet he quickly goes on to note that while, strictly speaking, intelligence activities should only relate to this task, other activities such as counter-intelligence and covert action have come to be considered examples of intelligence activity. The gap between official definitions and reality is also evident in the 1947 National Security Act which created the CIA. It assigned the CIA the following tasks:

1. To advise the National Security Council on intelligence matters of the government related to national security.
2. To make recommendations to the National Security Council for the coordination of intelligence activities of departments and agencies of government.
3. To correlate and evaluate intelligence and provide for its appropriate dissemination within the government.
4. To perform for the benefit of existing intelligence agencies such additional services as the NSC determines can be efficiently accomplished by a central organization.
5. To perform other functions and duties relating to national security intelligence as the National Security Council may direct.[15]

Absent from this definition are explicit statements authorizing the CIA to engage in covert action or to collect its own information. Both tasks, however, quickly became part of the CIA's organizational mission.

Definitions of intelligence found in recent presidential executive orders also are of little help in formulating a definition of intelligence that enlightens its readers more than it confuses them. Full citations of the Ford, Carter and Reagan executive orders can be found in the Appendix. Even a quick comparison reveals the extent to which they borrowed definitions from one another and the bureaucratic-legalistic nature of the language employed. For example, the Ford executive order defines intelligence as being composed of foreign intelligence and foreign counter-intelligence. The former is defined as 'information, other than counterintelligence, on the capabilities, intentions, and activities of foreign powers, organizations or their agents', and the latter is defined as 'activities conducted to protect the United States and United States citizens from espionage, sabotage, subversion, assassination, or terrorism'. The Carter executive order defines intelligence as being foreign intelligence and counter-intelligence, with somewhat more elaborate definitions being provided for each of these two component parts of intelligence. The Reagan order does not define intelligence but does

7

define foreign intelligence, counter-intelligence, and intelligence activities ('all activities that agencies within the intelligence community are authorized to conduct').

The approach taken here is that while the definition of intelligence should focus on its informational function, the history of US foreign policy in the post-war era, the activities of intelligence agencies within the United States, and the legacy left by the Office of Strategic Services (OSS),[16] a forerunner of the CIA which operated during the Second World War, requires that any discussion of controlling intelligence encompass covert action and counter-intelligence.

WHY IS INTELLIGENCE NEEDED?

The need for intelligence is rooted in the nature of the international system, and it is at once self evident and highly controversial. Roughly speaking, from the end of the First World War until the outbreak of the Second, the dominant school of thought in the United States concerning the nature of the international system was idealism. Idealism held that conflict was not an enduring feature of world politics. Rather, it was the product of decisions made by morally corrupt leaders and the absence of international restraints on the exercise of power. A peaceful international system was possible once leaders were controlled by their publics (who were assumed to be opposed to warlike policies) and checks on the use of power were put into place. Democracy, public opinion, international law and organization, and disarmament were at the top of the idealist's agenda as corrective measures that would ensure a peaceful international system. Little need was perceived for intelligence in such an international system. This attitude was summed up by Secretary of State Henry Stimson's often quoted 1929 statement that 'gentlemen do not read each other's mail'. He then proceeded to close the Black Chamber, the US's highly successful code-breaking unit which had solved more than 45,000 cryptograms. After the Second World War realism replaced idealism as the dominant perspective for studying international politics. It starts from a very different set of assumptions. Conflict, and the threat of conflict, is held to be a permanent and inescapable feature of world politics. In part this originates in human nature, which is held to be aggressive and far from perfect. More fundamentally, it arises from the anarchic nature of the international system. Power politics and not international law, organization, or morality govern the conduct of foreign policy. States are locked into a struggle for survival in which there are few, if any, rules. International organizations cannot compel their members to act in accordance with their decisions; allies cannot be forced to come to one's aid; treaties can be broken; rules of combat and diplomacy are observed because it is in one's own interest to do so (in the hope of encouraging reciprocity on the part of others); and the only true sanction for violations of international law is war.

Intelligence is a vital component of a state's foreign and defense policies in such a world. Unable to be totally secure in an ally's loyalty or know the extent to which a state is truly an enemy in a given situation, policy-makers need intelligence (defined in terms of analysed information) so that they are not surprised by the turn of events and to make the choice of a policy option something more than guesswork. Intelligence (defined in terms of counter-intelligence) is necessary in order to protect its secrets from falling into the hands of other states and so that policy-makers can feel confident about the accuracy of the information being used to make policy decisions.

Given the anarchic nature of the international system and the need for self-defense, the ability to manage power is of central importance for realists. The instruments of foreign policy through which the state exercises its power must be tailored to the challenge facing it. Not applying enough power will lead to policy failures and applying too much power runs the risk of leaving too little power available for the next challenge. Intelligence (defined as covert action) thus becomes a potentially important tool for policy-makers seeking a 'third option' between the application of large amounts of military force and doing nothing when confronted by foreign policy challenges or when they see opportunities for furthering state goals.[17]

Along with the need for intelligence comes controversy. Much of it centers on the proper relationship between intelligence and policy. These will be addressed in the following section. Two points of controversy, however, are germane to the question of why intelligence. The first deals with the location of the threat(s) against which intelligence is directed. Our discussion has defined the threat as external to the state, lying in the structure of the international system and the actions of others. Yet, intelligence can also be directed against internal threats to a state's security. One of the principal functions of the KGB is to investigate political crimes and exercise control over the Soviet people. Many third world intelligence services are as concerned with internal national security threats as they are with external ones. Even where it is not part of an intelligence service's charter to investigate domestic national security threats, such as in the United States, intelligence has been targeted internally against Black civil rights organizations and Vietnam war protesters. The second question deals with the priority assigned to protecting the national interest from the security threat in question. Is it an absolute goal or one which must compete with other goals in making claims on national resources and values? If security threat is treated as an absolute value then intelligence will proceed without any constraints being placed on it. While this may maximize the intelligence service's freedom of maneuver and its ability to contribute to the state's security it also brings with it the potential for abuse of power and excess. If security is approached as a relative value, intelligence must work within the context of respect for civil rights, free speech, the rule of law, checks and balances or other values held to be important by society. While this may complicate the task of intelligence professionals it may also be necessary to ensure control over the intelligence function.

THE RELATIONSHIP BETWEEN INTELLIGENCE AND POLICY

Stripped of its emotional and political rhetoric, different views of 'the intelligence problem' are basically disagreements over the proper relationship between intelligence and policy. Two competing positions exist on the question of linking together intelligence as information and policy. Both were forcefully articulated in the early years of the CIA. The majority view holds that intelligence and policy must be kept separate. The purpose of intelligence is to inform and warn policy-makers. The choice of what to do lies with the policy-maker. If intelligence is brought into too close a contact with policy making it runs the risk of being corrupted. That is, instead of presenting policy-makers with what they need to know, regardless of how unpleasant that information is, intelligence may end up simply providing policy-makers with what they want to hear. The proximity between the analyst and the policy-maker allows the latter to bring pressure to bear on the analyst to adopt positions in support of the policy-maker's preferred policy options and at the same time tempts the analyst to adopt the policy-maker's frame of reference in examining a problem when professional standards suggest that it is inappropriate. The terms 'intelligence to please' and 'backstopping' refer to this danger and have often been leveled at analysis produced by the Defense Intelligence Agency as well as other members of the intelligence community.[18] The minority view holds that separating intelligence and policy is unrealistic and unwise. While the danger of corruption is real, an even greater danger is for intelligence to be ignored by policy-makers as irrelevant to their concerns because it is too academic or fails to take into account their concerns or the pressures on them. To be effective intelligence must know what the policy-maker's worries and priorities are. This can only come about by bringing intelligence and policy into a close working relationship. Recent Directors of Central Intelligence (DCIs) have employed this view in justifying their involvement in (critics would say intrusion into) the estimating process. As William Casey put it, 'the estimates are my estimates . . . I'm responsible for drawing the conclusions and presenting them'.[19]

Embedded in this debate over the proper relationship between intelligence and policy are a number of other issues. First, policy-makers often treat intelligence as a free good. The costs associated with the collection, analysis, production and dissemination of intelligence go unrecognized. It is something which can be accessed at any time, turned on and off in accordance with the policy-makers' interest in the problem. Intelligence professionals tend to emphasize the costs involved. Furthermore, they point out that more is involved than monetary costs. Whether the investigation concerns a 'spy' or an overhead satellite, considerable lead time is necessary to get a collection system in place. Policy-makers cannot decide on Monday that they want currently unavailable information on a problem by Wednesday. Significant decision costs also arise in the process of building a consensus around the meaning and accuracy of piece of information.[20]

Policy-makers and intelligence professionals also tend to hold different expectations of what intelligence work is capable of. Policy-makers tend to see all events as knowable and treat information as self-interpreting. The former belief leads to charges of organizational or individual incompetence when events catch policy-makers off guard. In rebuttal, it can be argued that this view fails to take into account the inherent limitations of individuals and organizations in processing information and misunderstands the task of intelligence estimating. Producing an estimate involves artificially creating the future through the selection of starting assumptions and scenario creation. In doing so not everything may be known with equal certainty. Intelligence can have a high degree of confidence that it knows the number of Soviet divisions in Europe, but how or when those troops will be used is far more difficult to discover. Training exercises, doctrine, statements by Soviet military and political leaders, and past actions all provide insight but no firm answers. Plans are not always implemented, statements are made for many purposes, training exercises can be designed to deceive, and rarely does the present situation completely resemble the past. Soviet leaders themselves may not know how they would react to a concrete proposal to send Soviet troops into combat.

The belief that information is self-interpreting leads to a tendency to depreciate the value of intelligence. Seeing the meaning of events as obvious, policy-makers feel capable of serving as their own intelligence analysts. In the process they lose sight of the extent to which their interpretation of events is colored by the policies they are promoting or personal experiences and biases. Intelligence professionals and those who have studied intelligence failures are more likely to argue that information is inherently ambiguous.[21] Only with 20–20 hindsight does the meaning of raw data become clear. In fact, often it is

11

only after the fact that it is clear which data were information (signals), useful for making an estimate, and which were useless and irrelevant data (noise). Before the surprise Japanese attack on Pearl Harbor a great deal of evidence existed that supported all the wrong interpretations of the last-minute signals being picked up by US intelligence.

Finally, disagreement exists over who in the government intelligence should serve. One view, put forward by former DCI Richard Helms, sees intelligence as serving the President and the President alone. Former DCI William Colby has stated that the intelligence community should serve the entire government and not just the President.[22] For Colby, this means that if the intelligence community has information which contradicts the President's position, it must inform Congress. For Helms, no such responsibility exists and the intelligence community should remain silent.

Intelligence as covert action presents difficulties of its own in linking up with policy. On a most general level there is the question of whether covert action is a neutral instrument of foreign policy that all states can avail themselves of, or if it is a policy instrument suitable for realizing only aggressive, exploitive or imperialistic foreign policies. If it is a tainted or biased policy instrument then great care must be exercised in recommending its use. Questions can then legitimately be raised as to whether a state should even have a covert action capability.

On a more specific level, questions arise in linking different types of covert action to policy. In the public's view covert action is often equated with paramilitary activity. This is not the case. There is a wide choice of covert actions for a policy-maker who wishes secretly to 'influence the internal affairs of other nations', the working definition of covert action used by Richard Bissell, a former Deputy Director of Plans, in a 1968 discussion of intelligence.[23] He identified the scope of covert action as including: political advice and council; subsidies to an individual; financial support and technical assistance to political parties; support to private organizations propaganda; private training of individuals and exchange of persons; economic operations; and paramilitary operations. Assassinations may be added to this list.

The Church Committee investigated five cases where the CIA was allegedly involved in assassination efforts and found evidence linking it to plans to assassinate Fidel Castro of Cuba and Congo leader Patrice Lumumba. Assassination as a form of covert action was first officially forbidden by DCI Richard Helms in 1972 following the death of General Rene Schneider of Chile as part of the coup that overthrew the government of Salvadore Allende. That prohibition was repeated in all of the subsequent presidential executive orders on intelligence. Evidence that assassination continues to be considered a usable option arose in 1984 when the CIA was linked to the publication of a psychological warfare manual for the Contras which was widely interpreted as endorsing assassination.[24]

Each type or combination of covert action may present different problems for linking intelligence and policy. For example, large-scale covert action programs are not easily kept secret. The public nature of US 'covert' paramilitary assistance to the contras in Nicaragua and the Afghan rebels is just the latest manifestation of this problem. In recognition of this problem some suggest that these large-scale operations should be taken out of the CIA's jurisdiction and assigned to the Defense Department or some other organization where congressional and public scrutiny might be more readily realized. Small-scale covert action programs, while easier to keep secret, do not necessarily add up to produce concrete benefits for US foreign policy. Often they go forward out of institutional inertia or because key individuals have taken a personal interest in the operation. Integrating the various covert action programs that exist in a country so that they further US foreign policy goals is a demanding task and one which demands attention at all levels of the policy process from the CIA station up through the various policy making circles in Washington.[25]

Two sets of concerns need to be weighed in integrating counter-intelligence into the policy process: protecting national security and respecting individual rights. A balance is not easily struck. Individual rights are easily trampled upon in the pursuit of real or imagined national security threats, yet espionage, sabotage, and the infiltration of foreign agents into sensitive government positions do pose serious challenges to US national security interests. In pursuit of this balance distinctions have been made between domestic and foreign counter-intelligence. While legally appealing, this distinction does not readily conform with the nature of covert action or clandestine collection activities which show little respect for the sanctity of national boundaries. Bureaucratic wars have also been fought over whether to centralize counter-intelligence within the CIA, and where to put it in the overall structure of the intelligence community. The excesses of J. Edgar Hoover and James Angleton led many to oppose any effort to create a counter-intelligence czar, while the repeated revelations of spying that occurred in 1985, 'the year of the spy', led others to conclude that centralizing US counter-intelligence resources is the only way US national security can be protected.[26]

WHAT IS CONTROL AND HOW SHOULD IT BE REALIZED?

Controlling intelligence is an inherently difficult task for any political system. First, the secrecy surrounding the intelligence function makes exercising control problematic. Second, because intelligence remains more of a craft than a science, intelligence professionals must be afforded a certain area of discretionary authority within which to exercise their professional judgement in conducting covert operations, counter-intelligence programs or interpreting data. Third, policy-makers have found 'plausible denial' to be a valuable commodity when intelligence operations go awry. The desire to control is thus offset by the desire to disassociate oneself from too close a contact with intelligence.

The debate over how to control intelligence is complicated greatly by the fact that those involved in it have different definitions of the nature of 'the intelligence problem'. Some advocates of greater control over intelligence see the intelligence problem as one of preventing the CIA and other intelligence organizations from engaging in illegal activity. This version of the control problem has held a prominent place in efforts to write intelligence charters and found its way into the 1976 Democratic Party platform. Among its recommendations on intelligence were proposals that:

> ... assassination must be prohibited. There should be full and thorough Congressional oversight ... the constitutional rights of Americans can and must be fully protected, and intelligence abuses corrected without endangering the confidentiality of properly classified intelligence or compromising the fundamental intelligence mission.[27]

For others it is not so much a matter of ensuring respect for laws on the part of intelligence organizations and professionals as it is a question of bringing intelligence practices more in line with a given set of values. For example, those who hold this view of the intelligence problem and see terrorism as a major national security problem facing the US want to see an appreciation of this threat reflected in intelligence estimates, counter-intelligence programs, and covert action undertakings.

Formal-legalistic solutions to the problem of controlling intelligence have dominated the attention of reformers: intelligence charters, stricter budgetary oversight, executive orders, reorganizations, and specifically enacted congressional prohibitions on certain types of actions. An alternative approach to realizing control emphasizes the content of the informal norms and values which govern the day-to-day behavior of intelligence professionals within the intelligence bureaucracies. In this view formal-legalistic controls are limited by their reactive nature (rules are generally written to stop an unwanted behavior from taking place a second time) and by their inability to deal with the secrecy and discretion of intelligence work. Only by seeking to structure how intelligence professionals see their job can one hope to prevent abuses from occurring in the first place or ensure responsiveness.

14

There is still another dimension to the problem of controlling intelligence that often goes unappreciated. Control, like leadership, can be viewed as a 'reciprocal process of mobilizing ... in the context of competition and conflict, in order to realize goals ...'.[28] Control, then, requires not only something from the person or institution being controlled (legal behavior or responsiveness) but also something from those who exercise control. At a minimum a twofold obligation exists. First, intelligence organizations and professionals must be given adequate resources to accomplish the tasks assigned to them. This theme was central to the 1980 Republican Party platform which among other things called for 'legislation to allow intelligence officers to operate safely and efficiently abroad'; 'criminal sanctions against those who make disclosures of the identity of US intelligence officials abroad, sources, or methods', and 'provide a capability to help influence events vital to our national security interest'.[29]

Second, intelligence organizations and individuals must be provided with an area of autonomy within which to exercise their craft. The over-involvement of controllers in the intelligence process raises the possibility either that intelligence may become politicized, in which case the likelihood of intelligence to please or ill-conceived covert operations increases, or that through micromanagement intelligence professionals will be handcuffed and unable to exercise the discretion needed to carry out their assigned tasks.

CONTROLLING INTELLIGENCE IN THE 1990S

Like most policy problems, the question of controlling intelligence is not a permanent fixture high atop the political agenda. Once having come to terms with the issues outlined above, a type of normality returns to intelligence–policy-maker relations. Attention is refocused on perceived national security threats and the formulation of an effective foreign policy. Yet, each government must fashion answers to these questions even if those answers are grafted in one piece from the positions adopted by a previous government. The calm surrounding intelligence–policy-maker relations can be tenuous and easily shattered by a national security policy failure. In this altered policy environment calls for greater control over the intelligence bureaucracy frequently receive a great deal of prominence.

This is precisely the situation as we entered the 1990s. The Bush administration confronted control-oriented intelligence problems on several fronts in its first year in office. As a direct result of the Iran–Contra affair, in which the Reagan administration secretly transferred weapons to Iran in hopes of winning the release of American hostages in Lebanon and then used some of the profits from the sale of those weapons to aid the Contras at a time

15

when Congress had blocked all US aid, Congress gave serious consideration to two new intelligence control measures. The first would have altered presidential reporting requirements. In place of the existing requirement that Congress be notified in a 'timely fashion', the Chair and Co-Chair of the Senate Intelligence Committee (Senators David Boren and William Cohen, respectively) introduced legislation requiring notification with 48 hours of the onset of any covert action. President Reagan had kept the shipment of arms to Iran a secret from Congress for 10 months.

Bills tightening the reporting requirement had already been passed by both the Senate and the House in spite of predictions by the Director of Central Intelligence, William Webster, that President Reagan would veto any such legislation. In the end, House and Senate conferees dropped the more stringent reporting requirement because they were unable to agree upon mutually acceptable language and because of written assurances from President Bush that he would provide notification 'within a few days'. However, in that same letter Bush asserted that he possessed the constitutional right to withhold notifying Congress for as long as he wished.

The second control measure called for the creation of an independent inspector general within the CIA. Senator Arlen Specter, a member of the Senate Intelligence Committee, sponsored the bill. Proponents of the bill argued that the Iran–Contra affair not only demonstrated that the existing system in which the Director of Central Intelligence appoints an inspector general was inadequate, but that Congress was unable to oversee the CIA. Nineteen federal department's including the State Department and the Defense Department operate with independent inspector generals. Webster argued that the move would be counter-productive. He stated that because an independent inspector general might have access to secret information foreign and other sensitive intelligence sources would be reluctant to share information with the CIA for fear of leaks. House and Senate conferees did agree that an independent inspector general should be created and that the committee chairmen should have access to his reports. In December 1989 President Bush signed a funding bill which created just such an official.

Three other control-related issues made headlines during the Bush administration's first year in office. Unlike the above two pieces of legislation, these were the result of failed Bush foreign policy initiatives. The first involved the removal of the head of the CIA's Afghan Task Force. Webster made the change following congressional criticism of the way in which the covert arms transfer program was being run. Supporters of the mujaheddin asserted that an acute arms shortage existed and that because of this it was now possible that the rebels might lose the war. Part of the reason for the CIA's reluctance to transfer large quantities of weapons to the mujaheddin appears to have lain in the belief that the Afghan government would not remain in power for long following the Soviet withdrawal and that it would be unwise to leave the mujaheddin with a large quantity of unused sophisticated weapons that then might reappear elsewhere in the Middle East.

A second set of control-oriented issues surrounded the Bush administration's decision not to disclose secret information which a federal judge ruled was crucial to ex-CIA official Joseph Fernandez's ability to defend himself from charges stemming from the Iran–Contra affair. Fernandez served as CIA station chief in Costa Rica and was charged with lying to the Tower Commission about his role in Oliver North's operation to supply the Contras secretly with weapons. Under the terms of the Classified Information Act Attorney General Richard Thornburgh possessed the authority to block the release of such secret information, and, on the advice of the CIA, did so. Independent counsel Lawrence Walsh had appealed to President Bush to make the needed information public, arguing that by now they amounted to nothing more than 'fictional' secrets. Critics of the CIA maintained that the agency was only seeking to protect itself and that the documents sought by Walsh would show that, contrary to its official position, the CIA had extensive knowledge of North's Contra resupply operation.

Finally, control-oriented questions were at the heart of the Bush administration's revision of the ban on CIA involvement in assassinations. Following criticism of its handling of the failed Panamanian coup in October 1989, President Bush signed a finding authorizing the CIA to spend $3 million to overthrow Manuel Noriega. At issue was the long-standing prohibition on CIA involvement in assassinations. Administration officials had cited this ban as a reason for their caution in aiding the rebel military leaders. Under the new interpretation written by the Justice Department violence and assassination are not treated as synonymous and the CIA could legally support efforts to unseat a foreign leader even if that official was later killed accidentally.

The intelligence control issues encountered by the Bush administration in its first year in office serve to highlight the complexity of the task facing policy-makers in this area. Is the removal of the CIA official in charge of the Afghan Task Force an example of a measured response to effective congressional oversight or an example of bowing to political pressures brought on by congressional micromanagement of intelligence? To what extent will legislative curbs imposed on the CIA in the wake of the Iran–Contra affair provide control over intelligence operations when the primary force behind that operation was the National Security Council bureaucracy? In an era of overt covert operations at what point must the protection of CIA 'secrets' give way to the prosecution of individuals charged

17

with violating the law. Finally, who should be allowed to interpret restrictions on CIA activity? The Bush administration's Justice Department is hardly a disinterested party but because the prohibition on assassination is contained in an executive order, what role should Congress play? Should it, as is now the case with the INF Treaty, stipulate that no reinterpretation can take place without its formal consent or should it defer to the President as commander-in-chief?

PLAN OF THE BOOK

Because controlling intelligence is a complex task there are no easy answers. Solutions designed to solve one problem may only aggravate a problem elsewhere or bring new ones into existence. A necessary first step in addressing the many issues involved in controlling intelligence is to bring them into sharper focus. This is what the chapters in this book attempt to do.

In this chapter our concern has been with clarifying terminology and issues. In the next chapter, Stafford Thomas places the development of the CIA in a historical perspective. By doing so he helps provide a 'time-line' within which to place current issues and proposed solutions. An attention to historical context is vital if we are to overcome the tendency to treat the problem of controlling intelligence from the mindset of 'one problem at a time; solve it, get on to the next'.[30] Loch Johnson provides us with some additional context within which to view current and future control proposals. His chapter presents a critique of current safeguards against abuses by the CIA. He examines control mechanisms ranging from the National Security Council, ambassadors, and congressional oversight committees to the press, and parties and pressure groups. Johnson concludes that the US can have both a democracy and controlled intelligence organizations.

The next set of chapters provide overviews of the problem of controlling intelligence in its different forms. Arthur Hulnick, a career CIA professional, examines how the process of producing intelligence analysis is (or can be) managed so that the right questions are asked, that the product is relevant to policy-makers, and that it is delivered to them on time in a useful fashion. Hastedt's chapter also deals with the problem of controlling intelligence analysis. It starts from the assumption that too much attention has been given to the relative merits of competing formal-legalistic control mechanisms. He argues that meaningful control will only be realized if attention is first given to the values and norms which guide the behavior of the professionals working inside the intelligence bureaucracies. His analysis focuses on the behavior of DCIs in the production of intelligence estimates.

Gregory Treverton assesses the problems of controlling intelligence defined as covert action. His account provides both an analysis of the issues involved and a review of US covert action undertakings. At the core of his analysis is a paradox: by virtue of its traditions and values, secretly meddling in the affairs of other people offends the sense of America as unique; yet such a policy seems necessary given the nature of world politics and the types of enemies confronting the US. Marion Doss addresses the frequently overlooked question of controlling intelligence when it is defined as counter-intelligence. The central problem here is how best to protect the nation against threats to its security without abridging the fundamental liberties exercised by its people. In examining this issue, Doss identifies the key counter-intelligence bureaucracies and reviews past control proposals.

In the final chapter Stuart Farson provides us with a non-US example of a government's efforts to control intelligence. His focus is on the history and legacy of the McDonald Commission's investigation into the activities of Canadian intelligence. Farson's contribution is particularly valuable because it allows us to view US control efforts in a comparative context. In doing so it makes us aware that the problem of controlling intelligence is not unique to the US but is one with which all political systems must come to terms.

NOTES

1. On this point see Michael Handel 'Leaders and Intelligence', *Intelligence and National Security* Vol. 3, No 3 (July 1988), pp.1–39.
2. On this point see Shlomo Gazit, 'Intelligence Estimates and the Decision-Maker', *Intelligence and National Security* Vol. 3, No 3 (July 1988), pp.261–87.
3. Christopher Andrew, 'Governments and Secret Services: A Historical Perspective', *International Journal* (1979), pp.168–9.
4. The President's Special Review Board, *The Tower Commission Report* (New York, 1987), pp.87–99.
5. Kenneth Sharpe, 'The Real Cause of Irangate', *Foreign Policy* 68 (Fall, 1987), pp.19–41.
6. Harry Howe Ransom, 'Strategic Intelligence and Intermestic Politics', in Charles W. Kegley Jr., and Eugene R. Wittkopf (eds.), *Perspectives on American Foreign Policy: Selected Readings* (New York, 1983), pp.299–319.
7. Angelo Codevilla, 'Reforms and Proposals for Reforms', in Roy Godson (ed.), *Intelligence Requirement for the 1980's: Elements of Intelligence*, revised edition (Washington, DC, 1983), pp.93–110.
8. Harry Howe Ransom, 'Being Intelligent about Secret Intelligence Agencies', *American Political Science Review* 74 (1980), pp.141–8.
9. Harry Ransom, 'Review Essay', *American Political Science Review* 80 (1986), pp.990–91.
10. Roger Hilsman, 'On Intelligence', *Armed Forces and Society* 8 (1981), pp.129–41.
11. Sherman Kent, *Strategic Intelligence for American World Policy* (Princeton, NJ, 1949).
12. Harry Howe Ransom, *The Intelligence Establishment* (Cambridge, MA, 1970).
13. Roy Godson, 'Intelligence and Policy: An Introduction', in Roy Godson (ed.), *Intelligence Requirements for the 1980's: Intelligence and Policy* (Lexington, MA, 1986).

14. Quoted in Jeffrey T. Richelson, *The US Intelligence Community* (Cambridge, MA, 1985), p.53.
15. *National Security Act of 1947*, Title I. Section 102, *Stat*. 495.
16. History of OSS references.
17. Theodore Shackley, *The Third Option: An American View of Counterinsurgency Operations* (New York, 1981).
18. This position laid out by Kent in *Strategic Intelligence for American World Policy*. For examples of intelligence to please see Patrick McGarvey, *C.I.A.: The Myth and the Madness* (Baltimore, 1973) and Sam Adams, 'Cover-Up: Playing War With Numbers', *Harper's* (May 1975), pp.41–73.
19. The position is outlined in Wilmoore Kendall, 'The Functions of Intelligence', *World Politics*, 2 (1949), pp.542–52. Casey's quote is in John Ranelagh, *The Agency: The Rise and Decline of the CIA*, revised and updated edition (New York, 1987), p.687.
20. On the subject of decision costs see Loch Johnson, 'Decision Costs in the Intelligence Cycle', in Alfred C. Maurer, Marion D. Tunstall and James M. Keagle (eds.), *Intelligence: Policy and Process* (Boulder, 1985), pp.181–98.
21. On this point see Richard K. Betts, *Surprise Attack: Lessons for Defense Planning* (Washington, DC, 1982) and Michael I. Handel, *The Diplomacy of Surprise: Hitler, Nixon, Sadat* (Cambridge, MA, 1981).
22. These two competing views were put forward in congressional testimony and can be found in *The Washington Post*, 23 October 1979.
23. The Bissel philosophy is reprinted in Victor Marchetti and John Marks, *The CIA and the Cult of Intelligence* (New York, 1974), pp.357–76.
24. US Congress, Senate Select Committee to Study Government Operations With Respect to Intelligence Activities, *Alleged Assassination Plots Involving Foreign Leaders* (Washington, DC, 1976).
25. An example of the range of small-scale operations that *may* exist in a country can be found in Philip Agee, *Inside the Company: CIA Diary* (New York, 1976). Agee's book is highly controversial and should be read with care. A good companion book is David Atlee Phillips, *The Night Watch: 25 Years of Peculiar Service* (New York, 1977): Their careers overlap in many places and Phillips writes a 'pro-intelligence' memoir.
26. For examples of these excesses see Frank J. Donner, *The Age of Surveillance: The Aims and Methods of America's Political Intelligence System* (New York, 1981) and David G. Martin, *Wilderness of Mirrors* (New York, 1981).
27. *Facts on File*, 3 July 1976, p.477.
28. The definition of leadership is taken from James MacGregor Burns, *Leadership* (New York, 1978) p.425.
29. *Congressional Quarterly*, 19 July 1980, p.2051.
30. Richard Neustadt and Ernest May, *Thinking in Time* (New York, 1986), p.255.

APPENDIX

SELECTED DOCUMENTS ON CONTROLLING INTELLIGENCE ORGANIZATIONS

THE UNITED STATES

CONGRESSIONAL ACTION

Posse Comitatus Act: Section 1385 of Title 18 of the United States Code. Passed in 1878 it places restrictions on the use of military to enforce the civil and criminal law.

The National Security Act of 1947: The founding document of the CIA. It establishes the basic functions and duties of the CIA.

Central Intelligence Agency Act of 1949: This act modified the 1947 Act.

The Hughes-Ryan Amendment of 1961: Section 662 of the Foreign Assistance Act of 1961, the Hughes-Ryan Amendment prohibited any funds from being spent on behalf of the CIA covert operations in foreign countries without the President certifying that such an operation was in the national interest.

Foreign Intelligence Surveillance Act of 1978: Provided methods and procedures for engaging in electronic surveillance within the United States for foreign intelligence purposes.

The Clark Amendment of 1980: Section 118 of the International Security and Development Cooperation Act of 1980, the Clark Amendment prohibited the United States from engaging in covert operations in Angola.

Intelligence Oversight Act of 1980: This act cut back the President's reporting requirements to two committees and made it clear that Congress expected to be notified of all covert actions, and not just those carried out by the CIA.

The Boland Amendment of 1982: Section 793 of Public Law 97–377, the Boland Amendment prohibited the spending of funds by the CIA or the Defense Department for the purpose of overthrowing the government of Nicaragua or provoking a military exchange between Nicaragua and Honduras.

PRESIDENTIAL EXECUTIVE ORDERS

Executive Order 11905: Issued by President Ford on 18 February 1976, it is the first publicly released presidential order establishing the boundaries of permissible intelligence activities.

Executive Order 12036: Issued by President Carter on 24 January 1978.

Executive Order 12333: Issued by President Reagan on 4 December 1981.

Executive Order 12334: Issued by President Reagan on 4 December 1981, it established the President's Intelligence Oversight Board.

Executive Order 12537: Issued by President Reagan on 28 October 1985, it established the President's Intelligence Advisory Board.

INVESTIGATIONS

Domestic Security Investigations: Issued by Attorney General Levi on 10 March 1976.

The Attorney General's Guidelines on General Crimes, Racketeering Enterprise, and Domestic Security/Terrorism Investigations: Issued by Attorney General Smith on 7 March 1983.

The Attorney General's Guidelines for FBI Foreign Intelligence Collection and Foreign Counterintelligence Investigations: Issued by Attorney General Smith on 18 April 1983.

CANADA

Commission of Inquiry Concerning Certain Activities of the Royal Canadian Mounted Police:Commonly known as the McDonald Commission, it was in existence from 1979 to 1981 and issued three reports.

21

PLACING THE PROBLEM IN CONTEXT

The Canadian Security Intelligence Service Act of 1984: This act created a security intelligence agency (the Canadian Security Intelligence Service) separate from the Royal Canadian Mounted Police.

Security Intelligence Review Committee, Annual Reports. Under the terms of the Canadian Security Intelligence Service Act of 1984 a five-year review was mandated. A report was scheduled for release in 1990.

2

Intelligence and the American Political System

STAFFORD T. THOMAS

Three basic factors are important in analysing the evolution of United States intelligence. These three factors explain the changes in intelligence since America's founding, and help us to understand why there are many different views about when, how and why to control intelligence.

The most important factor concerns the world beyond our borders, sometimes called the external policy environment. The interactions we have with that environment, our foreign policy, are based in part on how policy-makers view it. If they perceive a threatening environment, the need for intelligence is obvious. The more obvious the perceived threat, the less debate there is over intelligence activities. When the perceived threat is extreme, and is shared by most of those in a position to influence policy, there is virtually no debate over intelligence control. However, when the perception of threat from the external environment is unclear or not commonly shared, intelligence control becomes a political issue, and the other two factors become important in analysing the resulting debate.

The second factor concerns the influence of intelligence institutions. If any governmental unit is small and designed to help *solve* a specific problem, it will quite probably be dissolved once the problem is solved. On the other hand, if the institution is intended to help *manage* a problem over a long period of time, it is quite likely to stay in existence indefinitely. In either case, the institution has rival institutions which seek to limit its influence. Like all governmental units, intelligence institutions become involved in such *bureaucratic rivalry*. The result is not only that they must justify the continuing need for intelligence as a basic policy tool, but also that they must compete with each other for funding and assignments. Thus, intelligence agencies are similar to other governmental units, and so the question of control of intelligence is only part of the larger question of control of government.

The third factor that is important in looking at intelligence as a control problem is the nature of the debate over the political agenda. When there is general agreement on the nation's foreign policy goals, the question of controlling intelligence depends on the factors of external environment and bureaucratic politics. However, when there is considerable debate over the scope and methods of US foreign policy, the question of controlling intelligence becomes a focal point of that debate.

The three factors are not of equal importance. The first, external environment, is the crucial one. If there is substantial agreement that the country's survival is threatened, control of intelligence becomes an irrelevant, if not treasonable, question. However, if there is not a clear threat to the nation, the factors of bureaucratic rivalry and policy debate help us to answer the question of intelligence control.

INTELLIGENCE BEFORE THE SECOND WORLD WAR

The history of US intelligence reflects the general foreign policy of which it is a part. Until the Second World War, the US deliberately sought to avoid confrontations with powerful countries. This policy was a rational consequence of the realities of international relations.

Beginning with the Revolutionary War and continuing throughout the nineteenth century, the United States was economically, militarily and politically weak compared with the much stronger nations of Europe. Furthermore, it had more important domestic goals, including developing the economy, settling the West, and adjusting to a new and untested form of government. During this period, there was little need for intelligence about potential foreign adversaries, simply because there were few adversaries, whether by design or fortune. The intelligence effort was minimal, and it was limited primarily to diplomatic and economic matters. This information usually was gathered haphazardly by people with no formal training in the art and science of espionage. In most cases, intelligence was collected coincidentally as a result of the normal activities of the Departments of State and Commerce, and its irregular and unsystematic nature meant that it was almost never part of general foreign policy, except by its absence.

The exceptions to this general pattern of intelligence neglect can be found in the direct and clear threats to the existence of the US. In times of national emergency, the necessities of war demanded knowledge of the enemy. George Washington recognized the critical importance of intelligence, and the Revolutionary War produced two of the most memorable spies in our history. Nathan Hale was an American espionage agent who was caught and convicted by the British and died a martyred hero. Benedict Arnold, one of Washington's most talented and successful generals, became a double agent, working for the British for money. He escaped to England and eventually died in poverty, a traitor to his country.

Intelligence became an almost totally neglected tool of policy following the War for Independence, but it became important again during the Civil War. Both sides relied heavily on intelligence to plan military campaigns and strategies, and new names were added to the list of intelligence heroes and heroines, or villains depending on one's sympathies. Perhaps the most memorable was Allan Pinkerton, who established an intelligence system to aid the Union military forces and later founded the Pinkerton Detective Agency.

The turn of the century coincided with a new thrust of United States foreign policy. Victory in the Spanish-American War of 1898 resulted in a very rapid and large expansion of US territory. The addition of the Philippines and other Pacific Ocean holdings greatly increased America's visibility in the world. Despite the apparent need for more regular and extensive intelligence about the rest of the world, it did not develop any significant ability to collect information about that world and process that information into intelligence useful to policy-makers. The major reason for this continuing neglect was the absence of any significant threat to US vital interests. Although America was making the transition from isolationism to unilateralism in world affairs, no nation could effectively threaten its physical security or economic vitality.

This fundamental relationship between threats to America's vital interests and its having a capable intelligence service is illustrated clearly by the rather startling fact that on 4 April 1917, when the country officially entered the First World War against Germany, the intelligence unit of the US Army's General Staff, which made its basic military strategy, was sparsely staffed with only four people. And while the First World War once again produced a growth in US intelligence, following the war most of the intelligence personnel were demobilized along with the rest of the military forces.

This pattern was broken with the approach of the Second World War. For the first time, there was a deliberate effort to gain knowledge of real and potential adversaries in a systematic and extensive manner *before* the onset of hostilities. A component of the State Department worked to 'break' the secret codes used by the Japanese to send messages from Tokyo to their diplomats in Washington. More significantly for the evolution of intelligence, on 11 July 1941, President Franklin D. Roosevelt authorized the creation of the Office of Co-ordination and Information (OCI). The name of this new governmental unit is not very important, but the date and event are highly significant since it marked the beginning of a conscious and consistent commitment by the United States to develop extensive capabilities in all of the fundamental activities or functions of intelligence: analysis (the relatively undramatic activity of producing estimates and predictions for policy-makers); protection of intelligence products and procedures (counter-intelligence and, more specifically, counter-espionage); collection (overt and covert, the latter more commonly called espionage or spying); and covert action (deliberate and active efforts to affect events clandestinely).

Despite these initial steps toward development of a peacetime intelligence apparatus, and despite a considerable amount of high-quality intelligence on Japanese intentions and activities, the attack on Pearl Harbor on 7 December 1941 was devastating. Its impact on the evolution of American intelligence was critical, primarily because it demonstrated so clearly and convincingly the necessity of being well-informed if the US were to play a major role in world affairs.

In terms of the structures and dynamics of American government and politics, the issue of intelligence was virtually non-existent before the Second World War. In times of real or perceived peril from foreign sources, the nation and its institutions responded with an overwhelmingly unified response. Consequently, there was no debate over either the utility or the propriety of the conduct of intelligence. This reflected the general relationship between President and Congress. While there was often disagreement between these two branches of government regarding domestic issues, foreign policy (of which intelligence was an infrequent and minor element) was not subject to prolonged and intensive debates. However, the low priority of intelligence before the Second World War was changed, probably for ever, by that war.

THE IMPORTANCE OF THE SECOND WORLD WAR TO INTELLIGENCE

The Second World War was a major event in the history of United States foreign policy. Previously, its relationships with other nations were either isolationist (avoiding relationships) or unilateralist (avoiding long-term and complicated relationships that restricted its options), depending on the situation. US participation in the war began a fundamental shift to the opposite extreme of a globalist foreign policy. The war greatly accelerated this shift, as did the immediate post-war period. Intelligence was part of this basic re-orientation of US foreign policy.

The fundamental policy goal was, obviously, to win the war. All other policies, domestic and foreign, were subordinated to this objective. As a

26

matter of military necessity, intelligence about the various enemies was of crucial importance. The problem was that the country lacked the capability to obtain the amount and quality of intelligence required to plan and implement a winning strategy. This weakness was overcome by an active effort to create governmental institutions that could help policy-makers and policy-implementers. One result of this effort was a dramatic increase in all kinds of military intelligence. This continued the traditional pattern of intelligence growth in response to security threats. However, the unique importance of the Second World War was the creation of a large, sophisticated *civilian* intelligence institution, the Office of Strategic Services (OSS), an updated version of OCI.

The OSS began as a small unit of government.[1] Its primary purpose, and original justification, was to carry out research on the wartime adversaries and produce analyses and estimates of their actual and potential capabilities. Significantly, it was not confined to just military matters. It was also asked to assess political, social, economic and other conditions abroad. Also, its focus was not restricted to enemy countries. Its geographical scope was world-wide, although it was concerned primarily with America's enemies and the countries they occupied. This unlimited intelligence agenda was new in the history of the United States, and it was significant because it represents the beginning of the 'modern era' of intelligence in American government. It is also noteworthy because both the executive and legislative branches agreed on its importance and missions.

The original idea of a governmental research and analysis unit devoted primarily to foreign affairs quickly evolved into a 'full-service' intelligence institution. Relying heavily on British intelligence, the OSS expanded its functions to include espionage, counter-intelligence and covert action. Once again, as in previous wars, the driving force for this increase in intelligence as a part of American government was the nature of the policy environment. In order to produce intelligence reports that policy-planners had to have, it became necessary to collect information from 'denied areas', a term that means places where the enemy is trying to keep secrets. It also became necessary to develop the counter-intelligence capabilities of securing US denied areas from enemy espionage efforts and of trying to confuse and mislead the enemy as to US plans and intentions. The OSS also engaged in a variety of covert actions, such as aiding resistance units fighting in enemy-held territory and using propaganda techniques to affect attitudes toward the enemy.

OSS activities were extensive and often effective. The organization became the subject of myth and lore, much of it genuine. It rapidly increased in stature, and, most importantly, it quickly gained political and institutional credibility in Washington. Due in large part to the enthusiasm and political acumen of its founder and wartime director, William J. ('Wild Bill') Donovan, the organization became an important part of the government's wartime effort. By the end of the war, OSS had become a large bureaucracy, and for the first time the United States had a group of people who were skilled in the work of intelligence. However, despite its record, expertise and bureaucratic importance, the OSS was disbanded in October, 1945. It had been created to help solve a problem, and victory over Germany and Japan meant the problem no longer existed.

Normally, the US would have waited until another military threat before reviving intelligence. However, the external environment after the Second World War was new and unique, and the result was the creation of a permanent intelligence service.[2] The world in 1945 represented new challenges to American foreign policy. Foremost among these was the perception by policy-makers that the US was faced with a massive, persistent and aggressive enemy which directly and imminently threatened its vital interests. Intelligence was essential to survival. The question of control of intelligence was not considered. Indeed, the demands of the Cold War focused attention on how much intelligence capability could be acquired, not on how little was needed. Although the military intelligence organizations raised serious objections to the creation of a large, permanent peacetime civilian unit, in 1947 the Central Intelligence Agency was created to deal with the threat posed by the Soviet Union and its ideological allies. Staffed to a large extent by OSS veterans, it began with a large mandate, a sizeable budget, and a threatening foreign environment that guaranteed its continuing necessity.

POST-WAR INTELLIGENCE: THE FIRST DECADE

America's permanent intelligence establishment began with the National Security Act of 1947.[3] The two years between the end of the Second World War (and the demobilization of the OSS) and the creation of the Central Intelligence Agency (CIA) were characterized by dynamic changes in the international environment and intense domestic bureaucratic rivalry among intelligence units within the US government. The basic external change was the shift by the United States to a globalist foreign policy to combat the perceived expansionism of the Soviet Union. US security interests were seen as threatened everywhere, and one major consequence was the recognized need for a permanent, large, 'full-service' intelligence capability. The domestic response to this new challenge was a contest among several institutions to become the focal point of the new US intelligence apparatus.

The Department of State, which had absorbed some OSS personnel, argued that it was the logical institution to perform the intelligence function since it was responsible for designing and implementing US foreign policy. The military intelligence units argued that they should lead the intelligence effort since the threat was a national security problem for which they were responsible. However, Donovan and others argued for the creation of a new institution that would perform all four intelligence functions: analysis, counter-intelligence, collection and, if necessary, covert action. Neither the State Department nor the military services was willing or able to provide a full-service intelligence capability, and because Donovan was such a persuasive person, his plan was adopted and the CIA became responsible for centralizing and co-ordinating the nation's intelligence work.

The CIA faced two basic challenges in its first decade. One was the problem of developing into a full-service intelligence organization that could meet the needs of those who were making and implementing US foreign policy. The other challenge was from the existing agencies of the US government that resisted the CIA's efforts to become the dominant intelligence organization. These two challenges were inter-related, and the result was a mutual understanding that some intelligence functions would be shared with other agencies while other functions would be performed primarily by the CIA.

The function of research and analysis was shared among several agencies. The most important of these were the CIA, the Defense Department and its separate Army, Navy and Air Force intelligence units, and the State Department. Each of these structures produced intelligence estimates independently, but they also co-ordinated their research efforts to produce National Intelligence Estimates (NIEs) on important issues, such as the Soviet military capabilities and worldwide economic trends and developments. Each NIE was co-ordinated by the CIA, since that unit was created to *centralize* intelligence for the nation. However, the co-ordination effort often was a difficult one because each participating agency had its own view of the issue or problem. So, the analysis and estimates function of intelligence became a shared activity, although the CIA was a major participant and often was successful in influencing the final versions of NIEs.

The domestic counter-intelligence function was performed primarily by the Federal Bureau of Investigation. Its director, the legendary J. Edgar Hoover, was especially protective of this activity, and he and the FBI dominated the effort to protect the US and its secrets from the espionage efforts of other countries, especially the Soviet Union. The CIA's relatively minor role in this function is also explained by the fact that it was prevented by law from conducting intelligence operations within the United States.

This restriction was intended by Congress as a control on intelligence, but it also reflected Hoover's persuasiveness during the 1945–47 period when the CIA was being created. The Agency *did* develop its counter-intelligence capabilities in foreign operations, however. While the distinction between foreign and domestic intelligence activities was sometimes blurred, the CIA and the FBI reached an understanding in most cases, although at times they failed to co-ordinate their counter-intelligence efforts.

Foreign espionage was another function that came to be shared among the various members of the US 'intelligence community'. (This is the term that is used most often to summarize all US intelligence agencies. However, the competition within the 'community' is so pervasive and often so intense that it is a misleading term. A more accurate term is US intelligence *apparatus*.) The military services collected information through its attachés in other countries. Likewise, the State Department used its embassies and consulates to gain knowledge of events and issues. (The intelligence collected by these attachés and diplomats allowed these agencies to produce their independent analyses and estimates, which explains why they were able to compete with the CIA in the production of NIEs and other intelligence reports.)

However, despite these espionage efforts by other agencies, the CIA dominated the collection function. Its espionage budget was substantial and it had a large number of people trained in the somewhat unique art of clandestine collection of other nations' secrets. The CIA's budget also allowed it to dominate collection of information from open sources, including newspapers, periodicals, journals, books, and radio broadcasts from abroad. (The collection of so much information from such varied sources also meant that the Agency could always have a relevant input to the NIE process. The result was that while it might not dominate the analysis and estimates function, it was always a major influence in the production of intelligence reports.)

In contrast to the other intelligence functions, covert action quickly became the almost exclusive responsibility of the Central Intelligence Agency. Within a year of its creation, the CIA was assisting non-Communist political parties in the Italian elections of 1948. This was the beginning of the use of covert action by US policy implementers. Given the dominant prevailing perception of the Cold War, that US global security and economic interests were being threatened by a hostile and pervasive adversary, covert action was seen as an appropriate and useful way of responding to that threat. It was viewed as a 'third option' between the extremes of traditional diplomacy (which often was not relevant to the antagonisms of the Cold War) and the use of military force (which was too costly and often not relevant to the problems the US was trying to solve or manage). Thus, the use of covert action by the United

States can be explained by the nature of the foreign policy environment. As we have seen, if that environment is perceived as threatening, as it certainly was during the Cold War era, covert action is viewed as a necessary tool of foreign policy. In these circumstances, there was virtually no debate in government over its utility, and there was no real concern over the need to control it or its major agency.

A second explanation for the frequent use of covert action by the CIA in the decade following the Second World War was the lack of involvement by any other agency in this intelligence function. Neither the military nor the State Department wanted to assume a significant covert action capability, and a group of people within the CIA was enthusiastic and motivated to do it. This combination of an absence of external bureaucratic functional rivals and internal bureaucratic zealotry meant that covert action became the CIA's most unique and characteristic governmental activity.

A third factor that helps us understand the CIA's use of covert action to support US foreign policy during the Cold War is Allen W. Dulles. In government service for decades, Dulles was a major figure in the OSS during the Second World War, during which he became involved with the intrigue of espionage and covert action. He was a principal supporter of the creation of the CIA, and became its Director in 1953. Adept at Washington politics, he had the ability to persuade most potential doubters that covert action was critically necessary for the nation and that the CIA was the institution to conduct it effectively.

The result of these three factors was the rapid incorporation of covert action into US foreign policy and the acceptance of the covert action function by the CIA. In its first decade, the Agency's covert actions became a major instrument of US foreign policy because it was convenient, appropriate and usually successful. It helped to achieve the general foreign policy goal of containment in Italy (1948), Iran (1953), Guatemala (1954), and other places where it appeared that Communist elements, possibly directed by Moscow, threatened regimes friendly to the United States. This record of success, together with the consensus in Washington that covert action was a viable way of dealing with the national security threat and the adroit portrayal of the Agency by Allen Dulles, meant that intelligence in general and covert action by the CIA in particular were recognized as necessary by nearly everyone of influence among the policy elite. This, in turn, meant that few people were even concerned about the question of control.

By the mid-1950s, the issue of control did surface, although it was not viewed with great alarm. In 1956, Senator Mike Mansfield led an effort to define the limits of US intelligence activities, especially the covert actions of the CIA.[4] There are several reasons for this first attempt to control intelligence, but the most plausible one is the traditional tension between the executive and legislative branches of government. Neither wants to concede complete authority to the other, and the Constitution's checks and balances reinforce this relationship. By 1956, Mansfield and a few others in Congress had begun to realize that intelligence had become an activity that was almost totally dominated by the executive. So, this initial and quite modest attempt to clarify jurisdiction of intelligence control was intended primarily to establish some claim to authority by Congress.

Mansfield focused on covert action in his effort to check the executive's almost exclusive dominance of intelligence. There were several reasons for this. One was the difference between covert action and the other intelligence functions. The collection of information, especially on adversaries, the protection of US secrets, and the analysis of the international environment were all accepted as legitimate and unquestioned needs of any country. However, because covert action attempted to affect conditions in other countries, it was viewed as qualitatively different. Reinforcing this distinction was the historical experience of America in the world. Even though the US had adopted a globalist foreign policy following the Second World War, the isolationist heritage suggested to some that it was none of America's business what other countries did as long as it was not directly affected.

Another reason for the doubt over covert action can be found in America's political culture, which includes the belief in the self-determination of other nations. Covert action contradicted this principle, and to some this suggested that it was not a proper and legitimate function of government. This concern with the ideals of the United States raised the philosophical question of control of intelligence.

A more realistic concern was the issue referred to previously, the need to specify the role of Congress in intelligence. The US government does not operate on the basis of the separation of powers so much as it does on the principle of separated institutions sharing power. The institutions are clearly separated by Articles I, II and III of the Constitution. However, checks and balances insure that most powers or functions of government are shared among the separate institutions. Mansfield's effort was intended to have Congress share the intelligence 'power' of government. He sought to do this by clarifying some language in the National Security Act of 1947.

In that portion of this sweeping reorganization of America's national security apparatus that dealt with the CIA, covert action was not mentioned specifically, but it was authorized by permitting the Agency to 'perform other functions and duties relating to national security intelligence as the National Security Council may direct'.[5] This ambiguous language is typical of most congressional legislation, which reflects the way the executive and legislative

32

branches normally share power. It allows Congress to make the general laws, but it also allows the executive branch to implement the legislation according to specific conditions. In the case of the covert action provision of the National Security Act of 1947, however, the language was so ambiguous that Congress had almost no way of affecting what the President chose to do. So, while historical roots and political culture were minor factors, the 1956 control efforts were basically motivated by the normal dynamics of American government. And, since covert action was so different and questionable, it became the focus of this first real effort at intelligence control by Congress.

Mansfield's efforts failed to gain a significant control capability for Congress. One reason was the view by most members of Congress that covert action was too important and necessary to the nation's security. The containment doctrine, which was the basis of US post-war foreign policy, demanded that it be vigilant and responsive to the efforts of Communism and Soviet expansionism, and the immediacy and pervasiveness of the threat justified covert action. Furthermore, some very influential members of Congress argued that control mechanisms *did* exist, and that control was being exercised.

The CIA, and most notably Allen Dulles, conducted regular intelligence briefings for the relevant congressional committees. Often Dulles would combine assessments that emphasized the antagonistic international environment with stories of daring espionage and covert action by CIA personnel. His effectiveness in testifying to Congress is shown by a general acceptance of his word that no laws were being broken and no principles were being transgressed. Thus, Congress technically could argue that these briefings constituted its control of intelligence, but its failure to challenge Dulles or actively seek information on CIA activities amounted to an abdication of control to the executive branch. As long as covert action was successful in containing the spread of Communism and protecting regimes friendly to the United States, control of intelligence was not an issue that was politically attractive. Mansfield's effort did not increase congressional control of intelligence, but it did have one major consequence – it focused the question of congressional control on covert action.

THE SECOND DECADE

The period 1956–66 was marked by changes in the international environment and changes in the US intelligence apparatus and its capabilities, but only a minor change in congressional attitudes toward intelligence control. For the first half of this decade, the Dulles era continued. His ability to satisfy, if not captivate, the most influential Senators and Congressmen on the feasibility and propriety of intelligence activities effectively muted any possible criticisms or concerns. However, the apparent unparalleled success of the CIA came to an end in 1960, and in subsequent years other failures became publicly known.

The 1960 event involved espionage rather than covert action, and it illustrates a major change in US intelligence capabilities. Espionage had depended historically on human agents using their wits and courage to obtain secrets held by the enemy. However, advances in technology decreased the risks of espionage and improved the reliability of the information collected. Technology such as secret listening devices and miniature cameras greatly enhanced the espionage profession. As more advanced technology was created, it became incorporated into intelligence collection.

By the late 1950s, CIA engineers had developed a remarkable espionage tool. The U-2 aircraft could cruise slowly at 70,000 feet for hours, beyond the range of any anti-aircraft guns or missiles. Furthermore, it contained an advanced camera that could take pictures from that height that were very clear and detailed. This enabled the United States to collect information on the most important national security problem of all: the Soviet Union's nuclear missile program. The CIA could fly over the USSR, take photographs of Soviet missile fields, and return safely with the film. Even if the Soviets became aware of the plane, they could not stop its espionage activities.

U-2 flights began in 1958 and they became critically important to intelligence analysts. Now it could be determined how many missiles the Soviets had and how quickly their missile program was developing. The risk to human life was minimized and the intelligence gain maximized. In addition, the Soviets could not complain since it would be too embarrassing to admit they were incapable of defending themselves against Western technology. The flights became a normal activity for the CIA, with the continuing approval of President Eisenhower. However, in May 1960 the U-2 program became an embarrassment to the US.

President Eisenhower and the Soviet leader, Nikita Khrushchev, had a summit meeting in Paris to discuss major issues between the two superpowers. Just before this meeting, on 1 May, the Soviets were finally able to shoot down a U-2 plane and to capture the CIA pilot, Gary Powers. At first, Eisenhower denied the plane was on a spy mission, but he later had to admit he had lied. Khrushchev cancelled the summit after humiliating the US President. The Soviets conducted Powers' trial in public, which further embarrassed the United States, especially when he admitted to spying for the US.

Although there was some public criticism of the CIA over the U-2 affair, the main focus was Eisenhower. He accepted responsibility for the inept handling of the event, but he did not apologize for the espionage. Nor was there a great demand for such an apology. To most Americans, and to most in Congress, espionage was necessary (especially if conducted against the Soviet Union), the CIA's activities were legitimate, and the US had just been unlucky to have its aircraft shot down. The event was seen by most as a case of questionable diplomacy rather than an intelligence failure by the CIA. The Agency would not be as fortunate a year later.

In January 1961, a new president occupied the White House. John Kennedy brought a vigorous approach to government, in terms of both his policies and his relations with Congress. His foreign policy continued the anti-Communist theme of his predecessors, and he inherited policies and plans endorsed by Eisenhower that were characterized by that theme. One of these plans involved an invasion of Cuba by Cubans who had left their homeland when Fidel Castro had taken over that government in January 1959. Castro had allied with the Soviet Union and had communized Cuba. Many people fled his regime and came to the United States. In 1960, the part of the CIA which conducted covert actions began to train some of the Cubans to go back to their country and overthrow Castro. This CIA plan was accepted by Eisenhower, and Kennedy approved it when he became President.

The invasion of Cuba took place in early April 1961, at the Bay of Pigs. It failed miserably and was a major embarrassment to the new administration. Kennedy publicly accepted responsibility for the fiasco, but privately he blamed the CIA. He had been assured by Allen Dulles that the plan would succeed, and he had trusted the CIA Director in his first major foreign policy action. Kennedy's reaction to the Bay of Pigs failure was to force Dulles to resign and to give the CIA notice that he intended to exercise greater control over its actions. This is an important point because it illustrates the first significant effort to control the Agency, and it was done by the President, not Congress. The reaction of Congress to the Bay of Pigs was quite modest, especially given how embarrassing it was. Normally, the President's political opponents in Congress would be expected to use a failure like this to call for greater control of intelligence by Congress. Instead, most members of the legislature praised Kennedy for accepting responsibility and argued that the invasion was consistent with containment. However, coming so soon after the U-2 affair, some in Congress began to question how proper it was for the US to be trying to overthrow a foreign government and whether the US should use secret methods to do it. Thus, while the majority in Congress continued to support covert action by the CIA completely, a few were raising questions that focused on the issue of restricting CIA operations.

Kennedy's concern with controlling the CIA focused on its covert actions. He wanted to be sure that the Agency would be responsive to his direction in performing that intelligence function. In effect, Kennedy realized that as long as Congress was not going to contest control of this governmental agency, it was *his* CIA and *he* would determine its activities. Again, this is important because control means more than constraint. It also means responsiveness within the constraints. Immediately after the Bay of Pigs, he was so angry with the CIA that he wanted to make his brother its Director so that his control would be direct. Instead, he made John McCone, a Republican businessman, head of the Agency. McCone was not an intelligence professional, as Dulles had been, so he owed no particular loyalty to the Agency, its personnel, or the intelligence profession. He owed his loyalty to the President, and this assured Kennedy that he could control the CIA, especially its covert action.

Kennedy also was upset over the CIA's dominance of the intelligence analysis function. Although NIEs and other intelligence reports were the result of compromise among the various units of the US intelligence apparatus ('community'), the CIA's estimate of the situation in Cuba just before the Bay of Pigs had been a major factor in Kennedy's endorsement of the plan. In effect, he blamed the Agency for a failure in knowledge as well as in execution. The experience caused him to distrust analyses and estimates that were either solely produced by the CIA or dominated by the CIA's position. As a way of controlling undue and possibly faulty CIA analyses, he authorized the creation of the Defense Intelligence Agency (DIA) in 1961. The purpose of this new unit was to centralize the intelligence efforts (espionage, analysis and counter-intelligence) of the Army, Navy and Air Force. The DIA did not replace the intelligence segments of the three services: it augmented them. From Kennedy's perspective, the DIA would compete with the CIA in the production of intelligence reports. In this way, the CIA would be restrained from dominating this function.

The creation of the DIA also reveals the extent to which bureaucratic politics had come to characterize intelligence by the 1960s. From the beginning of the post-war period, the CIA had rivals among other units of government. The Agency was created despite military, FBI and State Department objections that it was unnecessary. After 1947, each of these units continued to perform intelligence functions consistent with their bureaucratic *raison d'être*. In 1951, the National Security Agency had been created. Among the most secret of the publicly known units of the US government, it used the most modern technology not only to break the secret codes of other countries but also to make US secret codes unbreakable by others. Concerned primarily with national security information, it was connected with the Defense Department. Thus, the CIA had to compete with a number of other governmental structures to perform intelligence functions.

The competition between the intelligence bureaus and agencies grew in intensity as each became more established. By the mid-1960s, the CIA no longer dominated intelligence analyses. Its major competitors were the various intelligence elements of the military, although the State Department's Bureau of Intelligence and Research (INR) also was a major contributor. The Agency continued to have a contentious relationship with the FBI over performance of the counter-intelligence function. J. Edgar Hoover had a low opinion of CIA capabilities in this area, and collaboration between the Agency and the Bureau often was strained. The CIA conducted most of the nation's human espionage, but advances in technology meant that nearly all members of the US intelligence apparatus could acquire intelligence.

Only in the area of covert action was the CIA dominant, and while it continued to be vigorous in this area, its relevance to US foreign policy was being transformed by the growing importance of the Vietnam War. In 1966, the issue of control was debated again in Congress, as it had been ten years earlier. The outcome was the same, too, with no appreciable changes in the executive dominance of intelligence. The CIA conducted more briefings for Senators and Representatives, and thus Congress could argue that it was more cognizant of CIA activities. However, congressional 'oversight' (the commonly used term for legislative control) of intelligence was done by a small group of legislators who had great seniority and were in no way inclined to challenge or criticize Agency activities. Especially in the Senate, the Chairmen of the Foreign Relations and Armed Services Committees, to which the CIA regularly reported, had worked so closely with the Agency for so long that they preferred the status quo to any new arrangement of control that might cause a reduction in their influence. Reinforcing this status quo orientation was the seniority system that Congress had then. Under this system, a committee chairman controlled virtually all of his committee's activities, and junior committee members could not challenge his control.

By the end of its second decade, the US intelligence apparatus was subject to control, but not to any meaningful congressional oversight. The White House exercised control over the CIA's covert action in the sense that it made every effort to make the Agency respond to presidential directives. Also, the bureaucratic rivalry between the units of the apparatus exercised a form of restraint, especially on the CIA regarding shared functions. But control in the usual sense, exercised by Congress and focused on covert action, was restricted to a few senior members of that body who conducted their oversight responsibilities informally and tentatively. All of this would change radically over the next decade.

37

THE THIRD DECADE

For US intelligence, the last half of the 1960s was dominated by the Vietnam War. Indeed, US foreign policy became oriented around the war. Although its military was fighting openly, there was still a need for covert operations. The most notable of these were the secret war in Laos and the Phoenix Program in South Vietnam. For nearly ten years, the CIA conducted a war in Laos as part of the general US war in Southeast Asia. Generally regarded as one of the Agency's most successful covert actions, the secret war is credited with restricting the efforts of North Vietnam to supply its forces and allies in the South. The Phoenix Program in South Vietnam attempted to identify allies of North Vietnam (the Viet Cong) and either convert them or 'neutralize' them, which usually meant killing them. This effort, too, is generally recognized as a positive contribution to the war effort, although as attitudes toward the war began to change, evaluation of the Phoenix Program also changed.

Neither the secret war in Laos nor the Phoenix Program was common knowledge, even in Washington. They were not subject to congressional control, and in fact were not even subject to much White House control. In this regard they were typical of the Vietnam War in general, which was characterized by a lack of co-ordination among the many bureaucracies and agencies involved in the design and implementation of our war policy. In addition to a lack of constraint by either Congress or the White House, the CIA was not even severely limited by other bureaucratic rivals. The uniformed services obviously had enough military assignments and the State Department was busy, too. So, in the absence of restraints, the CIA's covert action unit, the Directorate of Operations, performed its basic function extensively.

On the other hand, that part of the CIA responsible for analysis and estimates, the Directorate of Intelligence, faced some major competition. The Vietnam War was probably analysed and studied more extensively while it was being fought than any war in history. The principal problem was to determine how successful US forces were. This was a difficult question to answer because different policy-makers had different definitions of success, and all of them interpreted the war's events from their own perspective. The result was a contest to influence the next policy decision by providing the most persuasive analyses and estimates. For instance, throughout the war, the CIA's Directorate of Intelligence consistently argued that the military objectives were inconsistent with the more fundamental social and political objectives of the war. Conversely, the military repeatedly argued that the military effort had to succeed before the other goals could be achieved.

This clash of perspectives and priorities between the CIA and DIA analysts was usually resolved in favor of the DIA. One reason for this was the predominance of the military when it came to resolving major disputes over intelligence estimates. Often these disputes featured the CIA view against the combined views of the DIA plus the intelligence representatives of the Army, Navy and Air Force. Another restraint on the CIA's estimates was the lingering doubts many administration officials had about the quality of CIA analyses. Most of these people had suffered with Kennedy through the embarrassment of the Bay of Pigs, and they remained skeptical of CIA assessments. So, while the Directorate of Operations was able to conduct its covert actions with little control, the Directorate of Intelligence was controlled by the elements of bureaucratic rivalry and its past mistakes.

The bureaucratic rivalry over estimates also can be seen in the other major issue of intelligence reports during this time period. While the Vietnam War became the focal point of US foreign policy in the 1960s, the arms race with the Soviet Union was also a major concern. It was clear that the Soviets were building a considerable nuclear force, and the basic questions were how threatening it was and how threatening it was likely to be. This was a classic problem of intelligence analysis and estimation. It also became a classic confrontation between the CIA and the military intelligence analysts. It became difficult to reconcile the conflicting views on how many missiles the Soviets had and how quickly they were building them for the future. Each side had a clientele of policy influencers, and there is still controversy over which side was most accurate, but this illustrates the point that by the late 1960s, the US intelligence apparatus had become so fragmented that control was a difficult problem, except for the restraints of bureaucratic rivals. This problem was a major concern to Richard Nixon.

In January 1969, Nixon became President and initiated a new foreign policy agenda. His plan of *détente* included ending our involvement in Vietnam in a reasonably respectable way, establishing a new relationship with the Soviets that would recognize opportunities for co-operation while continuing to frustrate their expansionism, and preserving relations with friendly regimes and opposing unfriendly regimes in the Third World. He and his chief foreign policy collaborator, Henry Kissinger, realized that the success of *détente* depended on control of the foreign policy machinery, including intelligence. This also meant not sharing control with Congress. In attempting to control intelligence, Nixon and Kissinger were to be frustrated repeatedly, as three examples show.

Nixon and Kissinger were never satisfied with the reports they received from the US intelligence apparatus, especially the CIA's Directorate of Intelligence. Each of these men was confident of his grasp of world affairs. The result was that they regarded intelligence reports that contradicted their views as flawed and worthless for their purposes. Those infrequent analyses and estimates that supported their perspectives were accepted, but both men regarded the intelligence products they received as too ambiguous or based on questionable assumptions. In effect, since they could not control the content of intelligence reports, they controlled the analysis function by often ignoring the intelligence products. This attitude was applied to all parts of the US intelligence apparatus, including the CIA, the military, and the State Department.

They also were disenchanted with the covert action function, performed by the CIA. Both regarded covert action as legitimate and appropriate in the right circumstances. The problem, as they saw it, was that the CIA's Directorate of Operations simply was not very adept in doing it. This is indicated in their frustration in trying to overthrow the Allende regime in Chile. Allende was a Marxist who became Chile's president in 1970. Nixon and Kissinger regarded him as a threat to US interests in South America, and they assigned the task of overthrowing him to the Directorate of Operations. After studying the problem, the Director of Central Intelligence, Richard Helms, reported that the CIA did not have the resources to accomplish the goal. Nixon and Kissinger insisted that a plan be developed and implemented. The result was a haphazard effort by the CIA, and while Allende was eventually overthrown, it was primarily by the Chilean military with only minor involvement by the CIA. This episode reinforced Nixon's skepticism of the CIA, and he became more convinced that the CIA should be controlled by the White House.

The final episode in Nixon's confrontation with intelligence, and especially the CIA, was Watergate. During the 1972 presidential campaign, the White House authorized an intelligence-gathering mission against the Democratic Party headquarters. It recruited some ex-CIA officers to break into the headquarters and plant listening devices. The plan failed when they were caught by police. Nixon tried to frustrate the judicial process, initially by telling Richard Helms to inform the FBI, which had jurisdiction, that the operation was for national security purposes and therefore not subject to further investigation. After some deliberation, Helms refused to go along with the White House in covering up its involvement in the crime. This was the final straw for Nixon. In the first place, he blamed the arrest on poor CIA training and general CIA incompetence. Secondly, with Helm's refusal, he had a clear indication that the Agency was not responsive to his orders. He

40

dismissed Helms and replaced him with James Schlesinger, who proceeded to remove nearly ten per cent of the CIA's employees, many of them in the Directorate of Operations.

The Watergate episode was the beginning of the end of Richard Nixon's presidency. It also began a two-year process that culminated in the most extensive public review of intelligence and its control in the history of any nation. By 1975, intelligence had become the most important political topic in America, and the basic question became how to control it. Hearings in both the Senate and the House plus an investigation by the White House revealed a number of violations of law as well as activities inconsistent with American principles. The CIA was the principal target of these public investigations, and covert action was the key concern.

There are several reasons why the United States reviewed its intelligence apparatus so publicly and thoroughly in 1975. The first was the dissent that now characterized US politics and foreign policy. The Vietnam War and Watergate had revealed that government leaders were not always trustworthy. The result of this revelation was the recognition that disagreement with the political establishment, especially the White House, could be a virtue, both morally and politically. Second, Congress had begun to change, especially with the demise of the seniority system. Junior members now could gain prominence by operating independently. Third, Vietnam produced a new generation of political elites who were willing to question America's role in the world, in terms of both goals and means. The CIA became a convenient and appropriate focus for this new generation, and the result of their investigations was a heightened awareness of the need to control the excesses of intelligence and especially covert action by the CIA.

THE FOURTH DECADE

Jimmy Carter's presidency coincided with the beginning of the fourth decade of modern US intelligence. Carter represented the new generation's view of intelligence, and in his 1976 campaign he specifically promised to exercise greater control over covert action. The 1975 investigations had revealed to nearly everyone the need for more specific statutory limitations on intelligence, and Carter moved quickly to replace the ambiguous and perhaps outdated language of the National Security Act of 1947 with a new charter for the CIA.

The idea of a charter was welcome even to most intelligence professionals.[6] They felt that the accusations of 1975 had not been supported by the evidence, and that intelligence was a noble profession that had been unjustly tarnished. They argued that a charter would protect them from

41

a recurrence of the problems of 1975. However, they generally disagreed with Carter on the scope of the limitations.

Carter wanted a very detailed list of prohibitions on intelligence activities. The CIA wanted a charter that would contain guidelines for action rather than restrictions. The debate over the charter continued throughout Carter's presidency. The Agency was able to mobilize enough support in Congress to defeat Carter's plan, but the President was successful in achieving his goal of control by prohibition. With Executive Order 12036, the President was able to bypass Congress and have his way.[7] Unlike legislation, executive orders are temporary and do not require congressional approval. Carter's action allowed him to control intelligence but it also meant that his successor could change those controls.

Executive Order 12036 reduced US intelligence activities abroad. Intended primarily to restrict covert action, it also restricted espionage, counter-intelligence, and even analysis. The pendulum had swung from the (perceived) excesses of intelligence before 1975 to a disenchantment with the basic notion of secrecy in the Carter years.

The pendulum swung back the other way under Ronald Reagan. One of his first acts as President was Executive Order 12333, which gave the intelligence professionals the kind of language and guidelines they preferred.[8] Reagan also indicated his attitude toward intelligence by appointing William Casey as Director. Casey, who had served in the OSS during the Second World War, was an enthusiastic advocate of covert action. Casey also had a narrow view of sharing secrets with Congress, which he generally distrusted on intelligence matters.

Under Reagan and Casey, intelligence activities were strongly endorsed as a way of aiding friends and opposing foes. It became the prime means of achieving a basic goal of the Reagan Doctrine, the overthrow of anti-Western, pro-Communist regimes. Intelligence operations were conducted vigorously, in Afghanistan, Angola, and most notably Nicaragua. In some cases, Congress supported these covert actions, but in the case of Nicaragua, the administration's support of the Contras became a matter of intense disagreement, and intelligence control was a focal point of the debate.

Those who supported the Contras argued that the CIA was the logical instrument of US policy. Those who opposed the Reagan policy in Nicaragua sought to restrain the CIA. Congress passed a series of restrictions, known as the Boland Amendments, but they were dismissed by the administration as too ambiguous and possibly unconstitutional. Casey further infuriated Congress by concealing certain covert actions from it, despite a legal requirement to inform members of such operations.

Attempts by the Reagan administration to circumvent control of intelligence by Congress were most notable in the Iran–Contra affair. In this case the White House did not even use CIA professionals, but instead relied on an intelligence amateur, Oliver North, to design, implement and manage an extremely complex and risky covert action. This appears to be an ultimate in control since it involved few people and had a single individual in charge of all phases of the operation. However, because North lacked intelligence expertise, the plan was not controlled in the professional sense.

The fourth decade of intelligence reflected the vacillation that characterized US foreign policy in general. In the period immediately following Vietnam and the Watergate scandal, American foreign policy sought to manifest virtuous principles, focused on the idea of human rights that was central to the Carter administration. The result for intelligence was a general agreement between the executive and legislative branches that intelligence, especially covert action performed by the CIA, should be controlled. The assumption was that the CIA had been, in the words of Senator Frank Church, a 'rogue elephant'. Consequently, a charter that greatly restricted intelligence activities was viewed as necessary and appropriate, as was the creation of permanent House and Senate intelligence 'oversight' committees.

The subtle power of intelligence careerists prevented the formal enactment of the Carter version of an intelligence charter, but he was able to restrain the CIA, both through administrative controls (personnel changes, budget allocations, etc.) exercised by his Director, Stansfield Turner, and by withholding approval for intelligence activities proposed by the CIA. The two congressional committees also controlled intelligence through hearings, briefings by intelligence personnel, and its confirmation power.

This harmonious effort to restrict intelligence activities was reversed by the Reagan administration, but the question of intelligence control remained a prominent one. The 1980s were the background to a continuing struggle between the President and Congress for influence over foreign policy and intelligence. Covert action in particular was viewed by the administration as a principal way to implement the Reagan Doctrine. Many in Congress disagreed with this view, and they tried to restrain the power of the President to use covert action. The contest was vibrant and constant, with Congress legislating controls and the President circumventing the intent, if not the letter, of these laws.

Now that we have entered the fifth decade of our modern experience with intelligence, it is important to assess the contemporary policy environment, which is so different from the 1940s. Foreign policy now is characterized by a lack of consensus among the various people and institutions which seek to influence intelligence policy. Furthermore, the power to influence intelligence is fragmented rather than centralized in the presidency. The current and continuing debate over the directions and means of intelligence is part of this dynamic. While the intelligence functions of analysis, counter-intelligence and espionage are rarely debated intensely or for long periods of time, covert action has become a useful measure of the dynamics of US foreign policy, especially the rivalry between the President and Congress (and, indeed, between various factions within Congress, which has become fragmented with the demise of the seniority system). The prospects for a return to earlier forms of control (or the lack of it) are unlikely, and it appears that the fifth decade will reflect the continuing evolution toward a greater sharing of the control of intelligence within the American political system.

CONCLUSION

US intelligence has evolved through several distinct eras, reflecting different modes and degrees of control. In the long period before the Second World War, intelligence was controlled through neglect. With sporadic exceptions, intelligence simply was not a matter of concern because it had a minimal existence. Following the Second World War, intelligence became critical to the nation's foreign policy, and in its early days it was subject to almost no control. This was followed by the Kennedy era in which the White House sought greater controls to reduce the embarrassment of intelligence failures. The Vietnam War produced a form of mutual control by competing intelligence units of American government. The Nixon–Kissinger approach was similar to Kennedy's in trying to regulate intelligence from the White House. Jimmy Carter attempted to control intelligence by reducing its assignments and placing detailed and specific restrictions on its activities at the same time that Congress was asserting its role in intelligence control. Ronald Reagan freed intelligence from many of these restrictions and challenged congressional attempts to control intelligence. This variety of control perspectives and mechanisms suggests several basic elements of the US experience with intelligence.

First, when there is consensus in government on the importance of intelligence to national security, its control is not a major political issue, whether the agreement is that intelligence is not important (until the Second World War) or that it is critically important (the first decade after the war).

Second, the issue of control of intelligence is similar to other political issues in many respects. It is subject to the usual contest between President and Congress, with each trying to gain as much influence as possible. Until Vietnam and Watergate the President prevailed, possibly because of a consensus on its importance. However, since then the contest for influence between the two branches has not been harmonious, and the prospects for intelligence have been uncertain.

Third, most intelligence functions are shared among so many governmental units that each is restrained by the others, which amounts to a form of control. This pluralism of American government applies to intelligence just as much as it does to other structures. The exception to this control by bureaucratic rivalry is covert action.

Fourth, covert action has become the focal point of the issue of intelligence control. To many observers, covert action and intelligence are synonymous, and the other functions are ignored or disregarded. While all intelligence functions require secrecy for success, covert action is the most legally questionable function and it has the greatest potential for clashing with basic principles of American political culture.

Finally, it is important to note that America is unique in its public concern over intelligence control. Almost every nation has an intelligence apparatus, and control of that apparatus is common concern. The irony of the issue in America is that while intelligence is viewed by some as uncontrolled and intrusive in our private lives, the openness of the debate over intelligence control may be the ultimate control.

NOTES

1. Many histories of the OSS have been written. One of the most objective, concise and accurate is Anthony Cave Brown (ed.), *The Secret War Report of the OSS* (New York, NY, 1976).
2. Thomas F. Troy, *Donovan and the CIA: A History of the Establishment of the Central Intelligence Agency* (Frederick, MD, 1981).
3. *National Security Act of 1947*, Title I, Section 102, *Stat.* 495.
4. S. Con. Res. 2, 84th Cong., 1st sess., 14 Jan. 1955.
5. 50 USC 403.
6. Sen. Select Committee on Intelligence, *National Intelligence Reorganization and Reform Act of 1978: Hearings* on S. 2525. 95th Cong., 2nd sess., 1978.
7. President, Executive Order 12036, *United States Intelligence Activities. Federal Register* 43, No. 18 (26 Jan. 1978), 3675–92.
8. President, Executive Order 12333, *United States Intelligence Activities. Federal Register* 46, No. 235 (8 Dec. 1981), 55941–54.

3

Controlling the CIA: A Critique of Current Safeguards

LOCH K. JOHNSON

Is it possible to have an effective secret service in an open society? That is the central question in this essay. The weight of the evidence suggests a positive answer – indeed, democracies in this perilous world must have a secret service. The United States could well perish at the hands of foreign enemies without the protection afforded by the eyes and ears of the intelligence community. But an important caveat has to be added immediately: democracies must also maintain strong safeguards to shield their citizens against the possible misuse of secret power at home or abroad. Various forms of self-protection have been tried, with imperfect results. The purpose of this analysis is to offer a succinct critique of the chief safeguards established as a check against abuses by the CIA.

The National Security Council

At the center of the control system for intelligence lies the National Security Council (NSC), or, more specifically, its subcommittees dealing with intelligence. These subcommittees have had responsibility for national policy on covert action, collection-and-analysis, and, least likely to be discussed at this level, counter-intelligence. The most prominent NSC intelligence subcommittees over the years have been the 5412 Committee (Eisenhower), the Special Group (Kennedy), the 303 Committee (Johnson), the 40 Committee (Nixon), the Operations Advisory Group (OAG, Ford), the Special Coordination Committee and the Policy Review Committee (SCC and PRC, Carter), and the National Security Planning Group (NSPG, Reagan).[1]

The purpose of the NSC is to provide a forum for the co-ordination of foreign-policy information prepared for the President, and for the discussion

46

of policy alternatives.[2] The Council was not created to make decisions; that is the President's job. Since the Eisenhower administration, the NSC staff has been expected to follow through on policy initiatives to insure that the President's decisions are carried out properly.[3]

The importance of the NSC lies in its statutory membership: the President, the Vice President, the Secretary of State, and the Secretary of Defense. The panel's co-ordinating secretary and staff director is referred to as the President's 'assistant for national security affairs' or, simply, the NSC director. The significance of this position for American foreign affairs is self-evident in the person of two recent incumbents: Henry A. Kissinger (under Nixon and Ford) and Zbigniew Brzezinski (Carter), men who clearly carried the job description far beyond the original conception of 'neutral policy co-ordination'.[4] Usually attending NSC meetings, too, over the years have been the Director, Central Intelligence (during the Carter and Reagan years, the DCI also met frequently with the President outside the NSC framework);[5] the chairman of the Joint Chiefs of Staff; and, less frequently, the director of the Office of Management and Budget (OMB), the Attorney General (AG), and other officials – though rarely members of Congress (never during the Reagan years).[6]

Precisely who is invited to attend NSC meetings, and who is influential during these deliberations, varies from administration to administration, as well as according to the issues before the panel. During the early years of the Reagan administration, the White House counsel (and later Attorney General), Edwin Meese III, often reigned over the NSC advisory system, because of the confidence the President placed in the judgement of this long-time political ally – an odd situation, for Meese had virtually no foreign policy experience.[7] Neither did another political confidant (and Attorney General) who played a prominent role in key NSC meetings during the Kennedy years: Robert F. Kennedy, the President's brother.

Despite its shifting configuration of dominant personalities, the NSC has managed to provide reasonably close control over intelligence activities – with some striking exceptions like the Iran–Contra affair of 1985–86. Since 1975, few important intelligence operations have taken place without prior review by the NSC and its stamp of approval – including, for covert actions, the President's authorizing signature.[8] The secret sale of arms to Iran, however, was based initially on a more flimsy oral approval by the President to his assistant for national security affairs, Vice Admiral John M. Poindexter, with no paper-trail of accountability leading to the Oval Office.[9] More flimsy still, if President Reagan's public statements and Poindexter's congressional testimony are accurate, was the authority relied upon by the NSC staff and the CIA for the subsequent diversion of the arms-sale profits to the Contras:

47

Poindexter's approval alone, without the knowledge of the President.[10]

The CIA assassination plots appear to represent another conspicuous exception to the rule of NSC control (though at least these schemes – carried out in the 1960s – have the excuse of preceding the enactment of the strong oversight statutes passed in 1974 and 1980).[11] The evidence regarding the plots remains murky, but the NSC was evidently unaware that the CIA had hired the Mafia for attempts against Fidel Castro's life and had resorted to other questionable *modus operandi*, including the shipment of murder instruments in diplomatic pouches to the US embassy in the Congo (now Zaire) for use against Patrice Lamumba.[12] Indeed, the details of operations aside, not a single living NSC principal recalled – under oath before Congress – any approval whatsoever, oral or written, from the White House for the assassination attempts.[13]

The Church and Pike Committees uncovered other instances of 'rogue elephantry' by the CIA and other intelligence agencies, but the list was short – at least in recent years. In earlier times, NSC controls over the CIA were much more lax. During the tenure of Allen Dulles as DCI (1953–61), the CIA seems to have had broad freedom of discretion, with Dulles running the Agency (according to a *New York Times* assessment in 1966) 'largely as he saw fit'.[14] The Church and Pike Committees found in 1975 that only a small percentage of the total number of covert actions had been sent to the NSC for prior approval during the early days of the CIA.[15]

The débâcle at the Bay of Pigs, however, stimulated more serious attention to the question of control at the NSC level; and, passage of the Hughes–Ryan Act in December of 1974 represented a giant stride toward tighter NSC supervision of covert action by stipulating the requirements of presidential authorization (implicitly in written form, a practice honored by Presidents Ford and Carter) and timely reports to Congress.[16] Since Hughes–Ryan and the further reforms stemming from the ensuing Year of Intelligence (which drew Congress more deeply into supervision over the NSC-control system – watchdogs watching watchdogs), the NSC as a safeguard against intelligence abuse has grown in reliability. This control system is hardly foolproof; the disclosures regarding the roles of DCI William J. Casey (1981–87), Admiral John M. Poindexter, and Lieutenant-Colonel Oliver L. North in the Iran–Contra operations are reminder enough of that.

Other White House Overseers

The NSC is assisted by two other White House entities established to monitor CIA activities: the President's Foreign Intelligence Advisory Board (PFIAB, pronounced 'piff-e-ab'), set up during the Kennedy administration (based on the model of an earlier Eisenhower administration Board of

Consultants on Foreign Intelligence Activities) and temporarily dismantled during the Carter administration; and the Intelligence Oversight Board (IOB), established during the Ford administration in a response to the congressional intelligence investigations of 1975.[17] In its early days, PFIAB provided some useful guidance to the President and the CIA, especially on technical matters related to intelligence collection via reconnaissance airplane and satellite since among its members (from nine to 21 in most administrations all civilians) were high-tech specialists like Edwin H. Land of the Polaroid Corporation. More recently, the Board has been less influential, though occasionally it offers a useful observation, even if ignored, as in the case of its warnings about possible counter-intelligence weaknesses at the US embassy in Moscow – well before US Marine guards there were charged with security breaches in 1987.[18]

On the whole, both PFIAB and the three civilian members of the IOB – 'three blind mice', concluded one knowing observer[19] – have been feckless participants in the intelligence-control process. Some members of both boards have been distinguished Americans, including over the years Clark Clifford, Henry Kissinger, William Scanton, and Albert Gore, Sr. Often, however, members have owed their appointments more to their political ties with successful presidential candidates than to any intelligence expertise they might claim. The boards have become, in too many instances, sinecures offered for presidential campaign support.

One of the more peculiar 'qualifications' on the curriculum vitae of one recent IOB member was his former experience as an officer in the CIA, where among other things he was in charge of the controversial covert operation to fund the National Student Association.[20] This considerable blemish for a would-be intelligence overseer apparently faded into insignificance in the light of what endeared him most to his White House benefactors: political help – notably proven acumen at fund-raising – during the presidential election. While 'hands-on' expertise can be useful for meaningful oversight, greater sensitivity should be exercised in the selection of overseers. Professional, non-partisan experience would improve the credibility of the IOB and PFIAB watchdogs.

Both panels rarely meet, and they have accepted a narrow view of their responsibilities. Neither, for example, routinely examines covert-action proposals. The members of the boards receive occasional, perfunctory briefings from the CIA and seem content to be 'participants' in White House affairs, with all the prestige that offices in the Old Executive Office Building confer – even if the boards deal more with shadow than substance. Staff assistance has consisted usually of only one person for each board, competent aides for the most part but unable to achieve meaningful supervision with

49

limited resources and an agenda tied to board members with the short attention span of distracted dilettantes. As intelligence scholar Harry Howe Ransom has observed, PFIAB resembles nothing so much as a friendly group of 'visiting alumni'.[21]

This harsh indictment is directed less against particular individuals on the boards (some, like Clifford, have been eloquent advocates of intelligence oversight), than against oversight as a part-time hobby for itinerant dignitaries. Needless to say, PFIAB never uncovered any of the CIA abuses revealed by the Church Committee and the Rockefeller Commission in 1975. When PFIAB asked to examine a copy of the Huston spyplan, the FBI and the Attorney General refused (according to the Church Committee investigative findings) – just as it had been denied access to 40 Committee minutes, which it sought in order to study the extent of CIA covert action in Chile.[22]

The IOB was established after the Church Committee inquiry was well under way and the Rockefeller panel already disbanded;[23] but its record since then has been lackluster at best and most recently, during the Iran–Contra affair, flatly pathetic. The IOB staff attorney during the Reagan years, Bretton G. Sciaroni, had the distinction of failing his bar exams four times before finally passing, and had never written a single legal opinion until the White House asked him to appraise the relevance of the Boland Amendment (prohibiting military aid for the Contras) to the activities of the National Security Council. None, he opined, in spite of weighty legal precedents to the contrary.[24] Learning by chance of the Iran–Contra operation, the IOB attorney began an inquiry. According to his testimony before the Inouye–Hamilton investigative panels in 1987, this probe consisted of a five-minute conversation with Colonel North and a 30-minute meeting with the NSC legal counsel. Assured by these individuals that there was nothing to worry about, he ended his 'investigation'. The Intelligence Oversight Board: three blind mice and a lamb.

Arguably (and the Church and Pike Committees settled on this view),[25] PFIAB's role should remain one of strictly advising the President on the quality and effectiveness of intelligence, abandoning altogether any 'watchdog' pretensions – a task it would leave to the IOB. The series of abuses uncovered by the Church, Pike, Rockefeller, Tower, and Inouye–Hamilton panels suggest, however, that two watchdogs – real ones, not pottery imitations – could be useful. At a minimum, the staff and personnel of the IOB requires new talent and a fresh sense of seriousness, including individuals with proven investigative skills and an air of curiosity – not to say skepticism. The same is true of PFIAB – doubly so if its job is to include oversight; but, even if it restricts itself to questions of quality control, this panel needs a better mix of experts (especially on technical matters) and thoughtful generalists not afraid of offering candid criticism.

Executive Budget Reviews

The CIA undergoes further review, of a more serious nature than that offered by the PFIAB and the IOB, at the hands of various budget panels whose members poke into the interstices of Agency spending. As well as sending a representative to some NSC meetings, the OMB has an office for national security affairs which is dedicated to the examination of CIA and other intelligence agency budgets.[26] These reviews by the OMB are real, not make-believe, and the intelligence agencies are required to justify their spending plans before gimlet-eyed budget examiners. Some improper operations in the past have slipped easily through this net, however (among them, the CIA domestic spying program codenamed CHAOS), for the simple reason that great mischief can be accomplished at little expense and, if necessary, funds can be shifted over from legitimate programs.[27]

The CIA also has its own budget auditors, along with those attached to the DCI's Intelligence Community Staff – the 'IC Staff', a community-wide group of assistants assigned to the DCI to help him co-ordinate the sprawling intelligence empire.[28] Both sets of auditors scrutinize the books at CIA Headquarters and at Agency stations around the world to monitor the flow of cash. The raising of covert-action funds by Colonel North through private channels outside the government – wealthy American citizens and foreign heads of state – held an added attraction beyond circumventing the Congress; here was a way to avoid the green eyeshades within the executive branch as well.

Internal CIA Overseers

The Agency itself conducts continuous inside inquiries over and above its budget audits. The Directorate of Administration sends inspectors (the dreaded 'Admin') to every station abroad and every office at home, to check on the proper functioning of the Agency.[29] The Counter-intelligence Staff and the Office of Security also have their own investigators who examine security problems and constantly test the CIA's defenses against hostile penetrations.[30] The Office of Legal Counsel churns out documents for the Agency on the propriety of planned operations.[31] The Legislative Liaison Staff reminds Agency personnel of various legislative strictures, as well as the personal views of leading legislators and staff on proposed intelligence operations.[32] The CIA Inspector General (IG) has an open door to hear from employees about alleged wrongdoing in their bureaus, and the 1980 Intelligence Accountability Act explicitly requires the CIA to report to the Congress 'any illegal intelligence activity'.[33]

51

The Agency, in short, has several in-house safeguards against abuse. It is sobering, however, to recall that Operation CHAOS was run out of the CIA's Office of Security itself and that the CIA's attorneys, budget examiners, and inspectors general apparently never knew about the Iran–Contra affair. Further, neither at the time of their occurrence, nor even very soon after, did these in-house entities know about the CIA wrongdoings disclosed by the Church Committee. Agency directors and other senior officials have simply by-passed these multiple checks when they wished – though always at the risk of another important internal bureaucratic check against malfeasance: the leak, like the one to *Times* reporter Seymour Hersh on CHAOS that led to the intelligence investigations of 1975.

The Station

The CIA has controls in the field, too, beyond periodic inspections by teams sent out from the Counter-intelligence Staff, the IG, and other Headquarters offices. The Agency's chief organizational entity in the field, the station (a few small countries have 'bases' and a few large ones have both), is supervised by the chief of station (COS). He or she is responsible for insuring that Headquarters directives are properly interpreted and carried out; that CIA officers assigned to the station ('case officers') and their local agents (often called 'assets', if they are paid) perform their duties within the bounds of legislative and presidential guidelines; and that a reasonably harmonious relationship is maintained with the overall chief of the American mission within the country, the US ambassador.[34]

The most difficult of these chores evidently is to control the assets and, sometimes, the case officers themselves.[35] Here is the business end of the CIA, the men and women who secretly plant the newspaper stories, pass the bribes, steal the government documents, smuggle the guns and ammunition, and, if necessary, pull the trigger. The more unsavory the deed, the more unsavory the asset the CIA might have to recruit for its execution. One Agency asset, codenamed WI/ROGUE, a potential recruit for the death-plot against Patrice Lamumba of the Congo, was described by his case officer as:

> aware of the precepts of right and wrong, but if he is given an assignment which may be morally wrong in the eyes of the world, but necessary because his case officer ordered him to carry it out, then it is right, and he will dutifully undertake appropriate action for its execution without pangs of conscience. In a word, he can rationalize all actions.[36]

Such individuals do not worry excessively about oversight legislation or executive orders.

52

Nor are many guerrilla 'freedom fighters' known for their devotion to the American Constitution. The Contras were intent on overthrowing the Sandinistas in Nicaragua by practically any means available – even when, in 1984, a majority of the Congress formally voted (in an early version of the Boland Amendment) to limit the CIA-funded operations of the rebels to the interdiction of weapons bound for left-wing insurgents in El Salvador supported by the Sandinistas. Rebels by definition are zealots, uneasily controlled and with their own agenda, their own deeply held beliefs, cultures, mores and allegiances – none of which may be necessarily in tune with instructions from their American overseers.

Case officers, too, have sometimes been difficult for Headquarters and the COS to contain. These individuals are not thugs, but rather well-educated individuals with long exposure to American cultural norms and the rule of law; yet, some have displayed a remarkable insensitivity to legal constraints. In 1984, a CIA case officer wrote and distributed an 'assassination manual' in Nicaragua; and, during the Kennedy years, an Agency case officer initiated ties with the underworld in the Castro murder schemes – by all accounts without the knowledge of the White House, the DCI, or other senior CIA officials.[37]

Nor have the station chiefs themselves been immune from lawlessness. During the Iran–Contra affair, for instance, the COS in Costa Rica facilitated air-drops of military supplies to the Nicaraguan rebels on the southern front, in clear defiance of the Boland Amendment.[38] Generally, the COS has been an effective overseer and most covert actions have been properly supervised. The record, though, reveals several examples of loose or non-existent supervision at the field level – probably the most consistently weak link in the hierarchy of controls.[39]

The Ambassador

The American 'chief of mission' – the US ambassador – is also expected to keep tabs on the COS and his operations within a country, providing yet another check upon the propriety of CIA activities abroad.[40] Since little has been published on the relationship between the ambassador and the COS, this safeguard warrants a more extensive examination here.

Personal interviews and public statements on the subject indicate that, by and large, the relationship has been smooth, with the COS accepting leadership and control from the ambassador.[41] Sometimes, though, the teamwork breaks down – usually when the ambassador fails to establish his or her authority forcefully, or when the COS has limited confidence in the experience and discretion of the ambassador (as when some misguided political appointees view the job of ambassador more as a social plum than a serious responsibility for protecting American interests abroad). On occasion, a strong-willed COS with backing from Headquarters will ignore ambassadorial instructions which the Agency finds disagreeable. The CIA, for example, continued to back Chinese nationalists in Burma in 1954, despite objections from the US ambassador (who eventually resigned in protest); supported Laotian Premier Phoumi Nosavan in 1960 over the instructions of the ambassador; and reportedly carried out a sensitive operation in Malaysia in 1960, which backfired, without bothering to clear the project with the ambassador.[42] When James Angleton served as CIA Chief of Counterintelligence, he conducted various aggressive operations around the world without informing ambassadors – or, often, even station chiefs.[43]

'The State Department through U.S. embassies and consulates offers the only external check upon CIA's overseas activities', stated the Church Committee report on State–CIA relations abroad. Yet, the Committee discovered, this check was far from satisfactory: 'uneven' was the best the investigators could say.[44]

The recent history of efforts to define the relationship between the ambassador and the COS begins on 29 May 1961 with a letter of that date from President John F. Kennedy addressed to each chief of mission. The President told his emissaries that he expected them 'to oversee and coordinate *all* activities of the United States Government' in their respective countries of assignment.[45] Kennedy's letter remained in effect until superseded by a similar one from President Richard M. Nixon on 9 December 1970. 'As Chief of the United States Diplomatic Mission,' Nixon's letter said,

> you have full responsibility to direct and coordinate the activities and operations of *all* of its elements. You will exercise this mandate not only by providing policy leadership and guidance, but also by assuring positive program direction to the end that *all* United States activities in [the host country] are relevant to current realities, are efficiently and economically administered, and are effectively interrelated so that they will make a maximum contribution to the United States interests in that country as well as to our regional and international objectives.[46]

Supplementing this message was a classified State Department–CIA communiqué further explaining the President's intent (State Department Circular Airgram 6693 of December 1970). In essence, the communiqué told the ambassador that any access he might have to information on intelligence sources and methods would be subject to the approval of the COS; if an argument over access arose, the disagreement would be reported to the Secretary of State and the Director of Central Intelligence for arbitration. According to the Church Committee, this communiqué 'may well . . . have had the effect of inhibiting ambassadors in seeking to inform themselves fully in this area'.[47]

The seemingly comprehensive authority given to the ambassador in the Kennedy–Nixon letters (diluted to a degree by the State Department–CIA communiqué) was set in legislative concrete four years later (1974) with Public Law 93–475.[48] According to this statute (emphasis added):

(1) the United States Ambassador of a foreign country shall have full responsibility for the direction, coordination, and supervision of *all* United States Government officers and employees in that country *except* for personnel under the command of a United States area military commander;

(2) the Ambassador shall keep himself fully and currently informed with respect to *all* activities and operations of the United States Government within that country, and shall insure that all government officers and employees in that country, except for personnel under the command of a United States area military commander, comply fully with his directives; and

(3) any department or agency having officers or employees in a country shall keep the United States Ambassador to that country *fully* and currently informed with respect to *all* activities and operations of its officers and employees in that country, and shall insure that *all* of its officers and employees, except for personnel under the command of a United States area military commander, comply fully with all applicable directives of the Ambassador.

A comparison of this law with the language of the Nixon letter shows that P.L. 93–475 went beyond even his considerable effort to strengthen the arm of the ambassador in the field; yet, neither the White House, the State Department, nor the CIA issued directives to implement this statute. The law, devoid of implementing regulations, remained (in the words of one ambassador testifying before the Church Committee) 'suspended.'[49]

It became clear through the testimony of its officials before the Church Committee that the CIA, in the words of the Committee Report, 'opposes giving the Ambassador the unrestricted access to communications and other operational information that the law would appear to authorize'.[50] A CIA deputy director for operations (DDO) told the Committee that, for example, 'individual agent recruitments are not cleared with either the ambassadors or the Secretary of State'.[51]

The CIA argues that the COS cannot freely provide the ambassador with all intelligence-related information, since the National Security Act of 1947 charges the DCI with responsibility 'for protecting intelligence sources and methods from unauthorized disclosure'.[52] This seems to be a gross over-reaction on behalf of the CIA, for seldom have American ambassadors engaged in 'micro-management' to the degree where they felt they had to know the specifics of sources and methods.[53] In one of the few documented cases where this occurred (in Portugal;[54] see below), the ambassador probably had good reason – in a country in the midst of revolution – to know the details of what the CIA was doing. While the debate over the meaning of 'unauthorized' remains lively today, the Church Committee concluded unequivocally in 1976 that, in its opinion, P.L. 93–475 'resolves any doubts as to whether disclosure to the Ambassador is authorized'.[55] Moreover, added the Committee, 'for CIA operations conducted within his country of assignment, the Ambassador should be a good judge of the risks of such operations, and of their possible usefulness to the U.S'.[56]

Three years after the adoption of Public Law 93–475 and seven years after the Nixon letter, a new President, Jimmy Carter, sent out to America's embassies a now familiar refrain giving US ambassadors around the world authority to supervise '*all* United States Government officers and employees in their countries' (emphasis added). Carter's letter, dated 25 October 1977, stated to each chief of mission: '[You] have the authority to review message traffic to and from *all* personnel under your jurisdiction' (emphasis added).[57]

The Carter initiative immediately triggered the release of a series of State Department and CIA explanatory directives to the field (just as Nixon's letter had done in 1969).[58] According to one correspondent, President Carter's letter, and the ensuing directives from the executive branch, reflected 'widely divergent interpretations' as to what the proper relationship ought to be between the chief of mission and the chief of station.[59]

The directives following the President's letter included:

1. A joint communiqué from Secretary of State Cyrus Vance and DCI Stansfield Turner to each ambassador and COS.[60] (This document is referred to privately in the intelligence services as the State Department–CIA 'treaty' on the role of the ambassador.)
2. A cable from Admiral Turner to all CIA stations, supplemental to the Vance–Turner 'treaty'.[61]
3. Two more CIA cables to all stations, supplemental to the Turner cable.[62]

Travelling from Carter's letter to the last two directives resembles a journey through a cave. First, with the President's letter, the ambassador stands at the entrance, which is wide and ample and filled with light. Then, with successive messages the passage narrows, the space for maneuvering grows cramped and the light turns to gray, becoming darker and more uncertain. Finally, the ambassador finds his pathway blocked altogether. While President Carter stated that 'all' in-country US government employees are under the ambassador's supervision, the Vance–Turner communiqué began the process of 'amplifying' or, more accurately, narrowing the meaning of the President's message. The ambassador would be notified in advance by the COS before certain – but not all – CIA activities.

The difference between the unclassified letter from President Carter and the increasingly restrictive directives from the CIA led to controversy. Learning about these differences through intelligence sources, an experienced *New York Times* correspondent concluded that the CIA apparently sought to 'undercut' the Vance–Turner treaty.[63] According to one Department of State source quoted by this correspondent, the CIA directives following in the wake of the Carter letter 'in effect . . . stated that the President's letter and the State Department guidelines do not apply to the CIA'.[64] In truth, claimed the source, ambassadors had greater leeway to monitor CIA clandestine operations before the Carter pronouncement.[65] A CIA officer concurred, suggesting that the kind of information the US ambassador to Portugal had reportedly been able to obtain from his COS in 1975 (regarding CIA assets in the Portuguese government) would no longer be forthcoming; with the new directives, the COS would no longer feel obliged to name his assets for an ambassador.[66] The correspondent concluded, with obvious understatement: '. . . several ambassadors have indicated unhappiness with the new arrangement'.[67]

Some observers suggest that, ultimately, the ambassador–COS relationship is reduced to personality.[68] If the ambassador is tough-minded, aggressive and interested in intelligence matters, he or she will receive most or all of what is requested from the COS – even when their views are at variance. While the COS may complain about 'micro-management' by the ambassador (as he did in the Portuguese case mentioned above), he will usually co-operate. If the ambassador would just as soon remain blindly ignorant (perhaps to avoid blame and embarrassment if an operation is exposed) or is more interested in the social and cultural activities of the United States Information Agency (USIA), he or she will receive minimal information from the COS.

In hearings before the Subcommittee on Oversight of the House Permanent Select Committee on Intelligence, former Ambassador William Porter agreed with Chairman Les Aspin's (D, Wisconsin) suggestion that a successful chief of mission who wants to know what the CIA is doing must be 'strong [so] he can impose himself on the system'.[69] Former Ambassador L.

Dean Brown pointed to another ingredient for success: an ambassador should possess 'a very suspicious mind'.[70] Despite the continuing tensions between the two offices, Ambassador Porter arrived at an optimistic conclusion. With P.L. 93–475, he testified, the ambassador 'has got the wherewithal today if he wants to use it'.[71]

While even the most perfectly written presidential directives would be of little use in the face of a passive or uninterested ambassador, those chiefs of mission who are energetic and dedicated to the full exercise of their duties none the less face an uphill struggle – Ambassador Porter's optimism to the contrary notwithstanding. The CIA has clearly sought in the past to circumscribe the spirit of White House directives designed to strengthen the hand of the ambassador.[72] By invoking its obligation to protect – in that slippery phrase – 'unauthorized disclosures' and through secret internal directives that skirt the ambassador, the CIA has been known to conduct its own foreign policy outside the vision of the nominal chief of mission. Testimony by Colonel North during the Inouye–Hamilton hearings gave the impression that DCI Casey hoped to achieve sufficient private funding for covert action that auditors, legislators, ambassadors, and other official nuisances could be by-passed altogether.[73]

Pressure Groups and Parties

One of the more venerable propositions in the literature of political science is that government is strongly influenced by a tripartite alliance of executive agencies, outside interest groups, and congressional committees – the so-called 'iron triangles' or 'subgovernments' of textbook fame.[74] Much evidence suggests that these three organizations develop a symbiotic relationship to enhance their respective goals: swelling budgets for the bureaucrats, federal largess for the interest groups, and re-election for the legislators. When the relationship operates in this mutually beneficial way, interest groups are unlikely to provide a check on agencies; they have been bought off – or, more often, the interest group has colonized or 'co-opted' the agency.[75]

In the myriad interest groups that exist in America's pluralist democracy (that is what 'pluralism' means), often competing groups become dissatisfied with the response of an agency to their demands and they make their dissatisfactions known to the public. In this public debate – or, less grandly, squabbling – over an issue and an agency's handling of it, a further check is placed on the bureaucracy; an alerted public and its representatives have an opportunity to take corrective measures in an effort to mollify the group conflict. This tension, and the useful publicity it engenders, can be seen dramatically in the periodic clashes of corporate and environmental groups over such policies as clear-cutting and strip-mining.

Such group dynamics are largely irrelevant, however, as a democratic control over intelligence policy. Few outside groups exist in this policy domain, and those that do are weak.[76] Moreover, most aspects of intelligence policy have been too concealed (and some have been genuinely too sensitive) to serve as subjects of public debate. This condition has changed somewhat since 1975, when the legislative investigations spawned both a pro-CIA advocacy group of retired intelligence officers (the Association of Former Intelligence Officers) and a civil-liberties group devoted to the prevention of further intelligence abuses (the Center for National Security Studies, CNSS). Other centers of intelligence inquiry and advocacy have cropped up, too, including the right-wing American Security Council (ASC), with Angleton among its founding officers, and the more scholarly, if still rightward-leaning, National Intelligence Study Center (NISC), with the former CIA deputy director for intelligence, now Professor, Ray S. Cline, among its founders, and the National Strategy Information Center – all located in Washington, DC.[77]

These groups provide expert testimony at congressional hearings and for the media, send out mailings, publish treatises on intelligence, and the like.[78] The CNSS, for instance, prodded the newly formed House committee on intelligence in 1978 to undertake extensive hearings on the relationship between the CIA and US domestic organizations.[79] But the groups have little influence over the shaping of intelligence policy – at least compared with the clout wielded over portions of the government by such groups as the AFL-CIO, the American Medical Association, and other giants in the constellation of Washington lobbyists.[80]

The political party stands as another entity in the American political system that sometimes attempts to set boundaries for the making of intelligence policy. Now and then, the parties have become involved in debates over intelligence controversies. Partisan wrangling over missile or bomber gaps (for which GOP attacked the Kennedy administration),[81] over scandals like the CIA involvement – however peripheral – in Watergate[82] and the Iran–Contra affair,[83] over unsuccessful *coups*[84] and battlefield reversals,[85] and other intelligence mishaps[86] (not to mention incidents of illegal domestic spying[87]), often carry at least an implicit allegation that the party in charge of the White House failed to make correct use of the intelligence agencies. The threat is always present that misuse of intelligence might be discovered and decried for partisan advantage by the 'loyal opposition'.

With the aggressive and more open resort to covert action by the Reagan administration (reportedly the backbone of the so-called 'Reagan Doctrine'),[88] partisan fissures over intelligence have become more conspicuous than ever, with clear-cut party votes occurring with some regularity on the congressional intelligence committees.[89] The Boland Amendment votes from 1984 to 1986 are prominent examples.[90] Though a source of acute discomfort for those who believe in 'bipartisan foreign policy' (a beguiling slogan with an often hidden agenda: defer to the President), the new tension between the two parties over intelligence policy may have had the salutary effect of encouraging closer legislative scrutiny over selected CIA operations.

The Media

In the modern history of American intelligence, the media has consistently provided the public with the most information on the abuse of power by the CIA.[91] The National Student Association scandal,[92] the CIA connection to Watergate (which proved to be slight),[93] Operation CHAOS,[94] even early reports (discounted) on assassination plots,[95] came to the attention of US citizens initially through the print media. Whether from leaks or from skillful investigative reporting (often both), the public has benefited from a free press able to warn Americans of transgressions and to prod the government into corrective measures.

Dependence on the media, though, is a less than fully reliable means to control the intelligence establishment. Correspondents have limited access to this secret world and must await, for the most part, tips from insiders (with all the biases they may carry). The media has been indispensable as a safeguard, but its reporters have hardly been a timely and infallible deterrent to abuse – or even a reliable chronicler of most abuses. The intelligence community is surrounded by too impenetrable a wall of secrecy for outsiders in the press corps to break through at will (a wall designed appropriately to keep the KGB and other US adversaries away from sensitive American secrets). Only the Congress among 'outsiders' has the formal powers (foremost among them the subpoena, budget review, and a capacity to focus public attention during controversial hearings) to wedge through this barrier – if its members have the motivation to use that power. Journalist Charles Peters sensibly recommends that the press concentrate more on stimulating the Congress to fulfill this obligation:

> What journalists could do is make the public aware of how little attention Congress devotes to what is called 'oversight,' i.e., finding out what the programs it has authorized are actually doing. If the press would publicize the nonperformance of this function, it is at least possible that the public would begin to reward the Congressmen who perform it consistently and punish those who ignore it by not reelecting them.[96]

The Congress

Potentially, Congress should stand high on the list of checks guarding against intelligence abuses. Indeed oversight, in the view of many, ought to be the primary focus of the Congress across the policy board.[97] Legislators, though, largely ignored their responsibilities for intelligence oversight until recently. From 1947 until 1975 the CIA received precious little attention from those legislative subcommittees supposedly responsible for intelligence oversight – probably less than 24 hours each year, and this time spent mainly in passively listening to briefings that carefully avoided issues of controversy.[98]

With the establishment of the two permanent Intelligence Committees in 1976–77, legislative oversight took a new vigor. Of particular importance has been the independent check on CIA spending provided by budget specialists on these two committees,[99] augmented by the intelligence subcommittees of the two appropriations committees.[100] Each of these units goes through the CIA annual budget line-by-line and supplements this audit with a series of closed hearings on whatever money requests the members decide to probe further, including special releases from the Contingency Reserve Fund outside the normal appropriations cycle.

Since 1976, the budget of the CIA (and other intelligence agencies) has risen steadily – indeed, by a factor of three according to one report.[101] This might lead some to conclude that the Intelligence Committees have actually failed to provide much of a check. Interviews with members and staff (current and former) of the committees suggest, however, that the funding increases have been merited by the need to improve the intelligence-collection capabilities of the United States and have been the subject of thorough examination by the legislative panels (though a handful of legislators worry that too much money is being spent on satellites and other hardware at the expense of HUMINT). The latest Boland Amendment, designed to shut off paramilitary funding for the Contras,[102] illustrates that the power of the purse will be used by the Congress against the CIA if legislators strongly oppose an intelligence activity (though forcing the executive to honor the legal prohibitions is another matter – the crux of the Iran–Contra hearings in 1987).[103]

Still, knowledgeable observers continue to question the steadiness and staying power of legislative oversight, and some have discounted its effectiveness all together – even before the Iran–Contra affair. For one senior intelligence official, oversight had descended by 1984 to a level of 'anarchy'.[104] Representative George E. Brown, Jr. (D, California) concluded baldly in October of 1985 that the new oversight 'is not working'.[105] A top staffer attached to the Center for National Security called the state of oversight in 1985 'absymal'.[106] A former Senate Intelligence Committee staffer noted, also in 1985, that at best oversight had been 'uneven'.[107]

Former DCI Stansfield Turner predicted – *before* the Iran–Contra scandal came to light – the death of the new oversight process unless, on the one hand, President Reagan discarded his 'indifference about whether his use of the CIA is supported by Congress' and, on the other hand, Congress 'takes the bit in its teeth and exercises the latent authority it has'.[108] Turner was especially critical of the relatively mild legislative reaction to the Nicaraguan assassination manual; the CIA's mining of harbors in Nicaragua (again accompanied by more sound than fury from Capitol Hill); CIA association with uncontrollable factions in Lebanon in 1984; and, the use of NSC staffer North to guide the Contras, despite the Boland Amendment prohibition to halt the support, 'directly or indirectly, [of] military or paramilitary operations in Nicaragua . . .'[109] Then, when the full force of the Iran–Contra scandal struck the nation in December of 1986, CIA-congressional relations reeled further backwards. The oversight process was now, according to the vice chairman of the Senate Intelligence Committee, 'fractured'.[110]

Yet, if a comparison is made with oversight in the pre-1975 period, when the congressional watchdogs were fast asleep and the CIA was content to let them lie, one would have to acknowledge the presence of greater watchfulness now – even counting the failure to prevent the unfortunate excesses of some NSC staffers and their CIA cohorts during the Iran–Contra episode.[111] One must avoid drawing general conclusions from exceptional, even if important, cases like this scandal. Though certainly imperfect, as revealed vividly during the televised hearings in 1987 of the Inouye–Hamilton Committee, the experiment in genuine oversight for intelligence policy only began, after all, in 1976. It seems premature to write this experiment off as a total failure already – especially when the record suggests many useful oversight results during this period, including (among several other examples) the Senate Intelligence Committee's thoughtful critique of CIA estimates on Soviet oil production; the House Intelligence Committee's demands (though not always consistent) for the details – sources and methods aside – of covert-action plans in order to evaluate them properly; and, within the CIA itself, the so-called 'A-team–B-team' critique of a key intelligence estimate on the Soviet Union – a review which, though biased toward an extremely bleak 'worst-case' view, at least had the merit of involving outside experts in the process.[112]

Another comparison is relevant: the state of intelligence oversight in other democracies. Though a systematic comparative analysis lies beyond the scope of this study, clearly most allied intelligence services have remained free of the restraints that have evolved within the United States. In Great Britain, the

Official Secrets Act sharply limits reliable monitoring of British intelligence by the press or even Parliament.[113] The French approach is equally slack from the viewpoint of maintaining safeguards against potential intelligence abuses.[114] In 1985, for example, a French intelligence officer sank the vessel *Rainbow Warrior* (an anti-nuclear protest ship belonging to a group called Greenpeace) in the harbor of Auckland, New Zealand, killing a person aboard. The French government freed the intelligence officer, choosing to arrest instead five individuals for leaking information about the incident to the press.[115] Under the present system of controls in the United States, one suspects that such a mission would never have been approved in the first place and, if approved and discovered, never so easily dismissed. As one CIA official has put it (with some dismay), 'We are the most carefully scrutinized intelligence agency in the world'.[116] Only Canada's new system of intelligence oversight, guided by a Security Intelligence Review Committee (SIRC), seems to keep comparably close tabs on its intelligence establishment.[117] The SIRC even has the authority, which it has exercised, to conduct surprise, random program-audits ('We want to look at files X, Y, and Z').

The meaningful practice of legislative oversight in the United States will probably have to be sustained by a few dedicated members on the two congressional intelligence committees. In the first decade of the new oversight (1976–86), several legislators on the Intelligence Committees provided the necessary leadership and integrity for oversight to work, including (among others) Les Aspin (D, Wisconsin), Wyche Fowler (D, Georgia), Lee Hamilton (D, Indiana), and Kenneth Robinson (R, Virginia), in the House (Fowler has since moved to the Senate), and William S. Cohen (R, Maine), David Durenberger (R, Minnesota), George J. Mitchell (D, Maine) and Daniel Patrick Moynihan (D, New York), in the Senate.[118] One must hope that others will step forward to assume this responsibility in the future. The special rotation system adopted by the Congress for the intelligence committees, whereby no member serves for longer than eight years on these panels, means a constant replenishment of personnel (at least above the staff level).[119] This ought to help avoid the co-optation that often occurs when committee members serve too long and grow too close to bureaucrats – though the unfortunate trade-off is the loss of corporate memory among the members.

It will take another decade or so to appraise how well this experiment in oversight is working. In its first decade, the intelligence partnership between Congress and the executive branch has been stormy – especially during the Iran–Contra affair – but far more healthy for democracy than the earlier ostrich-like posture of Congress with its head in the sand. Former DCI

63

William Colby has observed (with reference to covert action) that, in this new era, intelligence mistakes 'will be American mistakes. They will not be CIA mistakes, but mistakes of the administration *and* the Congress in power'.[120] While this proved untrue for the Iran–Contra operation, intelligence policy for the most part did become more of a partnership between the branches than ever before. This, one presumes, is how democracy in the United States is meant to work – not through reliance on the executive branch alone to determine the destiny of the nation.

The Courts

The role of the courts as intelligence overseers has been significant, but within a limited range. Occasionally the courts will adjudicate espionage charges or suits involving the public disclosure of classified information.[121] The most celebrated instance of the latter is the 'Pentagon Papers' case, in which the Supreme Court stood against prior restraint on the grounds that disclosure – in this instance at least – would not lead (in the words of Mr Justice Stewart) to 'direct, immediate, and irreparable damage to the Nation or its people'.[122]

The courts have also been involved in controversial cases based on contractual secrecy, in which the intelligence agencies have sought to prevent former employees from writing about intelligence policy without submitting their manuscripts to a CIA pre-publication review board.[123] The CIA has been successful through court action in preventing former employees from publishing without submitting first to this censorship process.[124] Its censors, though, have been arbitrary in their decisions about what materials must be cleared; former officers critical of the CIA have been hounded, while favoured individuals – including some retired senior officials who write newspaper columns without any clearance – are left alone.[125] In a landmark case, *Knopf v. Colby* (1975),[126] the Agency brought suit against one of its former senior administrators (Victor Marchetti) who had gone through the Agency's clearance process for his book-manuscript, but was unwilling to accept the extensive excisions requested by the CIA. The book (*The CIA and the Cult of Intelligence*, co-authored by John D. Marks) was eventually published, but with conspicuous gaps throughout – fascinating to the curious reader and no doubt a boon to sales – where the CIA censors had used their scissors.[127]

In one important case where the CIA was unaware of a forthcoming publication by a former employee (intelligence analyst Frank Snepp), the Agency moved after publication to block payment of royalties to the author.[128] The CIA was successful before the Supreme Court in establishing this precedent and in confirming its rights to pre-publication review [*U.S. v.*

Snepp, (1980)].[129] While the intelligence agencies seem to have a legitimate need to prevent former employees (like CIA defector Philip Agee) from revealing sensitive sources and methods, the method of pre-publication review currently in place has been widely criticized. Snepp persuasively argues: 'Congress should establish an independent review board to keep the C.I.A. and other intelligence agencies from overcensoring; clarify how, and under what circumstances, a censored author can challenge excisions in court; and set a time limit on post-employment censorship . . .'.[130]

Beyond these occasional suits, the systematic use of the court system for intelligence oversight is limited chiefly to its issuance of warrants for electronic surveillance by the intelligence agencies, as a result of the 1978 Electronic Surveillance Act.[131] The special court of district judges established for this purpose rarely refuses warrants;[132] but interviews with officials in Congress and within the intelligence agencies indicate that the court does actually serve as a serious check against poorly justified wiretaps by the federal government.[133]

Conscience and Opinion

The most important checks on the abuse of power in a democracy are, ultimately, the attitudes held by people in office and across the land. The Huston Plan, Operation CHAOS, covert actions in Chile and Cuba, and other controversial intelligence operations occurred because the climate of opinion in the country seemed to allow the use of extreme measures – even assassination and the violation of domestic law – to combat Communist-Marxist rivals. Bureaucrats are influenced by the example of their leaders in the executive branch, from agency directors to the President.[134] These leaders in turn must take into account the views of Congress and public opinion. If such views are unformulated or permissive, the executive acts accordingly and proceeds as it wishes; if Congress and the public set limits, the chances increase that limits will be honored, especially if it is clear that Congress intends to monitor the executive branch with serious intent. To tame the bureaucracy, then, the president, the Congress, and the public are obliged to make the boundaries of probity clear, and then to ride the fences. This clarity, as a former secretary of state has noted, ought to be made 'by insistence, not necessarily by legislation'.[135]

Prevailing opinion seems to oppose assassination as an instrument of American foreign policy (executive orders explicitly prohibit it – though, as the F-111 bombing of the home of the Libyan leader, Colonel Muammar el-Qaddafi, in 1986 demonstrates, at least one administration has been prepared to overlook such legal niceties).[136] It also seems to oppose US involvement in large-scale paramilitary operations of the magnitude conducted in Indochina during the Kennedy–Johnson years, as well as, it goes without saying, spying on American citizens.[137] The CIA, as a result, has curtailed such activities and is unlikely to acquire authority to resume them unless public opinion changes dramatically. The exception has been the CIA covert action in Afghanistan, which spiraled steadily toward the 'large-scale' category during the Reagan years, enjoyed widespread support in the Congress, and most likely contributed to the Soviet decision in 1988 to withdraw its army from this civil war.[138]

Changes in public opinion toward a broader support for major covert actions may occur if, for example, the Soviet Union attempted more direct, aggressive intervention in parts of the world considered vital to American interests, or if terrorism became a greater immediate problem within the United States. Former Secretary of State Dean Rusk has commented on the relationship between threat and the legal protections afforded American citizens against the intelligence agencies: 'If a president received what he thought was reliable information that a suitcase nuclear bomb had been hidden away in an American city, our constitutional provisions with respect to search and seizure, and wiretapping, and all of our freedoms would go out the window. Both authorities and citizens would turn that city upside down trying to locate such a device.'[139]

Following America's unhappy experience with Operation CHAOS and other transgressions, however, one would hope that a return to extreme intelligence measures would be preceded by debate (behind closed doors if necessary), meaningful prior consultation with Congress, the issuance of the appropriate written orders and warrants, and then careful monitoring to help assure fealty to the new boundaries – unless, as in the case of, say, a nuclear-terrorism threat, the President had no time whatsoever to consult and follow the letter of every procedure. Everyone recognizes, in the popular law-school phrase, that the Constitution is not a suicide pact. But for 99 per cent of the cases, prior debate, consultation, established procedures, and close monitoring can be honored. Indeed this is the democratic way. It will work, though, only if the press, the Congress, and the people refuse to allow – even when society is under pressure – a return to the pre-1975 era of permissiveness when intelligence policy lay in the hands of a few figures hidden in the shadows of government.

The Church Committee documented the relationship between the attitudes of intelligence officers toward their mission and the attitudes prevalent in the wider society.[140] FBI official William C. Sullivan told the Committee how contemporary intelligence officials had grown up 'topsy-turvy' during the Second World War, when sensitivity to the law was secondary to defeating the Nazi war-machine.[141] President Franklin D. Roosevelt himself stretched constitutional restraints to the breaking point, forcing Japanese-Americans into camp-like prisons and ignoring congressional prerogatives in the early stages of the war.[142] Obviously this rules-be-damned approach spilled over, for some, into the subsequent Cold War with the Soviet Union.[143]

Of overmastering importance, then, is the necessity to remind (or re-educate) intelligence officers – and the broader public to whom they must answer – of the central role oversight and accountability must play in a democracy. A significant number of professional intelligence officers still seem to reject the idea of legislative oversight, seeing it more as a hindrance to America's war against hostile foreign threats than a safeguard against the abuse of power at home.[144] 'Do you know why we all enjoyed reading [the 1984 Tom Clancy novel] *The Hunt for Red October?*' asked an intelligence officer of a visitor at a CIA seminar for senior intelligence managers held at Headquarters recently. His answer: 'Because in the book a senator and his aide are the villains and their culpability is uncovered by the Agency!'[145] Though said in partial jest, the point was made during a discussion of legislative oversight and was meant to convey the group's sense that legislators were a hindrance to their mission.

At another Agency seminar for senior officials, in 1987, a young officer displayed a brooding hostility toward a former legislative overseer partici-pating in the session. The officer attributed leaks over recent covert-action operations, notably in Afghanistan, to the involvement of Congress in the oversight process and was bitter about the danger leaks presented to case officers and their assets in the field.[146] Concern for leaks and the lives of intelligence personnel is warranted,[147] and shared by legislators and their staffs, who take such matters as seriously as officials in the executive branch (widely recognized as the source of most leaks); what this officer failed to appreciate is the importance of checks-and-balances in a democracy. Only when US intelligence officials accept within their own minds the legitimacy of executive and legislative supervision will the many safeguards against abuse truly work with reliability.

Officials in the CIA often find this Madisonian principle difficult to accept. They are driven each day by the vital mission to identify, describe, and help thwart external threats to the United States. 'Was it possible to lose the nation and yet preserve the Constitution?' asked Lincoln,[148] and the question resonates well in the halls of the CIA today. Yet, if the peril to the nation is less clear and immediate than in Lincoln's case, is it appropriate to dismiss the Constitution and the nation's laws?

Part of the dilemma for the intelligence officer resides in the changing nature of American foreign policy since the unambivalent confrontations with the Soviets during the Truman–Eisenhower–Kennedy years. Until recently a foreign policy consensus existed in the United States: the nation was in, if not a zero-sum conflict with the USSR, then at least a dangerous competition. Détente, however, illustrated the possibilities for some tempering of the steady animosity between the superpowers which had been the hallmark of the Cold War. Ransom offers a persuasive hypothesis linking threat and accountability: 'The greater the hostility between the United States and Soviet Union and the greater the consensus about the security threat, the less the public demand for accountability for secret intelligence agencies'.[149] As the consensus over the urgency of the Soviet threat diminished (at least compared with earlier periods of the Cold War), the new public mood seemed to place a greater emphasis on intelligence accountability.

Hence, just as legislators represent an aggravation to intelligence professionals, so, too, does the present uncertainty about American foreign policy objectives. Life was once much simpler with no congressional oversight to worry about and a monolithic, aggressive enemy to combat as the executive branch saw fit, few holds barred. Today, the modern intelligence officer must continue to provide the best warnings possible to protect the nation in a world more complicated and risky than in 1947, but must maintain as well a heightened appreciation and respect for the democratic process – from regulations in the executive branch to the advice of representatives in Congress. This is the difficult challenge confronting the US Secret Service. Can it honor democracy while protecting it from anti-democratic forces beyond these shores? Will the CIA live up to this twin obligation? The American people cannot afford for it to fail.

INTELLIGENCE AND ACCOUNTABILITY

'We must strive to assure the people that their intelligence agencies will not be turned against them,' said Griffin Bell in 1979, in the first address to CIA employees ever given by an attorney general.[150] This assurance depends upon redoubled efforts, at all the control points, to guard against abuse. The motivations of the men and women in key positions – their judgement, their respect for the law, their honesty – will continue to be of central importance. The recruitment of good people to positions of responsibility, in the CIA and throughout the government, has been and always will be a *sine qua non* for successful democracy.

In addition, members of Congress should demand to have continued (indeed, as the Iran–Contra affair revealed, improved) access to information about CIA operations through full and advanced briefings in all but the most extraordinary circumstances – and, even then, with at least a warning to key legislators (if not the Gang of Eight, then the Gang of Four: the top party

68

leaders in both chambers) that a finding has been signed and a full report will have to be delayed for a short period.

The former staff director of the Church Committee, William G. Miller, has emphasized recently the importance of the provision for *prior* notification in the 1980 Intelligence Oversight Act.[151] This law also uses the phrase 'in a timely fashion' as a reporting deadline, which seems to open the door to CIA lawyers for *ex post facto* briefings to Congress; but, Miller stresses, this phrase was meant to apply only narrowly to the most exceptional cases.

While an absolute insistence on prior reporting – without exception – has the virtue of clarity, it flies in the face of real-world complications. The 1979 rescue of a group of six American diplomats in Iran, with the indispensable help of the Canadian Embassy in Tehran, provides a useful illustration. According to President Jimmy Carter's chief counsel, Lloyd Cutler, Canada would have refused to co-operate in the rescue if Carter had had to report to Congress in advance about the covert action (which involved providing false documents and a safe house within the Embassy).[152] The Canadians, concerned about the security of the operation, demanded that the number of individuals who knew the details – what professional intelligence officers call 'the witting circle' – be sharply limited (only about ten American officials were allowed in this 'compartment' of information), or else they would not participate. Given this choice, President Carter elected to co-operate with the Canadians in order to rescue the Americans, then report later to Congress (which he did when the operation had successfully run its course over the next three and a half months).[153]

This centimeter of space allowed presidents could obviously be misused. To avoid mischief, Cutler suggests that a president might simply inform the Intelligence Committees straightaway that 'I have commenced an action' [i.e., signed a finding] and that, because of an extraordinary circumstance, a full reporting will have to be delayed.[154] Under this procedure, Congress would at least know that an operation was under way and that it could expect an accounting soon. Morton H. Halperin, a national security expert, would go further, requiring a slightly more detailed initial report to Congress, yet not so detailed as to jeopardize security, say: 'I have made a finding to help release hostages'. This brief description would then be followed by a full accounting to the Intelligence Committees after the operation.[155] Halperin also advocates for most covert actions a time-lag of at least a few days between the time of the finding and its implementation; this would allow the Intelligence Committees an opportunity to digest the the proposal before offering an evaluation to the President and the DCI.[156]

Senator Arlen Specter (R, Pennsylvania), a member of the Senate Intelligence Committee, reluctantly endorsed a 48-hour reporting requirement after concluding that prior notice simply has not worked in the past. He supports prior notice whenever possible, but, as an 'extra safeguard', he is willing to permit the President an extra two days to report to the Congress in extraordinary circumstances. 'If you're going before the court of public opinion [to accuse the CIA of violating its obligation to report to Congress],' he states, '[the time requirement had] better be clear and brief – in black-and-white so everyone can understand it.'[157] A 48-hour rule, he argues, has the virtue of satisfying that standard of clarity.

Beyond clarifying the reporting expectations, Congress must further insist on regular hearings, random program audits, and overseas inspections of CIA operations (*sans* fine operational details that might jeopardize sources and methods), written prior approval by the President for all important covert actions (with criminal penalties for those who disobey),[158] as well as an end to the privatization of intelligence operations and the establishment of secret funds outside the appropriations process – both of which have the effect of removing intelligence policy from proper constitutional checks and balances. The Reagan administration's new National Security Decision Directive on Special Activities (NSDD 268),[159] issued in the wake of the Iran–Contra revelations attempted to address some of these problems by prohibiting oral and retroactive findings in the future.[160]

Congress and the executive branch must create better criteria for determining whether the CIA is operating within acceptable bounds. This is a difficult assignment. What is *acceptable* covert action? Existing laws, as well as guidelines established by non-governmental organizations, have helped in this regard, but many unnecessary ambiguities remain. Foremost among them are the limits on the CIA's and FBI's use of surveillance techniques in the USA. President Reagan's omnibus executive order on intelligence seems to permit investigations of domestic groups. For example, such groups may be investigated if they might be tools of foreign powers or might possess information that could be relevant to US interests abroad.[161] This authority remains sealed in secret internal regulations. Unfortunately this situation is reminiscent of the notorious Huston Plan.[162] In a democracy, guidelines must be legislated (or at least carefully and regularly reviewed by the Intelligence Committees), not signed secretly within the executive branch and implemented without debate or review. Congress should codify guidelines for warrantless physical searches and the surveillance of Americans abroad.

All are necessary: dedicated individuals aware of the necessary balance between security and civil liberty; a steady flow of information to the congressional intelligence committees on all important operations; renewed efforts to define societal expectations more precisely through executive orders, laws and other guideposts; and, always so vital, a spirit of co-operation ('good faith', in the words of the Inouye-Hamilton investigative committee) between intelligence leaders in the executive and legislative branches. With this mixture – a challenging but reachable goal – the United States can have both democracy and a CIA.

NOTES

The author thanks Oxford University Press and the *Harvard Journal of Law and Public Policy* for allowing him to draw upon his earlier versions of this study.

1. See Rick Inderfurth and Loch K. Johnson, *Decisions of the Highest Order: Perspectives on the National Security Council* (Pacific Grove, CA, 1988).
2. Ibid.
3. Ibid.
4. Ibid.
5. Interviews with officials in the Central Intelligence Agency (CIA) and the NSC staff of the Carter and Reagan administrations (July 1980; June 1984; and March 1988), Langley, Virginia, and Washington, DC. Except when names are included, the officials interviewed in this study have requested anonymity.
6. Interviews, Reagan administration NSC staff aides (June 1984 and March 1988), Washington, DC.
7. See Leslie H. Gelb, 'Foreign Policy System Criticized by U.S. Aides', *New York Times*, 19 October 1981.
8. See 'Intelligence Oversight Act of 1988', *Report No. 100–705* (Part I), US House Permanent Select Committee on Intelligence, 15 June 1988.
9. *New York Times*, 15 January 1987; *Report of the President's Special Review Board*, 26 February 1987, Washington, DC at IV-5; the *Report of the Congressional Committees Investigating the Iran–Contra Affair*, Senate Select Committee on Secret Military Assistance to Iran and the Nicaraguan Opposition and House Select Committee to Investigate Covert Arms Transactions with Iran (hereafter, the Inouye–Hamilton Committees, chaired by Senator Daniel Inouye [D, Hawaii] and Representative Lee Hamilton [D, Indiana]), November 1987, S. Rept. No. 100–216 and H. Rept. No. 100–433, at 6–7.
10. *New York Times*, 16 July 1987; Inouye–Hamilton Committees, *Report*, p.379.
11. 'Alleged Assassination Plots Involving Foreign Leaders', *Interim Report*, US Senate Select Committee to Study Governmental Operations with Respect to Intelligence Activities (hereafter the Church Committee, named for its chairman, Senator Frank Church [D, Idaho], S. Rept. No. 94–465, 20 November 1975.
12. Ibid., pp.71–91 for Castro and p.24 for the murder instruments intended for Lumumba.
13. Ibid.
14. 28 April 1966, p.28; see also, Loch K. Johnson, *A Season of Inquiry: Congress and Intelligence* (Chicago, 1988), Ch. 1. p. 7.
15. 'Foreign and Military Intelligence', *Final Report*, Book I, Church Committee, Report No. 94–755 (23 April 1976), pp.56, 57.
16. Sec. 622 of the Foreign Assistance Act of 1961 (22 U.S.C. 2422); on the written reports, see 'Intelligence Oversight Act of 1988', loc. cit.
17. See *New York Times*, 28 April 1966; Church Committee, *Final Report*, Book I, pp.62–64; *Washington Star*, 25 February 1976; Martin Anderson, *Revolution* (New York, 1988), pp.361–62; 'The CIA Report the President Doesn't Want You to Read: The Pike Papers', (an unauthorized publication of the *Report*, US House Select Committee on

Intelligence, chaired by Representative Otis Pike [D, New York], hereafter the Pike Committee *Report*), *Village Voice*, 16 February 1986.

18. Remarks of panelists, 'Intelligence Oversight', Annual Meeting of the American Political Science Association, 28 August 1986, Washington, DC; see, also, comments of PFIAB member James Q. Wilson, 'Reducing Discord Over Foreign Policy', *New York Times*, 24 December 1986.

19. William Safire, 'The Iran–Contra Affair's "Three Blind Mice"', *New York Times* News Service, *Athens Banner-Herald* (Athens, GA), 12 June 1987.

20. Remarks to the author, IOB member, 16 December 1979, Washington, DC.

21. Interviews with intelligence community and White House staffers familiar with PFIAB and IOB, October 1975, July 1978, December 1979, and November 1980; for Ransom's observation, see his 'Secret Mission in an Open Society', *New York Times Magazine*, 21 May 1961, p.80.

22. Church Committee, *Final Report*, Book I, pp.62–4.

23. *Public Papers of the Presidents of the United States: Gerald R. Ford, 1976–77* (Washington, DC, 1979), 1, p.349; for the text of the order creating the IOB (Executive Order 11905), see *Weekly Compilation of Presidential Documents*, 12 (1976), pp.234–44.

24. See the Inouye–Hamilton Committees *Report*, p.132; for a legal opinion critical of Sciaroni's, see the remarks of former Senate Foreign Relations Committee counsel, Michael J. Glennon, 'The Boland Amendment and the Power of the Purse', *Christian Science Monitor*, 15 June 1987, p.16.

25. Church Committee, *Final Report*, Book I, pp.62–4; Pike Committee *Report*, p.82.

26. Interview with OMB and CIA officials, October 1980 and June 1984 Washington, DC.

27. See Burton Wides, 'CIA Intelligence Collection About Americans: CHAOS Program and the Office of Security', in Church Committee, *Supplementary Staff Report on Intelligence Activities and the Rights of Americans, Final Report*, Book III (23 April 1976), S. Rept. No. 94–755, 679–732.

28. See Jeffrey Richelson, *The U.S. Intelligence Community* (Cambridge, MA, 1985), pp.279–80.

29. Interviews with CIA officials, November 1980 and June 1984, Washington, DC.

30. Interviews with CIA officials, October and November 1975, Washington, DC.

31. Interviews with officials in CIA Office of Legal Counsel, Oct. 1978, Washington, DC.

32. Personal observations as staff director of the Subcommittee on Oversight, US House Permanent Select Committee on Intelligence, 1978–79, Washington, DC.

33. Remarks, CIA IG, Conference on US Intelligence, 12 June 1984, Langley, Virginia. For the quoted passage of the Intelligence Accountability Act (less formally known in Washington circles as the 1980 Intelligence Oversight Act), see Title V of the National Security Act of 1947 (50 U.S.C. 413, Accountability for Intelligence Activities), Sec. 501 (a) (3). In 1989, Congress established an independent Inspector General within the CIA – one subject to Senate confirmation.

34. Interviews with CIA officials, Nov. 1980, June 1984, and March 1988, Washington, DC.

35. For examples of assets difficult to control, see Church Committee, 'Alleged Assassination Plots', p.151; William E. Colby, 'Gesprach mit William E. Colby', *Der Spiegel* 4, 23 January 1978, author's translation, pp.103, 106; William E. Colby and Peter Forbath, *Honorable Men: My Life in the CIA* (New York, 1978), p.272; Loch K. Johnson, 'The Seven Sins of Strategic Intelligence', *World Affairs* 146 (Fall 1983), pp.194–5; and, Stansfield Turner, 'From an Ex-CIA Chief: Stop the "Covert" Operation in Nicaragua,' *Washington Post*, Outlook Section, 21 April 1983.

36. 'Alleged Assassination Plots,' p.259.

37. On the CIA assassination manual, see Stansfield Turner, *Secrecy and Democracy: The CIA in Transition* (Boston, 1985), pp. 168, 170–71; on the CIA-Mafia ties in the 1960s, see 'Alleged Assassination Plots'.

38. Remarks by Senator Sam Nunn (D, Georgia), McNeil–Lehrer Show, Public Television (21 May 1987), following closed hearings with the COS.

39. See the discussion of the Contras throughout Bob Woodward, *Veil: The CIA Secret Wars, 1981–87* (New York, 1987); and of some maverick mujahedeen factions in Afghanistan, Eqbal Ahman and Richard J. Barnet, 'A Reporter At Large: Bloody Games', *New Yorker* 11 April 1988, pp. 44–86.

40. Church Committee, *Final Report*, Book I, pp. 314–15; David D. Newsom, *Diplomacy and the American Democracy* (Bloomington, IN 1988), Ch. 11.

41. Personal interviews have included former Secretary of State Dean Rusk (21 February 1983, Athens, Georgia) and the following former US ambassadors: W. Tapley Bennett, ambassador to NATO (22 November 1987, Athens, Georgia), Martin Hillenbrand, ambassador to Hungary and the Federal Republic of Germany (25 May 1986, Athens, Georgia), and William Trueheart, ambassador to Nigeria (15 October 1975). For public statements on this topic, see 'The CIA and the Media, *Hearings*, Subcommittee on Oversight (chaired by Les Aspin [D, Wisconsin]), US House Permanent Select Committee on Intelligence (hereafter, Aspin Hearings), 29 December 1978, pp. 142–86; and the Church Committee, *Final Report*, Book I, pp. 305–17.

42. *New York Times*, 28 April 1966. For CIA instructions to bypass an ambassador during the Iranian arms-sale affair, see an account by Woodwood, *Veil*, p. 420.

43. Personal interview with James Angleton, 18 December 1975, Washington, DC.

44. 'Foreign and Military Intelligence', Church Committee, *Final Report*, Book I, p. 305.

45. Ibid., p. 311, emphasis added.

46. Ibid., emphasis added.

47. Ibid.

48. 22 U.S.C. 2680a.

49. Church Committee Report, Book I, p. 313.

50. Ibid.

51. Ibid., testimony taken on 10 December 1975.

52. Sec. 102(d)(4) [50 U.S.C. 403].

53. In the opinion of the experienced diplomats cited earlier (see note 41).

54. See David Binder, *New York Times*, 3 February 1978.

55. Church Committee Report, Book I, p. 313.

56. Ibid.

57. State Department Foreign Affairs Manual, November 1977.

58. Binder, op. cit.

59. Ibid.

60. State Department telegram, November 1977.

61. Interviews with CIA officials, July 1979, Washington, DC.

62. Ibid.

63. Binder, op. cit.

64. Ibid.

65. Ibid.

66. Ibid.

67. Ibid.

68. See the sources in note 41.

69. Aspin Hearings, p. 165.

70. Ibid., p. 163.

71. Ibid., p. 166.

72. Ibid., pp. 155, 165; also Church Committee, *Final Report*, Book I, pp. 313–14.

73. Testimony of Lieut. Col. Oliver L. North, *Hearings*, Inouye–Hamilton Committees, 7 July 1987.

74. See, for example, Kenneth Janda, Jeffrey M. Berry, and Jerry Goldman, *The Challenge of Democracy: Government in America* (Boston: Houghton Mifflin, 1987), pp. 520–21.

75. See Theodore J. Lowi, *The End of Liberalism* (New York, 1969).

76. Loch K. Johnson, 'Congress and the CIA: Monitoring the Dark Side of Government', *Legislative Studies Quarterly* 5 (November 1980), pp. 477–99.

77. Discussions with members of these organizations, 1980–88, Washington, DC.
78. See, for instance: the Aspin Hearings; James Angleton and Charles J.V. Murphy, American Security Council, 'On the Separation of Church and State', *American Cause, Special Report* (June 1976), Washington, DC; Roy Godson (ed.), *Intelligence Requirements for the 1980s* (Washington, DC: National Strategy Information Center, 1979; Marjorie W. Cline (ed.), *Teaching Intelligence in the Mid-1980s* (Washington, DC, 1985); Gary M. Stern, 'The FBI's Misguided Probe of CISPES', *Report No. 111*, Center for National Security Studies, Washington, DC, June 1988.
79. Observations as staff director of the Subcommittee on Oversight, which held the hearings (including the Aspin Hearings).
80. See L. Harmon Zeigler and G. Wayne Peak, *Interest Groups in American Society* (Englewood Cliffs, NJ, 2nd edn., 1972).
81. See Fred Kaplan, *The Wizards of Armageddon* (New York, 1983).
82. See Harry Howe Ransom, 'The Politicization of Intelligence', in Stephen J. Cimbala (ed.), *Intelligence and Intelligence Policy in a Democratic Society* (Dobbs Ferry, NY, 1987), pp. 25–46.
83. See the majority and minority reports in the Inouye–Hamilton Committees, *Report*. A popular slogan at the 1988 National Democratic Nominating Convention in Atlanta, Georgia, was 'Where was George?' – a suggestion that GOP front-runner, Vice President George Bush, a member of the Reagan administration NSC, must have known about the Iran–Contra decisions.
84. See, for example, Peter Wyden, *Bay of Pigs: The Untold Story* (New York, 1979).
85. On the Vietnam War, for instance, see Samuel Adams, 'Vietnam Cover-up: Playing War with Numbers', *Harper's* 250 (May 1975), pp. 41–44; and Robert W. Komer, 'The Tet Intelligence Flap: One Out of Step, or Many?' *Washington Star*, 16 November 1975.
86. For the political repercussions of the U-2 spyplane shoot-down by the Soviets in 1960 (and for other examples), see the history of the CIA by John Ranelagh, *The Agency: The Rise and Decline of the CIA* (New York, 1986), pp. 341–2.
87. See Seymour M. Hersh, 'Underground for the C.I.A. in New York: An Ex-Agent Tells of Spying on Students', *New York Times*, 29 December 1974, and the political repercussions examined in Johnson, *Season of Inquiry*.
88. Patrick Tyler and David B. Ottaway, 'Reagan's Secret Little Wars', *Washington Post* (Weekly Edition), 31 March 1986.
89. See David L. Boren, remarks, Association of Former Intelligence Officers, 28 March 1988, rpt. in *Periscope* (the Association's newsletter), Spring 1988; and interviews with staff aides on the two congressional intelligence committees (Sept. 1980; March 1987).
90. On the Boland Amendments, see Henry K. Kissinger, 'A Matter of Balance', *Los Angeles Times*, 26 July 1987. For the language of a key Boland Amendment, see P.L. 97–377, Sec. 793, the resolution making continuing appropriations in the Department of Defense appropriations act for Fiscal Year 1983, approved 21 December 1982. For a convenient collection of this law (and the others referred to in this article), see *Compilation of Intelligence Laws and Related Laws and Executive Orders of Interest to the National Intelligence Community*, US House Permanent Select Committee on Intelligence (April 1983).
91. See the accounts in Loch K. Johnson, *America's Secret Power: The CIA in a Democratic Society* (New York, 1989).
92. Sol Stern, 'NSA and the CIA', *Ramparts* 5 (March 1967), pp. 29–38.
93. Bob Woodward and Carl Bernstein, *The Final Days* (New York, 1976).
94. Hersh, 'Underground for the C.I.A'.
95. Drew Pearson and Jack Anderson, *Washington Post*, 3 March 1967.
96. Charles Peters, 'From Ouagadougou to Cape Canaveral: Why the Bad News Doesn't Travel Up', *Washington Monthly* 18 (April 1986), p. 31.
97. Ibid.; and, *Workshop on Congressional Oversight and Investigations* (22 October 1979), US House Document No. 96–217 (1980).
98. See Johnson, *Season of Inquiry*, Ch. 1.

99. See Johnson, 'Congress and the CIA'.
100. See Frank John Smist, Jr., 'Congress Overseas the United States Intelligence Community: 1947–1984', PhD dissertation, University of Oklahoma, 1988; and the author's personal observations as a congressional staff aide, 1975–79, at 504–07.
101. Leslie H. Gelb, 'Overseeing of C.I.A. by Congress', *New York Times*, 7 July 1986.
102. Kissinger, 'A Matter of Balance'.
103. Inouye–Hamilton Committees, *Report*; William S. Cohen and George J. Mitchell, *Men of Zeal: A Candid Inside Story of the Iran–Contra Hearings* (New York, 1988).
104. Quoted in the *New York Times*, 12 April 1984.
105. *New York Times*, 1 October 1985.
106. Author's interview, 15 November 1985, Washington, DC.
107. Gary J. Schmitt, 'Congressional Oversight of Intelligence', *Studies in Intelligence* (Spring 1985), an in-house CIA publication.
108. Stansfield Turner, 'Has Reagan Killed CIA Oversight?' *Christian Science Monitor*, 26 September 1985, p. 14.
109. Ibid.
110. Patrick Leahy (D, Vermont), 'The Week with David Brinkley', ABC Television (14 December 1986).
111. See Johnson, *America's Secret Power*, Ch. 11.
112. John P. Roche, 'Intelligence Estimates and a Grotesque Report', *Washington Star*, 10 March 1978.
113. Christopher Andrew, *Her Majesty's Secret Service: The Making of the British Intelligence Community* (New York, 1986), 63–4.
114. Interviews with CIA officials familiar with the French Secret Service, August 1987, Washington, DC.
115. Ibid.
116. CIA spokesman, Office of Public Affairs, 'Democracy and the CIA', panel discussion, annual meeting, American Political Science Association, Washington, DC, 1 September 1984.
117. Remarks by Canadian political scientists, panel on intelligence, Annual Meeting of the American Political Science Association, Chicago, 1 September 1987.
118. Personal observations and interviews with congressional and CIA officials, Washington, DC, 1978–88.
119. For the regulations that establish these unique rotational procedures, see U.S. House Rule XLVIII (1977) and Senate Resolution 400 from the 94th Congress (1976), reprinted in *Compilation*, pp. 337–51.
120. Participant, Roundtable Discussion, 'Should the CIA Fight Secret Wars?' *Harper's* (September 1984), p. 42, original emphasis.
121. See, for example, John Barron, *Breaking the Ring: The Bizarre Case of the Walker Family Spy Ring* (Boston, 1987); Morton H. Halperin, 'Secrecy and National Security', *Bulletin of the Atomic Scientists* (August 1985), pp. 112–17; Scot Powe, 'Espionage, Leaks, and the First Amendment', *Bulletin of the Atomic Scientists* (June/July 1986), pp. 8–10; Howard Morland, *The Secret That Exploded* (New York, 1979); and Jay Peterzell, 'Can the CIA Spook the Press?' *Columbia Journalism Review* (September/October 1968), pp. 29–34.
122. *New York Times Co. v. United States*, 403 U.S. 713 (1971), quote at p. 730. See the account in Sanford Ungar, *The Papers and 'The Papers'* (New York, 1972).
123. The central cases are *U.S. v. Marchetti*, 466F 2d 1309(1972), which supported the CIA's right to censor works written by its employees before publication; *Knopf v. Colby*, 509F 2d 1362(1975), which upheld the right of the CIA to demand deletions in censored works; and *U.S. v. Snepp*, No. 78–1871(1980), which awarded the government all royalties from a book published by one of its former officers (Frank Snepp) who did not honor the censor procedures on grounds that nothing in the book was classified (an argument the CIA maintained was moot).
124. *U.S. v. Marchetti*, ibid.

125. Interviews with present and retired CIA officers, 1980–88, Washington, DC and Boston.
126. See note 123.
127. Victor Marchetti and John D. Marks, *The CIA and the Cult of Intelligence* (New York, 1974).
128. *New York Times*, 20 February 1980.
129. See note 123.
130. Frank Snepp, 'Protect Rights of All Privy to U.S. Secrets', *New York Times* (22 February 1984).
131. Foreign Intelligence Surveillance Act of 1978 (P.L. 95–511, signed 25 October 1978; 92 Stat. 1783).
132. Interview with Senate Intelligence Committee staff aide, 2 Sept. 1985; also, *Report No. 98–665*, US Select Committee on Intelligence, 98th Cong. (10 Oct. 1984), pp.35–37.
133. Ibid., as well as interviews with other aides on the congressional intelligence committees and CIA officials, 1980–87.
134. See Victor Thompson, *Modern Organization* (New York, 1961), 91. As Wyden has put it with reference to high-level meetings in the White House, 'Nothing permeates the Cabinet Room more strongly than the smell of hierarchy', *Bay of Pigs*, p.315.
135. Testimony of Dean Rusk, 'Oversight of U.S. Government Intelligence Functions', *Hearings*, Committee on Government Operations, 22 January 1976, p.77.
136. For the latest executive order prohibiting assassinations, see *Public Papers of the Presidents of the United States: Ronald Reagan, 1981* (Washington, DC, 1982), pp.1128–9; on the Qaddafi bombing, see Seymour M. Hersh, 'Target Qaddafi', *New York Times Magazine* (22 February 1987), p.16ff.
137. See the poll reports in *Public Opinion* (Summer 1986), citing CBS/*New York Times* polling results of 6–10 April 1986; and James Chace, 'A Quest for Invulnerability', in Sanford J. Ungar (ed.), *Estrangement: America and the World* (New York, 1985), pp.248–9.
138. Ahmad and Barnet, op. cit.
139. Interview with author, Athens, Georgia, 21 January 1985.
140. See Frederick A. O. Schwarz, Jr., former chief counsel of the Church Committee, 'Intelligence Activities and the Rights of Americans', address, New York Bar Association Meeting, New York City (16 November 1976), rept. in the *Congressional Record*, 28 January 1977, pp.51627–9, a summary of the Committee's findings, and 'Recalling Major Lessons of the Church Committee', *New York Times*, 30 July 1987. See also, Loch K. Johnson, 'National Security, Civil Liberties, and the Collection of Intelligence: A Report on the Huston Plan', in Church Committee, *Supplementary Detailed Staff Reports on Intelligence Activities*, pp.921–86.
141. Formal deposition, Church Committee files, 10 June 1975.
142. On the Japanese-American internment, see James MacGregor Burns, *Roosevelt, 1940–1945: The Soldier of Freedom* (New York, 1970), pp.214–17; on Roosevelt's decisions during the years immediately preceeding America's entry into the Second World War, see 'National Commitments', Committee on Foreign Relations, *Report No. 91–129*, US Senate, 16 April 1969.
143. See, for example, the testimony of former CIA Chief of Counterintelligence, James Angleton, before the Church Committee, 'The Huston Plan', *Hearings*, 24 September 1975.
144. The author's periodic discussions with CIA professionals from 1975 to 1990, Washington, DC and various conferences of the American Political Science Association and the International Studies Association during this period. See James Angleton's views in Johnson, *Season of Inquiry*, p.193; and PFIAB member, Professor Paul Seabury, who opines that it is an act of 'cowardice' for intelligence officials 'to regard congressional oversight as of equal if not greater importance than White House oversight', in 'A Massacre Revisited', *Foreign Intelligence Literary Scene* 7 (May–June 1988), p.2.
145. Author's personal observation, 16 March 1986, Langley, Virginia.

146. Author's personal observation, 12 March 1987, Langley, Virginia.
147. On 23 December 1975, CIA officer Richard S. Welch was murdered by terrorists in Athens, Greece. While his identity was not a government leak (but rather appeared in an underground newspaper and various Marxist publications overseas), the tragedy further emphasized how vulnerable American diplomatic, military, and intelligence personnel are abroad and how carefully 'sources and methods' must be treated. On the Welch murder, see Johnson, *Season of Inquiry*, pp.161–2; on the question of government leaks and how they are rarely from the legislative branch, see George Lardner, Jr., 'Moynihan Unleashes the C.I.A.', *Nation* (16 February 1980), 177, citing an internal CIA study to this effect; Allan E. Goodman, 'Reforming U.S. Intelligence', *Foreign Policy* 67 (1987), p.132; Gelb, 'Overseeing of C.I.A.', and Johnson, *Season of Inquiry*, pp.206–7.
148. Letter from Abraham Lincoln to A.G. Hodges, dated 4 April 1864, cited in Wilfred E. Binkley, *President and Congress* (New York, 3rd ed., 1962), p.155.
149. 'CIA Accountability: Congress As Temperamental Watchdog', paper, annual meeting of the American Political Science Association, Washington, DC, 1 September 1984, p.26. See also, Ransom, 'The Politicization of Intelligence', pp.43–4.
150. Cited by John T. Elliff, 'The Legal Framework for Intelligence Activities', paper, annual meeting of the American Political Science Association, Washington, DC, 1 September 1984, p.22. See also, Griffin B. Bell, with Ronald J. Astrow, *Taking Care of the Law* (New York, 1982), Chs. 5 and 6.
151. Remarks, Symposium on the Management of Intelligence, School of Foreign Service, Georgetown University (3 March 1988); see also, Harold Hongju Koh, 'Why the President (Almost) Always Wins in Foreign Affairs: Lessons on the Iran–Contra Affair', *The Yale Law Journal* 97 (June 1988), p.1331.
152. On the details of this operation, see 'Intelligence Oversight Act of 1988', *supra* note 8, at 54, 78–9.
153. Remarks, Covert Action and Democracy: A Tufts University Symposium on Secrecy and U.S. Foreign Policy, Tufts University Experimental College, 26 February 1988.
154. Cutler, remarks, ibid.
155. Halperin, remarks, ibid.
156. Remarks, Symposium on the Management of Intelligence.
157. Ibid. In an understandable reaction to the Iran–Contra affair, Senator Specter may have overstated the failure of the prior-notice reporting requirement. At the same symposium, William G. Miller of the Senate Intelligence Committee observed that prior notice had been the case throughout his term as staff director (1976–81), with the exception of the Canadian-assisted rescue in Iran. Specter rested his case on the observation that during the Reagan administration prior notice had been less well honored by the CIA. [According to a recent House report ('Intelligence Oversight Act of 1988', p.59), only four violations of the prior-notice expectation have occurred since passage of the 1980 Intelligence Oversight Act in the fall of that year: three associated with Carter administration operations in Iran designed to rescue US diplomats in hostage and, during the Reagan years, the Iran–Contra affair.] Specter, it turned out, stood in strong company with his endorsement of the 48-hour provision. On 15 May 1988, 70 of his colleagues in the Senate joined with him to approve the 1988 Intelligence Oversight Act (with 19 nay votes), which urged prior notice in most circumstances but gave the executive branch a 48-hour leeway. The Reagan administration opposed the bill because of the strict time-limit, preferring the formula in its National Security Decision Directive on Special Activities (NSDD 286) – that is, discretionary reporting based on the inclinations of NSC members ('Intelligence Oversight Act of 1988', see note 8). The House failed to vote on this proposed legislation in 1988. By 1990, the Senate Intelligence Committee had retreated altogether from the 48-hour provision, embracing instead a 'timely manner' rule – though with the understanding that this meant no more than a couple of days.
158. On the desirability of criminal sanctions against those who violate national security statutes, see the testimony of Clark M. Clifford, *Hearings*, Permanent Select Committee

on Intelligence, US House of Representatives (24 February 1988), pp.6–7; and various expert witnesses testifying on H.R. 3665 (the 'Official Accountability Act'), Subcommittee on Criminal Justice, Judiciary Committee, US House of Representatives (15 June 1988).
159. 'Intelligence Oversight Act of 1988'.
160. See ibid., p.5; and 'Intelligence Oversight Act of 1988', *Report No. 100–276*, U.S. Senate (27 January 1988), p.9.
161. Executive Order 12333, signed on 4 December 1981.
162. Stern, 'The FBI's Misguided Probe'; on the Huston Plan, see Johnson, *America's Secret Power*, Ch.7.

PART TWO

POLICY AREAS

4

Controlling Intelligence Estimates

ARTHUR S. HULNICK

Managing and controlling intelligence production – the part of intelligence that actually delivers information to policy-makers – is the 'end game' in the intelligence process. It may not have quite the glamor, excitement or mystery of espionage, but if this end game is played badly, the value of the expensive, complicated and highly secret intelligence apparatus of the nation could be dissipated.

Concern with intelligence failure is one of the major forces that drives the system to play the game correctly. No one has forgotten the lesson of the failure to predict the Japanese attack on Pearl Harbor in 1941 or the North Korean attack on South Korea in 1950. More recently, intelligence analysts were blamed, in part, for missing the Arab attack on Israel in 1973 and the fall of the Shah of Iran in 1978. In each case, enough data were available to predict the correct outcome, but the end game was misplayed. These failures continue to haunt US intelligence.

At issue, then, is how this process can be managed to ensure that the right questions are directed at analysts, that the scope and direction of the analysis is relevant to policy-makers, that the product is packaged and delivered on time, and that it takes a form that consumers find useful and easy to understand. Further, it must be free of personal or political bias, it must encompass divergent views without burying ideas, and it must be policy-neutral in the sense that it must not push or direct decisions toward specific policy options.

The neutrality of intelligence analysis is critical if the product is to be believable as well as useful. The founders of the Central intelligence Agency understood that they would have to create a system that was free of the kind of political pressure that was commonly accepted in the rest of government.[1] At the same time they realized that useful analysis – especially if more than one intelligence agency was involved – would require a way of co-ordinating or joining different views without forcing analysts to argue and water down their

81

conclusions until some rather weak and useless agreement was reached.

The analytic system that exists today had its roots in the Research and Analysis section of the Office of Strategic Services (OSS) in the Second World War. The OSS was America's first independent intelligence organization, and while it was part of the military establishment, it was really run by civilians in uniform, including its leader and founder, Major General William 'Wild Bill' Donovan. While it may have been based on the British model, the Americans quickly adapted a more flexible design to include the capability to carry out espionage, as well as covert action, and with a unique capability for research and analysis. This carried over into the CIA. In the early days of the Agency, there was heavy emphasis on current, event-driven analysis, along with very formal set-piece estimates or forecasts. Demands from policy-makers led to the creation of a system for more basic research, and today the analytic elements of the US intelligence community deliver an incredible variety of intelligence products to consumers.

In order to assist readers who have little experience or knowledge of the inner workings of the intelligence profession, it would probably be useful to try to define what we mean by 'products' before discussing how the production process in general is controlled or managed. They will be examined in greater detail later, but for now a simple classification might be helpful. There are several ways of dividing these reports. In general, they are considered to be 'finished' intelligence. That is, they have been assembled from various kinds of raw or unevaluated data by analysts who have compared the new material with an existing data-base, have applied some kind of analytic methodology and have added conclusions derived from methodology, expertise and wisdom.

Intelligence products may be divided by subject, or format, or intended audience, but the most commonly used division relates to the kind of material the products are trying to deliver. Products may be thought of in the following categories:

Warning or alerting intelligence. These kinds of reports are supposed to tell policy-makers that an event is either about to take place or has already occurred. This usually relates to an event that requires at least close attention, if not some kind of policy response. Typical examples of such reports might be the warning that a government friendly to the US is about to be overthrown, or that some world leader has been assassinated.

Current intelligence. These are composed of some form of daily or periodic reports that are quite journalistic in nature. They are meant to provide intelligence reporting and analysis to supplement the daily news to which most policy-makers are regularly exposed, and to cover events that have just happened, are happening, or are about to happen. In some sense, current intelligence is a form of intelligence newspaper, and, in fact, for several years at the CIA, a newspaper format was used. A typical current intelligence item might provide an update on a battle being fought, or on a political campaign in a country in which the US has particular interest.

Basic intelligence. These are research reports that are usually not event-driven, but are painstaking examinations of some issue or subject. They usually take months to research and write, they are quite long and detailed, and they may be used more by professional staff officers than senior policy officials. They are designed to provide a resource for policy officials as they go about formulating and implementing policy. A typical research report might examine in painstaking detail the economic infrastructure of a country to include, perhaps in an annex, the economic model on which the research was based.

Estimates. National Intelligence Estimates have been the most enduring of intelligence products. Professionals consider them the most important of all products because they are supposed to be highly policy-relevant, and they require a formal approval process before being delivered to the White House. This formal process was developed during the Second World War by the OSS, and the present system retains some of the flavor and even some of the arcane language of the early days. Among the most well-known estimates are those that examine each year the state of Soviet strategic capability, although most estimates focus on the outlook for some world leader, or political system.

Another way of looking at intelligence products relates to content in a different way. Intelligence reports, especially finished intelligence, contain several basic elements:

They must contain facts or learned data and they must explain in some way how the data was obtained. Was it from a reliable human source (a spy perhaps), or from a technical sensor, or from open material?

They must indicate the assumptions that the analyst has used in drawing conclusions or in manipulating the data.

They must reach some conclusions about the data and the events under consideration.

The process of 'estimating' or judging what the data mean lies at the very heart of the intelligence analysis process. In order to understand how that process works, and how this 'estimative' or analytic process is controlled or managed, we must examine the process itself. A good way to do this is to consider the various parts of the process in some detail, because it will

83

POLICY AREAS

FIGURE 1
INTELLIGENCE PROCESS MATRIX

COLLECTION	PRODUCTION	SUPPORT AND SERVICES
MANAGEMENT	MANAGEMENT	ADMINISTRATION
REQUIREMENTS	REQUIREMENTS	SECURITY
TASKING	TASKING	COUNTER-INTELLIGENCE
COLLECTION	ANALYSIS	COVERT ACTION
COLLATION	PRODUCTION	INSPECTION AND AUDIT
DISSEMINATION	DISSEMINATION	LIAISON
EVALUATION	EVALUATION	

become apparent that this is a highly complex, multi-variate system, with a good deal of subjectivity built into it. Thus, the problems of control and management are far from simple.

For many years, writers about intelligence have described the process as a cyclical pattern, in which policy-makers provide intelligence managers with requirements, data are then collected and analysed, the final reports are delivered to the consumers, and either decisions are made, or more questions are asked, thus starting the cycle over again. While this notion of the 'Intelligence Cycle' is still regularly taught in courses on intelligence, most professionals would probably be willing to admit that it does not describe reality at all. It is much more useful to consider the intelligence process as a matrix of interconnected, mostly autonomous functions.[2] The complete matrix is shown in Figure 1, although we will only be concerned here with the production functions.

In the production process, it is quite possible to follow intelligence material as it passes through the various stages or functions of the matrix. In order to understand how control is applied, it is necessary to examine in detail each of the functions. Control, as applied here, means applying an agreed standard to the production process to ensure that the quality of work and the quantity of output is achieved. In that sense, intelligence control is no different than the standards of control applied in any production process. But, control in intelligence also involves the steps that ensure that the product is timely, relevant, useful and free of bias.

MANAGEMENT

More so than in industry or other types of production processes, management in intelligence is heavily involved in the actual substance of the work. Of course, management must be involved in resource utilization, but because of the unique nature of intelligence, managers are forced to become and remain rather expert in the activities of the units they oversee, since they are inevitably the final arbiters of the substantive output.

Intelligence managers are forced to become experts, in part, because at the most senior levels it is they, and not their working analysts, who are expected to give the briefings at the White House, or attend meetings with cabinet officers. Thus, managers of analysts traditionally are drawn from the ranks of analysts, and they tend to retain their interest and expertise. This would explain why the Deputy Director for Intelligence at the CIA has almost always come up from the analytic ranks and has been well schooled in the production process.

Clearly, managers should be giving resource guidance to their working elements and should be carrying out the usual tasks of managers anywhere. But, should they be giving substantive guidance as well? And, if so, of what kind? Managers have to be careful not to intimidate analysts, or try to dictate the analytic conclusions their analysts will reach. Managers who have been analysts never seem to lose their lust for reading incoming reports, and analysing the material. It is extremely hard to rein in managers who become impatient when analysts do not draw the same conclusions as themselves from the data. And, it is quite common to see managers pick up the editorial pencil when writing styles do not match their own classic prose.

Managers in intelligence also play a key role in acting as a link with policy-makers. In the days when analysts were more independent and had individual country accounts, many of them were able to deal effectively with policy elements at their own level. Today, however, with the fusion of political, economic and military analytic units into geographic offices in CIA – a situation that mirrors the way the policy community is organized – and with the proliferation of specialties, analysts no longer are country desk officers. Rather, they are part of teams that work on countries or accounts. In such a situation, it becomes almost impossible for a working analyst to be able to find a counterpart in the policy realm. Thus, the necessary liaison falls to managers at various levels. Managers should be seeking out their counterparts to learn what policy-makers are worried about, what kind of analysis would be useful to decision-makers, when it should be delivered, and even how it should be packaged.

REQUIREMENTS

In the cycle theory of intelligence, requirements are supposed to come to the intelligence community in much the same way that intelligence flows to policy-makers. In fact, policy-makers rarely take the time to tell intelligence managers what they want or need to know. This is understandable, given the enormous pressure on the average policy-maker, especially when he or she is operating in some kind of crisis mode. We also have learned that policy-makers do not always know how to tap the intelligence community, and in some cases, may not want to ask certain questions of intelligence because they already know that they will not like the answers.

Requirements for analysis are generated in several ways. Policy-makers do provide some clues, sometimes through their staffs, sometimes by the public or official statements they make, and sometimes because they have actually sought out an intelligence contact and have asked questions.

Requirements are also self-generated within the intelligence system as analysts ask themselves what kind of material they ought to be providing to the policy community. The analysts need to consider what policy-makers want, as well as what they probably do not want but ought to have. This creates the very real possibility that the product, when delivered, might be quite useful but rather unpopular.

The third category of requirements are generated by events. Usually, these are activities that neither policy-makers nor intelligence officers had anticipated, but because they have taken place, it becomes obvious that some sort of coverage – beyond regular daily reporting – must be undertaken to put the events in perspective.

It is important to understand that requirements for analysis are not finite. Because many intelligence inputs to policy are incremental in nature – they are delivered as situations are developing, or as policy initiatives are tried and modified – initial assessments may change as the situation changes. Thus, managers must understand what was done with initial intelligence inputs to know what to deliver next.

Despite pressures to deal with current events, analysts and managers must always be thinking and planning for longer-term research and assessments. The key to knowing how to do this lies in establishing and maintaining a good working relationship between intelligence producers and policy consumers. This is more difficult than it sounds, and becomes increasingly a problem at higher levels in government. Yet, when such relationships are good ones, intelligence managers can find out with relative ease what their consumers want and need. At the highest levels, the relationship works best through staffs or executive officers who often know the issues that their bosses are dealing with, and can give good guidance on what kinds of estimates or judgements are likely to be the most useful.

We know from experience that this producer-consumer relationship has to be established at the initiative of the intelligence side; consumers just will not do it. Some intelligence managers may be reluctant to spend the time and resources to make the relationship work, and they may also be reluctant to 'turn their analysts loose' to talk with consumers if it leads to additional requirements, or ends up upsetting a carefully crafted research plan. Nevertheless, when managed properly, effective producer–consumer relations will almost always lead to more effective and useful intelligence products.

TASKING

Some professionals in intelligence would probably argue that tasking and requirements are all part of one function, but in looking at the matrix arrangement, it proves useful to examine the two separately. Requirements involves deciding what to do; tasking involves deciding who will do it. At one time, deciding who would undertake a particular piece of analysis was easy at the CIA because the Agency's analytic units were arranged functionally. Political analysts were in one unit, economists in another, military analysts in a third and so forth. They were then further divided by country assignment or subject account. The result was a system in which each analyst had particular specialized 'turf' and when it came time to do analysis, it was easy to see who would do the work. There was, of course, considerable collaboration, but each analyst had a unique account.

In the modern era, things have become more complex. The CIA's Directorate of Intelligence is now divided along geographic lines, with political, economic, military and other analysts located together.[3] This has forced analysts to produce multi-disciplinary analysis, but it has also blurred the accounts. Today, it is rare to find an analyst who has total control of particular 'turf'. This more sophisticated management system has complicated decisions about tasking, perhaps, but has led to more usable and more interesting analysis. Team approaches to problems make it less likely that mistakes will be made, but managers must ensure that the right analysts are chosen to 'work' the problem at hand.

There is no question that personalistic elements enter into some tasking decisions and it must be recognized that there is no perfect way to assign analytic work. The great danger, in terms of control, would be to have a system in which certain analysts were excluded from participating in a project because of their known views or their anticipated inputs. Fortunately, this has not been a problem. At CIA, analysts are always encouraged to come up with ideas that defy the conventional wisdom, or that provide new insights into old issues. Managers never know when the key analytic judgement will come from the reserve players rather than the first team.

ANALYSIS

The analytic process would be worthy of a book all by itself, although none has ever been written. How an analyst sifts through ambiguous, fragmentary, contradictory information, some of it gathered at second or third hand, to arrive at some estimate of why an event has happened, and what is likely to happen next is perhaps one of the most intriguing aspects of the intelligence profession. The data may very well be clouded by deception or disinformation – false data intentionally planted by an adversary to deceive or confuse an analyst. The challenge for the intelligence researcher goes well beyond that faced by an academic scholar. The academic may not have all the data, to be sure, but usually does not have to worry about deception.

The art of intelligence analysis involves a number of control decisions and each is worth discussion. They include:

Deciding when there is sufficient data so that an analyst can make more than an educated guess about an issue. Analysts should not be operating without enough material to draw reasonable conclusions. At the same time, analysts should not be reluctant to make an estimate even when they have only a percentage of the information they think they need.

Determining the terms of reference of the analysis so that the topics are covered in ways that will prove useful to consumers.

Choosing a methodology that will take advantage of the data at hand, as well as the knowledge and skill of the analyst.

Establishing a review procedure that will knock out bias, prejudice, politics, poor analysis, poor writing and weak organization.

Are the Data Adequate?

Modern electronic message systems guarantee, for the most part, that analysts throughout the intelligence system receive data at about the same time. Usually, analysts are starting to deal with most issues using an established data-base, so the new material provides an incremental input to an already existing file. It is rare that an analyst has to start from scratch on a particular subject.

With automatic delivery systems for most raw or unevaluated intelligence, there is a tendency for analysts to wait passively for the material to pop up on the computer screen, or turn up in the in-box. It is easy to be lulled into thinking that the incoming mail provides all the data needed. In fact, there is usually more material available if the analyst is willing to hunt it down. Sometimes this means seeking out informal reporting that has not got into the established channels, such as memos of conversation or debriefing reports. It may also involve seeking out particularly sensitive cables or reports that can be accessed only with special clearances. Analysts have to establish and maintain good contacts with collectors or with control offices to find out about such information and to be able to use it.

While some analysts may be prepared to draw conclusions from scanty data and are eager to get their thoughts into print, others seem always to be waiting for the next cable or agent report to make a murky picture clear or pin down some elusive bit of information. Managers may be forced to prod reluctant analysts into drawing conclusions, while at the same time reining in those who are plucking conclusions out of thin air.

Analysts have to be able to justify their assessments to their superiors, so they must be able to cite the information on which their analysis is based. The managers, exercising their right of substantive judgement, may well try to play devil's advocate to make sure that the analyst really believes in the assessments that are being made, or may challenge the analyst with an alternative view. Analysts have to be prepared to stand up to these attacks on their wisdom and should not be intimidated by their bosses if they believe strongly in the assessments they have made.

Are the Terms of Reference Correct?

Terms of reference – essentially the questions to be addressed by intelligence analysis – are very important in shaping the end product. Establishing the terms of reference ought to be an interactive process in which producers and consumers agree, at the beginning of a project, about the nature, the timing and the format of the work that is to be done. This may not be so important in producing current intelligence, but it certainly counts for a lot in basic research, and is critical in creating estimates or other products that are keyed directly to policy considerations.

Different policy-makers will have varying interests in intelligence analysis, and it is helpful, in establishing terms of reference, to include questions that will serve all the potential users. Experience shows that policy consumers will not usually create their own terms of reference, but are often willing to comment or revise those submitted to them by analysts. It is essential to solicit comment at the beginning of the work, so that analysts can avoid discovering, as they near the end of a project, that they have failed to deal with some aspect of a problem that turns out to be quite important to their consumers.

Is the Methodology Effective?

Advances in analytic methodology seem to have grown remarkably in the last decade. There are almost always a variety of approaches to understanding any problem. Managers in intelligence must ensure that analysts are trying

89

different techniques and they can do this by seeking out methodological expertise from outside the unit, by bringing together analysts from disciplines to investigate the same problem, or even by asking academics, consultants or other units within the intelligence community to attack the issue.

The most famous case of 'competitive analysis' is probably the A-Team–B-Team exercise of the 1970s in which two different groups, the A-Team of regular analysts and the B-Team of outside appointees, were asked to draft an estimate of Soviet strategic capability. The conservative institutional and political biases of the B-Team were so great that it turned what might have been a constructive effort at competitive analysis into an exercise that became highly politicized, and one in which the conclusions of the B-Team were as much based on their preconceived ideas as on the data.

Actually, competitive analysis goes on all the time within the Intelligence Community because units at CIA, State and Defense are almost always analysing similar problems. If lines of communication are good, and if analysts are talking informally with each other, as well as co-ordinating their analysis, they will all benefit, even though they develop different approaches and answers to some of the issues. These differences sometimes confuse consumers, but they also ensure that the issues are carefully examined.

Is the Review Process Instructive?

The process of having several layers of management review a product is perhaps the most painful one for most analysts. The goal of intelligence analysis is to produce an institutional product – one that the institution supports. Policy-makers are always interested in expert opinion, but they also want to know if the material they are getting reflects the views of the CIA or some other agency as a whole, and has official approval.

Over the years, CIA has tended to develop a system of review and approval that might be considered a kind of 'group-think'. It means that, at each level, managers are going to be examining the analysis carefully, often based not just on experience, but also on their own expertise, to make sure that they can accept or at least live with the language as well as the conclusions of the analyst. It is thus inevitable that, at each level, the writing will undergo subtle changes and that analysts will find themselves defending their work to a whole series of critics. While this may make analysts uncomfortable, it also tends to focus their prose, sharpen their insights, and give them expert advice as they go through the process.

While most work moves rather rapidly through the review process, poor writing, faulty analysis or poor presentation is not likely to survive. Analysis that is out of step with the conventional wisdom may raise lots of questions and require that the analyst or line supervisor spend more than the usual amount of time defending the work, but this is quite necessary. Analysts should not allow themselves to be intimidated if they think they have the right answers, but clearly they must know the subject well and be able to prove their conclusions.

This process of defending analysis to substantive managers at various levels tends to eliminate personal biases, prejudice and policy advocacy. The system tends to 'zero out' such things, while creating a product that may be a bit more bland than if authors had complete freedom to write as they pleased. If this means a neutral product, then the system will have served its purpose.

PRODUCTION

It is important to draw a distinction between analysis and production. The former involves a judgemental process, while the latter describes a process of packaging that has as much a mechanical as an intellectual content. Production means creating a vehicle for intelligence analysis so that consumers recognize what they are getting and can use the material easily.

The production process is steeped in tradition. If consumers from the Second World War period or the early days of the CIA were invited to review the works of finished intelligence produced today, they would probably remark – as, in fact, some have actually done – that today's intelligence products do not look very much different from those of their own era. Through standardized packaging and delivery systems, consumers come to recognize intelligence products quite readily. This is essential, not only because intelligence managers want consumers to use the material, but also to remember that most of it is quite sensitive and its material must be carefully protected. It should not become the stuff of cocktail party conversation or casual phone calls.

At the beginning of this chapter, several categories of product were outlined. Now, we can look more carefully at the control issues relating to each category:

Warning Intelligence. This type of product tends to be highly stylized if there is time to print something at all. Often, the warning has to be given by phone or in a special cable message, and it is only afterward that the warning is put into a printed format. These publications are kinds of situation reports, heavy on descriptions of events, with only short-term analysis because that may be all that is possible or meaningful.

The key control issue is making sure that policy consumers actually receive the warning and the follow-up publication. This means that delivery systems have to work properly, that crisis management teams have materials ready to go when crisis strikes, that maps, photos, and other such aids are readily

91

available when the policy-maker rushes into the alert center in the middle of the night for a briefing. Warning analysis cannot undergo the careful review of longer estimates or research. Analysts are pretty much on their own when it comes to the putting their conclusions into a warning notice or a situation report. If analysts have done their homework and have anticipated the crisis, then defending the work will not be a problem. In fact, having to deal quite rapidly with a fast breaking situation, when there is certainty that the most senior officials of government will read the unexpurgated work of junior analysts, is one of the great thrills of the intelligence profession.

Current Intelligence. The control problems inherent in producing current intelligence would be quite familiar to any newspaper editor, TV anchorman or radio personality.

Here producers are working with fixed formats, tight deadlines and serious competition from the media. In the early days of intelligence production, there might have been some notion that it was possible to 'scoop' the press. Today, that rarely happens. Almost nothing goes on in the world where intelligence gets the story so early that it leaves the media behind. But, intelligence can often obtain insights or information that is unique and that is the true service of current intelligence in the modern era.

Intelligence managers have to decide how they will use the current intelligence publication to take advantage of the 10–15 minutes policy-makers are likely to devote to such a product. It will inevitably be cursory and simplistic, but managers hope that a properly crafted item, even if it is only a paragraph, will motivate senior officials to have their staffs obtain more fulsome materials from their intelligence contacts. Current intelligence is not designed for the experts on an issue as much as for those who have a peripheral interest or for those who are generalists and need to be brought up to date in a hurry.

Basic Intelligence. Producing the encyclopedic data and analysis demanded by policy consumers makes up the great bulk of intelligence production these days. The analysis takes the form of detailed and complex studies and research papers, many of which take months to write and produce. Clearly, they are far too long, too detailed, and perhaps too formidable for the average senior official, but for the working level policy official enmeshed in formulating or implementing a plan of action for the government at State, Defense, Treasury, or some other department, this kind of analysis may be essential.

Basic research is designed to serve a great variety of needs and is not usually tailored for individual users. It may sit on a shelf or in a safe for months before being used as a reference work, but usually it will be produced in a time frame so that it meshes with some policy issue under review. It must be packaged in such a way that it contains the appropriate maps, charts, photos or other such aids, and it must contain a summary so that a busy user can see what is inside without having to peruse the entire text.

While basic research often involves a good deal of factual material, it also should contain a considerable amount of analysis to explain what the data mean. This tends to be interspersed through the text, but most such publications end with some sort of outlook section that is mostly an estimate by the researcher about the future. A good analyst will see that this outlook makes its way into the executive summary of the paper.

Estimates. When journalists and academics write about 'intelligence', estimates – judgements about the future – are really what they mean. While most finished intelligence contains some sort of estimate, National Intelligence Estimates – the formal products through which the Director of Central Intelligence sends the judgements of the Intelligence Community to the President – have a special place in the American system. These kinds of formal papers were among the first products developed during the Second World War years, and the formal process of creating them carried over into the CIA.

Today, estimates tend to be more flexible and less stylized than they were at first. They take general forms. For example, in some estimates, analysts outline the most likely scenarios of future events, with clues or indicators suggested so that policy-makers can tell when things are beginning to break. Other estimates tend to outline what seems to be an agreed forecast, if the data point clearly in one particular direction. Some estimates tend to be full of research, but will include the outlook for the future as well.

Intelligence professionals ascribe particular power to estimates and consider them the premier product of the intelligence system. Policy-makers do not hold them in such awe, and usually criticize them when the agreed judgements do not match the policy consumer's own views. When they are wrong – and it is inevitable that some will be – it usually causes a fuss and leads to some sort of examination of what went wrong.[4] When they are right – and most have proven to be pretty accurate – it is accepted as the norm, no fuss is made, no medals are given, and no press coverage is devoted to such success. Intelligence professionals learn from success as well as failure, and this has gained more attention from managers in the modern era.

DISSEMINATION

Dissemination is a professional term for distribution and delivery. Early writers about intelligence – especially those who advanced the 'cycle' theory of intelligence – did not place particular emphasis on this part of the intelligence process, believing that it took place more or less automatically. In fact, intelligence managers must pay careful attention to intelligence delivery systems, because failure to ensure that the appropriate consumers actually receive the intelligence materials they need can destroy the value of the entire intelligence process.

Intelligence materials are delivered to policy-makers today in much the same way as 40 years ago – publications are taken by couriers to mail rooms where clerks sort them and send them out to consumers. That provides no guarantee that those consumers who really need the material will actually receive it. This has forced managers to develop some alternatives that often prove more effective. Most units will find, over time, that there are a handful of consumers who are avid readers of the unit's product. In those cases, personal delivery by working analysts or managers not only makes certain that the analysis gets into the right hands, it also cements a good working relationship between producers and consumers.

It seems likely that this system will become increasingly automated in years to come. Intelligence will adopt the same systems used in private industry and various forms of electronic delivery will likely become the norm. This has happened more slowly in intelligence than in the private sector only because of security considerations. Electronic or automated delivery may very well speed up the process, but if it destroys the producer–consumer relationship that now exists, the benefits of efficiency will be questionable.

Managers also have to be sure who their consumers really are, no matter how delivery is made. Sending analysis to policy-makers who have no interest in the subject may only cause them to become disinterested in intelligence in general and overlook some particular estimate or judgement that they really need. The temptation is to make as wide a distribution of a research paper as possible. This may be cost-effective but counter-productive. It is probably better to find out who really wants or needs the material and tailor the distribution accordingly.

EVALUATION

The development of a systematic effort to evaluate the intelligence product is a relatively recent development in intelligence management. This step was not considered by those who espouse the 'intelligence cycle', and analysts have long complained that they need more feedback from consumers. But evaluation is more than feedback. Consumers may not always be the best judges of how good the material is, although they will understand the utility to themselves. Developing methodologies to evaluate the relevance, utility

94

and effectiveness of intelligence analysis has proven to be a real challenge for intelligence managers.

It is difficult to provide some realistic assessment of an intelligence judgement after the fact because evaluators almost always have more information than the analyst had when making the judgement being evaluated. Assessing yesterday's events in light of today's information will yield a skewed result. It is more important to learn lessons than give grades, if analysts are to learn from success as well as failure.

Methodologies that have proven useful in evaluating finished intelligence include:

An internal evaluation by managers to see if the product met the terms of reference, fulfilled the requirements for analysis and was delivered on time in a useful format to the proper consumers.

Evaluation by outsiders, perhaps scholars or other consultants, who can provide a disinterested perspective. Sometimes it is better to have such advice before the product is completed, but experience shows that independent views can often be helpful no matter when they are obtained.[5]

An evaluation by the consumers. This usually requires some sort of broad survey, and consumers are known to be less appreciative of intelligence than intelligence managers think is justified. Nevertheless, if consumers do not find intelligence useful, it is better to know it than ignore it.

In the end, there is probably no perfect way to evaluate the intelligence product, but a combination of the steps outlined is likely to provide managers with a sense of 'how they are doing' while enabling them to correct problems before serious intelligence failures result.

The research and analysis elements of US intelligence rarely get much attention unless there has been some egregious 'failure' to predict what in retrospect should have been obvious. The intelligence 'failures' cited at the beginning of the chapter should not mask the fact that there have been a significant number of successes in intelligence, although they usually go unheralded. For example:

Intelligence analysts realized that the standing assessments of North Korean Order of Battle were too low. This enabled President Carter to reverse an earlier decision to withdraw American troops from what might conceivably have become once again a battle zone.

Analysts advised President Reagan that his plans to try to stop the Soviet construction of a natural gas pipeline from Siberia to Western Europe would likely be counter-productive, an assessment the administration eventually adopted.

Assessments of the situation in Central America during the Reagan period were on the mark, despite enormous political pressure to push the analysis in favor of ruling regimes or insurgents.

Most successes will probably remain hidden until well after the events because the intelligence community does not publicize its victories, and it does not ask anyone else to do it either. Still, House and Senate Oversight Committee reports consistently give the Community high marks for its judgements and its presentations.[6]

The thrill and challenge of intelligence analysis lies in the ability to understand, from ambiguous fragments of data, events that affect the security and interests of the United States, and to communicate assessment and estimates about those data in a succinct and understandable fashion. The rewards lie in knowing that policy-makers – including the President and the other most senior officials in government – are receiving and reading these judgements.

NOTES

1. For insights into the founding of the CIA, see Ray S. Cline, *Secrets. Spies and Scholars* (Washington, DC, 1976); and Thomas F. Troy, *Donovan and the CIA* (Washington, DC, 1981).
2. The matrix model was first suggested by the author in Arthur S. Hulnick, 'The Intelligence Producer-Policy Consumer Linkage: A Theoretical Approach', *Intelligence and National Security'*, Vol. 1, No. 2 (May, 1986), pp.212–33.
3. A detailed organizational chart of the Directorate of Intelligence is contained in the CIA Fact Book, available on request from the CIA's Public Affairs Office.
4. The most insightful work on this issue is Richard K. Betts, 'Analysis, War and Decision: Why Intelligence Failures Are Inevitable', *World Politics*, Vol. XXXI, No. 1 (October, 1978).
5. See, for example, Walter Laqueur *A World of Secrets* (New York, 1985)
6. Both House and Senate Select Committees have issued periodical reports evaluating, among other things, the products of the Intelligence Community. The most recent are *Report by the Permanent Select Committee on Intelligence* HR99–1033, 1987 and *Report of the Select Committee on Intelligence* SR98–665, 1985.

5

Controlling Intelligence: The Values of Intelligence Professionals

GLENN HASTEDT

Almost exclusively, the controversy over controlling intelligence has focused on the relative merits of formal-legalistic solutions. Measures to enhance congressional control, formalize executive control and reorganize the intelligence bureaucracy have been particularly popular subjects of debate. Largely unexamined is a second avenue for realizing control. Its focus is on the values and norms which guide the behavior of the professionals working inside the intelligence bureaucracies. The two approaches are not incompatible with one another. In fact, it can be argued that the success of formal-legalistic solutions is dependent upon the existence of a given set or mix of informal organizational norms and principles which will allow them to be effective. In this chapter, we (1) examine the shortcomings inherent in formal-legalistic controls, (2) present a role orientation typology which is focused on the question of control, and (3) illustrate the typology by looking at several past Directors of Central Intelligence (DCIs).

SHORTCOMINGS OF FORMAL-LEGALISTIC CONTROLS

Formal-legalistic control mechanisms are limited in their ability to control intelligence by the realities of the American political process, the nature of world politics, and the assumptions that this approach makes about the relationship between intelligence professionals and policy-makers. Four problems are paramount.[1]

First, external controls operate retroactively and address only a portion of organizational behavior. For example, budgetary restrictions are the product of earlier policy decisions and existing priorities. The Clark Amendment, conclusions until some rather weak and useless agreement was reached.

The analytic system that exists today had its roots in the Research and Analysis section of the Office of Strategic Services (OSS) in the Second World War. The OSS was America's first independent intelligence organization, and while it was part of the military establishment, it was really run by civilians in uniform, including its leader and founder, Major General William 'Wild Bill' Donovan. While it may have been based on the British model, the Americans quickly adapted a more flexible design to include the capability to carry out espionage, as well as covert action, and with a unique capability for research and analysis. This carried over into the CIA. In the early days of the Agency, there was heavy emphasis on current, event-driven analysis, along with very formal set-piece estimates or forecasts. Demands from policy-makers led to the creation of a system for more basic research, and today the analytic elements of the US intelligence community deliver an incredible variety of intelligence products to consumers.

In order to assist readers who have little experience or knowledge of the inner workings of the intelligence profession, it would probably be useful to try to define what we mean by 'products' before discussing how the production process in general is controlled or managed. They will be examined in greater detail later, but for now a simple classification might be helpful. There are several ways of dividing these reports. In general, they are considered to be 'finished' intelligence. That is, they have been assembled from various kinds of raw or unevaluated data by analysts who have compared the new material with an existing data-base, have applied some kind of analytic methodology and have added conclusions derived from methodology, expertise and wisdom.

Intelligence products may be divided by subject, or format, or intended audience, but the most commonly used division relates to the kind of material the products are trying to deliver. Products may be thought of in the following categories:

Warning or alerting intelligence. These kinds of reports are supposed to tell policy-makers that an event is either about to take place or has already occurred. This usually relates to an event that requires at least close attention, if not some kind of policy response. Typical examples of such reports might be the warning that a government friendly to the US is about to be overthrown, or that some world leader has been assassinated.

Current intelligence. These are composed of some form of daily or periodic reports that are quite journalistic in nature. They are meant to provide intelligence reporting and analysis to supplement the daily news to which most policy-makers are regularly exposed, and to cover events that have

98

of facts is clear. The imposition of assumptions or conclusion on analysts, or a priori declaring certain assumption, sources of information, or conclusions unacceptable may enhance the policy-maker's control over intelligence but does little for the quality of that intelligence. Similarly, there is little evidence that organizational changes in the structure of intelligence estimating and analysis have much impact on the quality of the intelligence produced.

Further limiting the ability of many formal-legalistic measures to control intelligence is the basic nature of Congress as a political institution.[2] By nature, Congress is a reactive body. As the public mood changes, its attention to issues and policy positions changes. The early congressional reluctance to investigate the CIA was in large part due to the existence of a national consensus that fighting Communism was of the highest priority in the conduct of US foreign policy and that the CIA was an important tool in this struggle. Similarly, the inability to pass a legislative charter controlling the CIA can be traced in part to the public's declining interest in 'the intelligence problem'.

Congress is also a highly decentralized institution. Attempts to establish oversight procedures have repeatedly run into jurisdictional and partisan road-blocks. In 1956, Senator Mike Mansfield introduced a measure calling for the establishment of a joint committee on the CIA which would be kept 'fully and currently informed' by the CIA and be authorized to investigate its activities. At that time, CIA oversight was conducted by subcommittees of the House and Senate Appropriations and Armed Services Committees. The proposal was defeated on the Senate floor with all those sitting on the existing oversight committees voting against it. In 1966, Senator Eugene McCarthy introduced a resolution calling for the Senate Foreign Relations Committee, on which he sat, to undertake a 'full and complete study with respect to the effects of the CIA on the foreign relations of the United States'. His proposal ran into opposition from the members of the Senate Armed Services Committee who saw it as an attempt to muscle in on their jurisdiction. Senator Richard Russell, chairman of that committee, implied that if the proposal passed intelligence, leaks would soon follow. In the end, McCarthy's resolution was sent to Russell's Armed Services Committee for further study, thereby effectively killing the reform initiative.

Lastly, Congress has only blunt policy instruments at its disposal. Budgetary controls such as the Boland Amendment barring the spending of US intelligence funds to overthrow the Sandinista government in Nicaragua or provoke a war between Nicaragua and its neighbors are exercised only at the cost of a confrontation between the Congress and the President. Congress's 'big guns' such as its subpoena power are only brought out in the face of an absolute refusal to co-operate by the executive branch.

In the daily 'war of attrition' between the two branches, the executive is able to dominate by manipulating classification systems and the wording of memorandums of understanding which set the conditions for the exchange of classified information, and claiming that it is only protecting intelligence sources and methods as required by law.[3]

A third limitation of external controls is that they are effective only to the extent that they are used properly. Policy-makers have exhibited a persistent unwillingness to carry out their intelligence oversight responsibilities. Early congressional CIA oversight hearings are more aptly identified as briefings rather than hearings. Congressional overseers were there to learn, not to restrict or monitor.[4] Additionally, the appropriations process long served to protect the CIA more than restrain it. While Congress annually approved the CIA budget, the actual figures were not revealed to the full Congress. The fiction of congressional budgetary control became evident to all when in 1971 Senator Stuart Symington introduced an amendment placing a government-wide cap on intelligence spending. His proposal was defeated, but in the course of the debate, he asked Senator Alan Ellender, Chairman of the Senate Appropriations Committee, if it had approved funding of a 36,000-man secret CIA army in Laos. Ellender replied, 'I don't know anything about it . . . I never asked . . . it never dawned on me to ask about it. I did see it published in the newspaper some time ago'.[5]

Neglect is not the only possibility. Equally dangerous is the situation where policy-makers become over-zealous and seek to impose their will on the intelligence community. Instructive here is the distinction between militarism and the military way. The latter concentrates on achieving specific objectives with the utmost efficiency where the former focuses on prestige and custom, and displays the qualities of caste and cult. Alfred Vagts, in his study of militarism, concludes that militarism is often found among civilian leaders and is not the monopoly of military professionals.[6] We need look no further than the Iran–Contra affair to see that a similar situation holds true for intelligence. A major complaint voiced by Lieutenant-Colonel Oliver North was the apparent unwillingness of the CIA to provide him with the resources he needed to engineer a hostages-for-arms swap. The CIA also warned policy-makers against placing any trust in Manucher Ghorbanifar, one of the key middle men in North's plans.

The fourth limitation of formal-legalistic controls centers on the assumption they make about the policy-maker–intelligence professional relationship. It is taken as a rule that policy-makers and intelligence professionals form two internally coherent and separate groups with different sets of values. As we noted in discussing militarism, this cannot be assumed to be the case. Numerous studies of the intelligence community also point to the existence

100

of multiple value systems within and between intelligence organizations. For example, within the field of intelligence estimating and analysis, Hughes identifies three different value structures: the butcher (who is consumed with current intelligence and cutting 'juicy morsels' out of the flow of the intelligence process), the baker (who concentrates on producing a finished intelligence product), and the intelligence-maker (who functions as a middleman, quality control inspector, salesman, or production manager ensuring that all of the pieces of the intelligence process come together as they should).[7]

Because it dichotomizes the policy-maker–intelligence professional relationship, formal-legalistic controls are insensitive to the informal sources of power held by the intelligence community. It fails to appreciate that control involves a relationship between those exercising control and those being controlled, and that it is not a one-way process. Among the most significant sources of power enjoyed by intelligence are its ability to control information, to play a major role in defining the situation confronted by policy-makers, and to control as well as present options.

A TYPOLOGY OF INTELLIGENCE ROLES

The limitations inherent in formal-legalistic control measures lessen somewhat if they are accompanied by an attention to the values, role orientations, and norms held by those working within the intelligence community. A number of choices need to be made in constructing a framework for categorizing the views of those involved in intelligence work. What aspect of intelligence are we concerned with (covert action, counter-intelligence, or analysis and estimates)? Whose behavior are we concerned with (high-ranking intelligence officials with community-wide responsibilities, intelligence professionals running major programs or individual intelligence bureaucracies, or middle and low-level intelligence careerists)? What do we mean by control (is the focus on explaining illegalities, or specific behavior patterns that hold implications for control)?

To illustrate the ways in which a concern for role orientations furthers our understanding of how to realize control of intelligence, we focus on how Directors of Central Intelligence (DCIs), who are simultaneously the head of the CIA and the entire intelligence community, have defined their role in the production of analysis and estimates. The five-part typology to be employed is based on the work of F. F. Ridley who developed a typology of subjective senses of bureaucratic responsibility.[8] He defined subjective responsibility as the beliefs of officials regarding to what or to whom they feel a sense of loyalty, and what principles motivate their behavior.

101

The first role orientation is *loyalty to the President*. The DCI sees himself or herself as the anonymous and confidential servant of the President. Policy-making and intelligence analysis are treated as separate areas of activity with the President and DCI recognizing each other's dominance and expertise in their respective spheres of influence. In return for political support and protection from outside pressures, the DCI loyally serves the President, offering advice when asked and carrying out his policies in an efficient manner regardless of his or her personal view. While a change in presidents might change the nature or content of the analysis being produced, it would not change the relationship between the two offices.

A second role orientation is *loyalty to one's profession* or the organization for which one works. Here the DCI's loyalty is primarily to protecting the CIA as an organization and intelligence as a profession. Alternative courses of action are weighed in terms of their potential impact on the future autonomy, health and stature of these two bodies. An especially important component to loyalty to the profession is defending the profession's ability to define its own terms of reference with regard to proper conduct and its definition of national interest.

The third role orientation is *loyalty to a political cause*. This category is best subdivided into two parts: the zealot and the advocate.[9] The DCI as zealot is intensely loyal to a narrow set of policies on the political agenda and uses his or her position to further these goals both in their dealings with the President and their subordinates. The advocate is also a policy activist but directs his or her attention to a wider range of issues and is likely to abandon a cause if the prospects for success appear to dim.

The fourth role orientation is *loyalty to the law*. In this role orientation, the DCI is primarily concerned with the lawfulness of the action. Did officials have the legal right to request a course of action? Were the proper procedures followed? In carrying out the action, did illegal behavior occur? Were rights violated? Do those requesting information have the legal right to it?

The fifth role orientation is *loyalty to the public at large and Congress*. Here, the DCI recognizes the legitimacy of multiple political masters and seeks to balance competing claims placed upon intelligence. Intelligence is seen as the property of the entire government and not as just belonging to the President. When the President and Congress are in agreement, this role orientation presents the DCI with few problems. When they disagree, the DCI is faced with conditions that threaten to undermine his or her overall effectiveness. Is information or analysis which contradicts the President's policy to be made available upon demand to Congress? How often can the President be opposed? Personality, situational, and policy variables are key additional factors that need to be looked at in these cases.

DCI ROLE ORIENTATIONS

In this section, the intelligence analysis and estimating role orientations of four of the most prominent DCIs are examined. They are Allen Dulles, John McCone, Richard Helms and William Casey.[10]

Allen Dulles served as DCI from 1953 to 1961. His interests and expertise as DCI were rooted in his OSS experience with the consequence that operations dominated his attention. Intelligence analysis and community-wide co-ordination concerns were of lesser importance to Dulles as was personal input into policy making. Powers goes so far as to suggest that Dulles had 'something of a fetish of neutrality' in this regard.[11] In his approach to intelligence analysis and estimates, Dulles displayed a role orientation which stressed loyalty to the CIA as an organization and intelligence as a profession. The former was revealed in his avoidance of bureaucratic battles that might threaten the CIA while the latter was revealed in a deference to the expertise of subordinates.

Dulles did not seek to impose himself on the agency. Typically, he did not interject his views on a matter until the analysis was in its final stages and being made ready for presentation to the US Intelligence Board. Deference to professional expertise can also be seen in his unwillingness to impose desk-to-desk co-ordination within the CIA between the Deputy Directorate of Plans and the Deputy Directorate of Intelligence.

Even more significant from the perspective of control-related problems was Dulles' recalcitrance to exert CIA influence on intelligence matters which required dealings with other intelligence agencies for fear that an activist approach would be interpreted as a unilateral effort to expand agency authority and invite counteraction. Two examples highlight Dulles' unwillingness to act forcefully. First, it took two years to create an inter-departmental guided missiles intelligence committee. The Air Force regarded this as a military intelligence question in which the CIA had no jurisdiction. Dulles only pressed the concerns of the CIA's Office of Scientific Intelligence for a voice on this subject after political pressures for co-ordination began building within the government. The Hoover Commission had criticized the organization of Air Force Intelligence, Congress was supporting an interagency approach, and Eisenhower was reportedly interested in having non-military input into the problem. Together, these forces led the Air Force to reverse its position and Dulles to champion an interagency committee.

A second case involved Dulles' rejecting a proposal by the CIA's Economic Research Area (ERA) to establish a Military Economic Branch. By 1956,

ERA was spending a considerable portion of its time analysing Soviet strategic matters. The Military Economic Branch would have centralized this work in one office. Dulles' failure to act led to a situation where the CIA's production of strategic intelligence went formally unrecognized within the intelligence community. Anne Karalakis characterized Dulles' unwillingness to act as a lost opportunity for the CIA and DCI to establish its role as intelligence co-ordinators.[12]

From a control orientation, even more significant consequences followed. A 'dead zone' was created between policy-makers and the intelligence community as intelligence failed to address policy-makers' concerns. A 1956 survey of National Intelligence Estimates (NIE) readers found many to be dissatisfied with the product and that senior policy-makers were not reading it. Professional and bureaucratic concerns replaced policy-maker concerns as the guiding force in the production of intelligence.

John McCone was appointed to replace Dulles and served from 1961 to 1965. An outsider to the intelligence profession, he did not share Dulles' sense of loyalty to the CIA as an organization or intelligence as a profession. Instead, he was very much Downs' policy advocate. While not the first to be offered the post of DCI by Kennedy, McCone took the position 'with the intent of becoming a power in the administration' and by all accounts he was a vigorous participant in policy debates.[13] In fact, McCone's downfall in part may be attributable to having played the role of advocate too intensely. McGeorge Bundy is reported to have uttered that he was 'so tired of listening to McCone say he was right'.[14]

The role of policy advocate led McCone to treat intelligence as a resource to be used, molded or discarded as the situation required. It also led him to involve himself actively in the production of intelligence estimates and to challenge their assumptions and conclusions. The best remembered example of McCone's approach to intelligence as analysis and estimates came during the Cuban missile crisis. Going on what is best described as instinct, McCone was convinced that the Soviet Union was placing offensive missiles in Cuba long before other policy-makers or the intelligence community came to that conclusion. Initially, the Board of National Estimates (BNE) disagreed with McCone. Sherman Kent, its head, insisted that the information then available did not support McCone's thesis.

McCone continued to press his case, and as additional information became available, the BNE produced a new estimate. SNIE 85–3–62 explicitly considered McCone's thesis but concluded by rejecting it. McCone did not accept this as the end of the matter. Even though away on his honeymoon, he cabled the BNE that it should do a special estimate. Its conclusions also disappointed McCone, and he urged that yet another estimate be undertaken, because the BNE had failed to consider the increased bargaining power which the Soviet Union would realize from placing missiles in Cuba. During the crisis itself, McCone's preferred policy option was an air strike. This line of argument was supported at least indirectly by two SNIEs. The tone of SNIE 11–18–62 produced on 19 October encouraged a US military response by minimizing the danger of a Soviet response and by concluding that lesser non-military responses would not be effective. SNIE 11–19–62, produced the next day, again argued that a Soviet military response was unlikely. John Prados argues that the October SNIEs showed indications of the intelligence community searching to get back on board with McCone in the wake of the failures of the September estimates. He argues that had not other members of EXCOM opposed the air strike option the result of the October SNIEs would have been to 'significantly narrow the options available to President Kennedy'.[15]

McCone was selective in his use of the intelligence professionals expertise in playing the role of a policy advocate in the 1963 controversy over ratifying the Partial Nuclear Test Ban Treaty. McCone opposed the treaty because of his concern over the military potential of the ballistic missile defense system around Leningrad and his belief that the Soviet Union would use the treaty to further its lead in this area. Opposition senators used information supplied by McCone to advance their case. McCone even had a CIA analyst temporarily posted to Senator Stennis' office to help with the opposition case. The intelligence community did not fully share McCone's views although a national estimate prepared during the Cuban missile crisis did speak to the future potential of an ABM system. Other CIA officials and representatives from the State Department, Defense Department, and the Arms Control and Disarmament Agency all disagreed with McCone. It required the strong intervention by the Kennedy White House to blunt McCone's opposition to the treaty.

A final example of McCone's advocacy and his willingness to take positions that outdistanced the intelligence community's analysis of an issue comes from Vietnam. During the Johnson administration, McCone spoke out vigorously and his views often clashed with those held by Johnson. McCone had little doubt about the need for victory and pressed Johnson on the need for strong military action, including a major US intervention. At the same time, the CIA's position evolved into one of consistent pessimism over the prospects of victory. Earlier, while Kennedy was still President, McCone had also staked out a position different from that held by many CIA officials in his support for South Vietnamese President Ngo Dinh Diem. In fact, his opposition to Diem's ousting continued after Kennedy had indicated a willingness to have Diem replaced.

McCone's wide-ranging activism is typical of the policy advocate who is not so much committed to a cause as he is to the game of policy making. Also highlighted in these examples is the major control-related problem inherent in this role orientation. The policy advocate's use of intelligence will be selective and designed to push deliberations in directions compatible with personal convictions rather than ones consistent with analysis and estimates. In the process, intelligence loses its ability to serve its intended purpose of clarifying policy options by identifying areas of certainty, ambiguity, and places where crucial information is lacking.

Richard Helms was DCI from 1966 to 1973, serving in that position longer than anyone except Allen Dulles. Like Dulles, Helms adopted a role orientation which stressed loyalty to the CIA as an organization and to intelligence as a profession. And like Dulles, Helms showed little interest in estimates or management-related problems, preferring to focus on the operational side of the CIA's activities. He also shared Dulles' reticence toward expressing his personal views on policy matters. Powers, in his biography of Helms, notes that President Johnson never asked Helms for his opinion on Vietnam, and Helms never volunteered it.[16] Helms showed a similar sense of detachment in his approach to evaluating covert action programs, opposing them or toning them down not because he felt they were wrong but because they were ineffective and disruptive. Unlike Dulles, Helms maintained a low profile as DCI and did not seek to establish a public reputation for himself.

On the basis of the earlier discussion of this role orientation, the major control-related problems were identified as centering on the substitution of organizational and professional survival concerns for the policy-makers' need for intelligence. In Dulles' case, it took the form of a failure to pursue co-ordinated intelligence efforts. Under Helms, it took the form of withholding or suppressing intelligence because of opposition from other policy-makers. A first case involved the debate over Soviet strategic capabilities. Against a backdrop of criticism from the Nixon administration for underestimating the magnitude of the Soviet threat, pressure was applied on Helms to get the CIA back on board as the administration pressed its case that the SS-9 had a MIRV capability. Secretary of Defense Melvin Laird publicly stated that the SS-9 was such a missile. At the time of Laird's statement, the intelligence community was drafting an estimate on this question. The estimate was approved by the USIB on 12 June 1969, and an intelligence memorandum based on it was presented to the National Security Council the next day. The conclusion reached was that the Soviet Union might be trying to achieve something more than nuclear parity but that it was not seeking a first strike capability. Also, the SS-9 was judged to be functionally equivalent to a MRV and not a MIRV. As such, it could hit only one target.

Kissinger reacted negatively to these conclusions and asked Helms to send it back for revisions. Helms complied with the request and the estimate was sent back to the BNE for 'editorial revision'. While the estimate was being reworked, administration officials continued to state publicly that the SS-9 was MIRVed. When it finally emerged in August, the new NIE still contradicted administration policy stating that:

> We believe that the Soviets recognize the enormous difficulties of any attempt to achieve strategic superiority of such order as to significantly alter the strategic balance. Consequently, we consider it highly unlikely that they will attempt within the period of this estimate to achieve a first strike capability, i.e., a capability to launch a surprise attack against the U.S. with assurance that the USSR would not itself receive damage it would regard as unacceptable. For one thing, the Soviets would almost certainly conclude that the cost of such an undertaking along with all their other military commitments would be prohibitive. More important, they almost certainly would consider it impossible to develop and deploy the combination of offensive and defensive forces necessary to counter successfully the various elements of U.S. strategic attack forces. Finally, even if such a project were economically and technically feasible the Soviets would almost certainly calculate that the U.S. would detect and match or overmatch their efforts.[17]

Once again, pressure was brought to bear on Helms to remove the contradictory statement from the estimate. On 4 September, Helms did so. In explaining his actions, Helms stated that when the DCI 'clashes with the secretary of defense, he isn't a big enough fellow on the block'.[18]

It should be stressed that while Helms did give in to administration pressure, he did present the CIA position on the SS-9 to Congress. The discrepancy between his testimony and that of Laird troubled many senators and brought Kissinger's wrath down upon him. Powers argues that 'at this point Helms was about as far out on a limb as a DCI can get and that in the end it may have been only his reputation for integrity in dealing with Congress that saved him'.[19]

In this case, the intelligence pulled by Helms from the NIE found its way back in as a dissenting footnote at the insistence of State Department officials. Such was not the case regarding CIA analysis relating to the invasion of Cambodia. In spring 1967, the CIA's office of National Estimates was working on a paper which addressed the long-term future in Indochina. Helms read an early draft of the report, complemented the work, and stated that he wanted a good paper 'even if I have to make the controversial judgements myself, we owe it to the policy makers'.[20] A second draft sent to Helms on 13 April judged the probable effects of a US invasion and found them to be neither crippling nor permanent.

Later that month, Helms learned for the first time of the Nixon administration's plans for invading Cambodia. He was also warned to keep the plans secret even from the CIA. In subsequent policy meetings dealing with the invasion, Helms did not introduce the CIA's conclusions, and on 29 April, he sent a note to ONE with instructions to wait and look at the problem again in June. Cambodia was invaded later that month. Helms' rationale for withholding this intelligence from policy-makers was strikingly similar to that he put forward in the SS-9 dispute: policy-makers had their minds made up, and it would have done no good to put up a fight. He also argued that it would have been unfair to the analysts who knew nothing of such plans in putting together their estimate.[21]

Counter-examples also can be found where Helms did push the CIA's position against outside opposition. He challenged the Defense Department's plans for a military orbiting satellite and for constructing an over-the-horizon radar in Great Britain. What these counter-examples suggest is that the impulse to protect the CIA as an organization or intelligence as a profession does not dominate all instances where intelligence becomes controversial. The nature of the issue is perhaps central to determine whether it will appear. Those issues that appear only once or are not closely tied to other issues offer the greatest potential for using intelligence to challenge policy options without endangering the autonomy of the organization or intelligence as a profession. Where the issue is highly visible, reappears frequently, or is tied to other issues, opposition is less likely to be tolerated. As many have observed, there are only so many times in which negative or contradictory information can be presented to policy-makers before it will become unwanted or made to fit existing policy preferences. Given these political realities of injecting intelligence into the policy process, a concern for protecting intelligence organizations and professionals cannot be characterized fairly as deviant behavior. The difficult judgement is one of when to stand and fight.

William Casey was appointed DCI by Reagan at the beginning of his presidency and held that position until forced to resign for reasons of health in February 1987. In terms of the role orientation typology developed here, Casey was a zealot. His background provided him both with an exposure to intelligence work as a member of the OSS and a commitment to politics. He served in the Ford and Nixon administrations, including a stint as chairman of the Securities and Exchange Commission, and was campaign manager for Reagan in his 1980 presidential campaign. His

108

appointment as DCI was generally regarded as a reward for his service in that position.

From the very outset, Casey was a controversial DCI. Widely credited with restoring the morale of the CIA, he was also sharply criticized for his perceived politicization of intelligence estimates and his activist policy-making role. His approach to combining intelligence and policy-making has been described as 'solutions now'. *The Washington Post* observed of Casey that he had 'an abiding confidence that an intelligence agency could be used to make a difference in the world, and he set out to do so'. Casey, himself, remarked that 'a person with a lot of ideas is going to make some mistakes . . . I don't get terribly upset about mistakes'.

Two focal points of Casey's activism were the struggle against Communism in Central America and the situation in the Middle East, especially the problem of terrorism. His critics charge that in his zeal to produce intelligence that supported Reagan policy initiatives, he undermined the integrity of the estimating process. Said one former intelligence official: 'He does not ask us for a review of an issue or a situation. He wants material he can use to persuade his colleagues, justify controversial policy, or expand the Agency's involvement in covert action'.[22]

NIEs on Lebanon were repeatedly returned by Casey for revision. According to one former intelligence official, many analysts concluded that Casey's objections centered on the conclusion that the Gemeyal government was not viable even with the presence of US Marines. Press reports suggest that early CIA estimates on terrorism met a similar fate. In 1984, a National Intelligence Officer resigned because of what he felt was pressure to produce the 'right' estimate on Mexico. Not all estimates were politicized but consistent with the expected behavior of a zealot, where 'the political heat is particularly high', CIA estimates adopted a 'more partisan tone'.[23]

Casey's zealot role orientation also came through in his dealings with congressional oversight committees. Committee members repeatedly expressed frustration with Casey over his unwillingness to brief them fully and honestly on intelligence matters. Casey is reported to have once told a CIA associate 'don't brief, limit disclosures'. Nowhere was this more evident and congressional reaction more intense than in his testimony regarding CIA operations in Nicaragua.

Nowhere was Casey's zealot role orientation more evident or better documented than in his participation in the Iran–Contra affair. Where Secretary of State Schultz and Secretary of Defense Weinberger disagreed with the concept of using weapons as an opening to Iran, Casey strongly endorsed the idea. The Tower Commission Report concluded that Casey appears to have been 'informed in considerable detail about the specifics of the Iranian operation', and that he acquiesced in Lieutenant-Colonel Oliver North's exercise of operational control over the initiative. The Report also criticizes Casey for his failures in the decision-making process, failures that are readily attributable to his zealous commitment to the project: he failed to make clear to the President that the CIA was not running the operation; he did not urge a thorough discussion of the assumption behind the Israeli plan; he did not push for a careful investigation of the intermediaries used in the operation in spite of the fact that one was considered unreliable by the CIA; he failed to assess the impact of transferring arms and intelligence to Iran; and he failed to keep Congress informed of the operation.

To this list can be added other actions and omissions by Casey which reveal the extent to which he was committed to the operation and subordinated his responsibilities as DCI to realizing its success. Shultz told the Tower Commission that while attending the Tokyo Economic Summit, Casey told him that the operation had ended and the people involved had been told to 'stand down'. It was DDCI John McMahon, and not Casey, who after the fact found out about the Iranian operation and insisted that a presidential finding be produced. Casey also supported the sending of intelligence to Iran, something objected to by McMahon. And finally, in his post Iran–Contra testimony to Congress, Casey's statements were found to be misleading and incomplete.

Other DCIs. Case-studies of the four most prominent DCIs reveal that only a narrow set of role orientations have been adopted. Other role orientations have surfaced. More than any other DCI, William Colby adopted a role orientation emphasizing a sense of responsibility to the government and public. According to Karalekis, 'well before the public disclosures and allegations regarding CIA activities, Colby was committed to reconciling the agency's priorities with changing public attitudes and expectations'.[24] This general attitude also characterized Colby's approach to intelligence analysis. In testimony before Congress, Colby asserted that intelligence belonged to the entire government and was not to serve just the executive branch. He continued that he also felt the intelligence community had a responsibility to present to Congress intelligence that contradicted administration policy.

Two control-related problems grow out of this role orientation. First, this DCI is likely to find his authority and legitimacy challenged (or at least questioned) from within the intelligence community. This happened with Colby, who was considered by some a traitor for turning over 'the family jewels' to the Church Committee. Second, he is likely to be frozen out of key policy deliberations. Few presidents have shown a willingness to tolerate opposition from their DCIs. Even Stansfield Turner, who is said to have welcomed a policy support role for the CIA, recounts the opposition he encountered from the White House when he made public a study on the health of the Polish economy. Zbigniew Brzezinski in particular was 'livid' and asserted that the DCI had no business publishing intelligence on his own authority.[25]

George Bush, in his brief tenure as DCI, gave evidence of adopting a role orientation stressing quiet loyalty to the President and the administration. Though a partisan figure, Bush did not use his position and intelligence analysis to lobby for personal influence or particular causes. He saw his role as a mediator and buffer between the CIA and Congress and the President. The primary control-related danger growing out of this role orientation is excessive deference. Under Bush, the danger became a reality with the establishment of the 'A-team–B-team' study into Soviet military expenditures. Team B was made up of leading conservatives who felt that the CIA (Team A) had systematically underestimated Soviet military spending. While establishing Team B was a deft political move designed to reduce conservative opposition to President Ford's policies, it guaranteed future problems for the CIA. Given the predictability of Team B's conclusions and the atmosphere of an upcoming presidential election campaign, the absence of Team C, D, or E studies based on differing assumptions meant that the CIA would come under heavy unidirectional pressure to change its estimates.

SUMMARY

Controlling intelligence requires more than formal-legalistic measures. A prerequisite for control is to change the basic nature of the assumptions away from a formal-legalistic perspective to the control problem to one sensitive to the informal aspects of organizational behavior. In the analysis presented here, DCIs were found to have adopted a relatively narrow set of role orientations. Dulles and Helms acted consistently with a role orientation based on loyalty to the CIA as an organization and intelligence as a profession. McCone and Casey acted as a policy advocate and zealot respectively. No one role orientation is necessarily superior to any other, and each presents control problems. The goal, therefore, should be not only to seek out a particular role orientation but to insure a healthy mix of role orientations among top administrators. The case-studies also point to the need to address the question of presidential role orientations regarding intelligence. The selection of a role orientation is in large part based on the expectations that relevant others have regarding an office or position. The most relevant 'other' for a DCI will always be the President. So long as

111

presidents expect policy support or obedience from intelligence, it will be impossible for DCIs to adopt role orientations other than those emphasizing advocacy, protection or loyalty.

NOTES

1. This analysis is based upon that presented in Glenn Hastedt, 'The Constitutional Control of Intelligence', *Intelligence and National Security*, Vol. 1, No. 2 (1986), pp.255–71.
2. See Ann Karalekis, 'Intelligence Oversight: Has Anything Changed?' *The Washington Quarterly*, 6 (1983), pp.22–30.
3. Michael Glennon, 'Investigating Intelligence Affairs: The Process of Getting Information for Congress', in Thomas Franck (ed.), *The Tethered Presidency* (New York, 1981), pp.141–52.
4. Ray Cline, *Secrets, Spies, and Scholars: The Essential CIA* (Washington, DC, 1977), p.247.
5. Quoted in Victor Marchetti and John Marks, *The CIA and the Cult of Intelligence* (New York, 1974), p.324.
6. Alfred Vagts, *A History of Militarism: Civilian and Military* (New York, revised edn., 1959).
7. Thomas L. Hughes, *The Fate of Facts in a World of Men: Foreign Policy and Intelligence-Making* (New York, 1976).
8. F. F. Ridley, 'Responsibility and the Official: Forms and Ambiguities', *Government and Opposition*, 10 (1975), pp.444–72.
9. For a discussion of these two subtypes see Anthony Downs, *Inside Bureaucracy* (Boston, 1967), p.88.
10. These case-studies were originally presented in Glenn Hastedt, 'Controlling Intelligence: The Role of the DCI', *International Journal of Intelligence and Counterintelligence*, 1 (1986–87), pp.25–40.
11. Thomas Powers, *The Man Who Kept Secrets* (New York, 1979), p.206.
12. Anne Karalekis, *History of the Central Intelligence Agency* (Lagune Hills, CA, 1977), p.48.
13. Lawrence Freedman, *U.S. Intelligence and the Soviet Strategic Threat*, second edition (Princeton, 1986), p.18.
14. Powers, *The Man Who Kept Secrets*, p.205.
15. John Prados, *The Soviet Estimate* (Princeton, 1986), p.134–7.
16. Powers, *The Man Who Kept Secrets*, p.225.

6

Controlling Covert Action

GREGORY F. TREVERTON

The idea of conducting secret operations in a democratic society is a paradox, especially when the secret operations are designed to influence – sometimes dramatically – the politics of a foreign country.[1] The paradox is reflected in the deeply ambivalent attitudes of the American people: on the one hand meddling in other people's politics, especially secretly, offends the sense of America as unique; on the other hand, the world *is* a nasty place and sometimes the United States, it seems, must be just as nasty as its adversaries.

The paradox and the ambivalence, as old as the Republic, have been sharpened by the post-war competition with the Soviet Union. Indeed, the post-war history of covert action is the history of the attempt to cope with the paradox in the context of perceived threat from the Soviet Union. The Iran–Contra scandal of the mid-1980s is the latest reminder that the paradox cannot be made to go away, only managed, more or less successfully.

More than a decade earlier, when the Senate created the first Select Committee on Intelligence – often called the Church Committee after its chairman, Senator Frank Church (D, Idaho) – it did so very much under the shadow of another scandal, Watergate. Former intelligence officers, such as E. Howard Hunt, the man who had been in charge of propaganda for PBSUCCESS, the covert overthrow of President Arbenz of Guatemala in 1954, were among the Nixon administration's 'plumbers'. The press was full of intimations, many of them unfortunately true, that intelligence agencies had been involved in a wide variety of activities outside the law – illegal wire-tapping, domestic surveillance, harassment of anti-war and civil rights groups, and more.

Still more troubling was the impression that the intelligence agencies had become kingdoms of their own, operating beyond the ken of Congress and outside the control even of presidents. Some of the CIA's internal investigation into its own involvement in plots to assassinate foreign leaders already had found its way into the American media, evoking Senator Church's metaphor

113

of the CIA as a 'rogue elephant' on the rampage.

Then, the Committee, which I served, did not find much evidence of rogue elephants in the CIA. (We did find some in the domestic counter-intelligence operations of the FBI, another kind of illustration of the paradox.) Yet if the Committee did not find 'rogue elephants', it did find that so-called, 'plausible denial', as it had been practiced, sometimes created a troubling looseness in the Executive Branch's review and control of covert action, even as in a pinch it seldom protected administrations in power. And in the early days, the Congressional role amounted to the 'buddy system' – that is to say, informal conversations between the CIA Director and a few senior members of Congress.

Plausible denial and the buddy system did not emerge because the CIA had broken free of its political masters. They emerged because that was how both administrations and Congress wanted it at the time – an illustration that how the American body politic and its leaders strike the balance between secrecy and accountability has changed over time.

'PLAUSIBLE DENIAL' AND THE 'BUDDY SYSTEM'

When Richard Helms testified before the Church Committee in 1975 about charges that the CIA had tried to kill Fidel Castro, he was vivid in describing plausible denial and almost plaintive in drawing its implications:

> ... it was made abundantly clear ... to everybody involved in the operation that the desire was to get rid of the Castro regime and to get rid of Castro ... the point is that no limitations were put on this injunction ... one ... grows up in [the] tradition of the times and I think that any of us would have found it very difficult to discuss assassinations with a President of the U.S. I just think we all had the feeling that we're hired out to keep those things out of the Oval Office.[2]

If he had ever thought he would later have to testify before Congress about what he had done, Helms reflected, he would have made sure that his orders were clearly in writing.

By their own testimony, not a single member of the National Security Council outside the CIA knew of, much less authorized, those plots.[3] Even within the CIA, it remains unclear exactly how much John McCone knew of the plots while they were going on during his tenure as Director of Central Intelligence (DCI).[4] As Richard Bissell, the Deputy Director for Plans (DDP, later labelled, less disingenuously, Deputy Director for Operations, or DDO) at the time of the first plots, puts it, even within the CIA 'there was a reluctance to spread, even on an oral record, some aspects of this operation'.[5]

As a result, CIA officials spoke to each other only in riddles about these operations. And if they spoke of them at all with those outside the CIA charged with approving covert operations, they did so 'indirectly' or in 'circumlocutions'. Thus, in 1975 the Church Committee spent hours trying to unravel whether terse references in documents to 'disappear' or 'direct positive action' or 'neutralize' referred to assassination. It could not be sure. And that was precisely the point of plausible denial. Those CIA officials who spoke in circumlocutions could feel they had done their duty as they understood it. Their political superiors could understand what they would, ask for more information if they desired, but also forbear from asking. If things went awry, they could, if they chose, disclaim knowledge, and do so more or less honestly.

These effects of plausible denial are extreme in the instance of the Cuban assassination plots, but similar effects ran through covert actions of the 1950s and 1960s. Dean Rusk, who served Presidents Kennedy and Johnson as Secretary of State, has observed that he routinely knew little of CIA operations: 'I never saw a CIA budget, for example . . .'.[6] Of thousands of covert action projects between 1949 and 1968, only some 600 received consideration outside the CIA by the National Security Council body then charged with reviewing covert operations.

In practice, the CIA sought broad grants of authority for covert action, which spawned small projects, many of which, arguably, were sensitive enough in political terms to merit specific NSC approval. Through the major covert operations in Iran and Guatemala in the 1950s there was no NSC body charged with reviewing covert action, and even after the first such group, the 5412 Committee, was created in 1955, it met infrequently. Then, and later, the initiative remained with the CIA. Its officials were the only ones in a position to make judgements about whether a given project was covered by a previous authorization or was large and sensitive enough to merit special consideration outside the CIA.

When a project did come before the NSC body for approval, only the briefest of notations was recorded, in keeping with plausible denial. The President's special assistant for National Security Affairs – in the Eisenhower administration more of an executive secretary than the policy-maker the holders of that job became in later administrations – noted in a memorandum: CIA project number 75A was approved.

Beginning in 1959, the 5412 Committee's successor, the Special Group, began to meet weekly. Yet even when proposed covert actions came before NSC review, those outside the CIA were in a weak position to assess it. That fact is striking in the run-up to the Bay of Pigs invasion of Cuba in 1961. The initiative remained with the CIA. Senior political leaders who had doubts about

115

the project could hardly address its operational details: hence the Bay of Pigs grew from a guerrilla uprising to an amphibious invasion, and the invasion site changed.

They were only slightly better positioned to question the presumptions and implications of any other covert action. In the few years leading up to the Bay of Pigs, those officials confronted the legacy of CIA success in Iran and Guatemala and the formidable personality of Allen Dulles, then the DCI. The CIA had succeeded; it had done so with tolerable 'deniability'. Who were they to say it could not be done again, particularly when Dulles said it could? Moreover, criticism, especially in the Kennedy administration, could easily be mistaken for insufficient energy in the war on Communism – and so, perhaps, Rusk refrained from voicing any doubts he had about the Bay of Pigs.

For its part, the US Congress was more interested in making sure the CIA had what it needed in the fight against Communism than in overseeing its operations. The fate of several Congressional initiatives for improving oversight that came to naught in these early years is eloquent testimony to that mood of the times and temper of the Congress. In early 1955 Senator Mike Mansfield, later Chairman of the Foreign Affairs Committee, introduced a resolution calling for a Joint Oversight Committee; his resolution grew out of a Congressional review of Executive Branch procedures. The resolution had 35 co-sponsors. It also had the strong opposition not only of the Executive but also of the 'club' of senior members. In hearings on the resolution, Mansfield elicited the following comment from Senator Leverett Saltonstall, the ranking Republican on the Armed Services Committee and its Defense Subcommittee:

> ... it is not a question of reluctance on the part of the CIA officials to speak to us. Instead, it is a question of our reluctance, if you will, to seek information and knowledge on subjects which I personally, not as a Member of Congress and as a citizen, would rather not have, unless I believed it to be my responsibility to have it because it might involve the lives of American citizens.[7]

In April 1956 the resolution was voted down, 59 to 27, with half a dozen co-sponsors voting against.

The debate did, however, result in the creation of formal CIA subcommittees in both Armed Service Committees. Yet the 'buddy system' remained largely unchanged. Dulles, the near legend, was still DCI; relaxed and candid with senior members, he had their absolute trust. In the Senate Armed Service Committee, Senator Richard Russell appointed to the formal subcommittee those senators with whom he had been meeting informally on CIA matters: Saltonshall and Robert Byrd. Later he added Lyndon Johnson and Styles

Bridges. When, in 1957, the Appropriations Committee formed a subcommittee for the CIA, its members were Russell, Byrd and Bridges. They did both 'authorization' and 'appropriation', often at the same meeting.[8] Most CIA business continued to be conducted as before – by Dulles and Russell, meeting informally.

'FAILURE' AND ITS AFTERMATH

The Bay of Pigs marked the end of an era for the CIA. It was a stunning defeat for an agency that had been known only for success. President Kennedy took responsibility for the débâcle, but Dulles and Bissell were eased out of their jobs, to be replaced by John McCone as DCI and Richard Helms as DDP. The Dulles era was over.

Yet neither Executive procedures for, nor Congressional oversight of, covert action changed all that much. Plausible denial seemed threadbare after the Bay of Pigs: Kennedy did not feel he could make use of it; nor had his predecessor, Eisenhower, when the Soviet Union shot down a CIA U-2 reconnaissance aircraft over Russia in May 1960. In the wake of the Bay of Pigs, the Taylor Report – after General Maxwell Taylor, who became the President's Military Advisor – redefined the membership of the Special Group to improve co-ordination of paramilitary operations. Later, the administration created two additional variants of the Special Group, one for counter-insurgency and one to handle the covert war on Cuba.

By 1963 the CIA and the Special Group had developed criteria for which covert action proposals should come before the Group; until then, that decision had been left to the discretion of the DCI. The criteria were never written down and were not – could not be – all that precise. Twenty-five thousand dollars came to be agreed as the dollar threshold, and CIA officers also estimated three kinds of risk: chances of exposure, chances of success and degree of political sensitivity.

In February 1970, National Security Decision Memorandum (NSDM) 40 replaced the 15-year-old NSC 5412/2 as the governing document for covert action. Apart from changing the NSC authorizing group's name to the 40 Committee, it affected process in the Executive only by mandating a yearly 40 Committee review of projects previously authorized.

The Bay of Pigs and a decade of covert action afterward, including the big expansion in Asia as the war in Vietnam heated up, did lead to somewhat more formal procedures in the Executive Branch. For instance, the 40 Committee considered Chile on 23 separate occasions between March 1970 and October 1973.[9] Not all those occasions were meetings; some were merely the collection of clearances by telephone. Yet major decisions were debated. The range of

117

that debate was constricted, but within those limits, the debate sometimes was sharp: the US decided not to give covert support to a particular candidate in the 1970 Chilean elections, as it had in 1964; and later it set limits on support to opposition forces.

Still, in numbers of projects, most covert action projects continued not to be approved by anyone outside the CIA. In this sense the Cuban assassination plots were unusual even within the unusual. Most were small, often propaganda projects, deemed not risky by the rough guidelines in effect. By the early 1970s only about a fourth of all covert actions came before the NSC review body.[10]

Moreover, the authorization process also was – and is – made more difficult by the fuzzy line separating covert action from espionage or counter-intelligence. Covert actions of the political kind – support to labor unions, political parties or media organizations – often used links to foreigners ('assets' in the language of the trade) that had been developed to provide intelligence. That intelligence-gathering provided wherewithal for covert action, yet typically it was not reviewed outside the CIA. In the extreme, it might itself *be* a kind of covert action: for example, after CIA efforts had failed and Salvador Allende became President of Chile in 1971, there were grounds for concern that the Chilean military officers being cultivated by the CIA for intelligence purposes would also construe that contact as implying support for *their* purposes – unseating Allende in a military coup.

More committees of Congress received more information from the CIA than in the early days. In 1967, 13 committees in addition to the four with oversight responsibilities were briefed by the CIA.[11] Most of those briefings, however, concerned intelligence products, not clandestine operations. About those operations, the CIA did not often volunteer information, and Congress did not frequently ask. The role of Congress had not moved from receiving information to overseeing operations. In 1961 after the Bay of Pigs, and again in 1966, Senator Eugene McCarthy attempted to revive the idea of a CIA oversight committee, but it was still an idea whose time had not yet come.

American covert operations in Chile both illustrate this pattern and suggest the beginning of a change in attitude, especially on the part of Congress. According to CIA records, Chile was the subject of 53 CIA briefings for Congress between 1964 and 1974.[12] Covert actions were discussed at 31 of these, and of those, 23 concerned special releases from the CIA Contingency Fund – a fund designed to permit the Agency to respond quickly to changing foreign circumstances. Of the 33 covert action projects the CIA undertook with 40 Committee approval during that period, Congress was briefed in some fashion on eight; those eight comprised about half of the 13 million dollars the CIA spent in Chile during that period. Many of those briefings did not come until quite long after the fact, and, needless to say, Congress was not informed of sensitive operations that did not go before the 40 Committee.

Before 1973 most of the meetings with Congress were confined to the designated oversight committees – the appropriate subcommittees of armed services and appropriations in each house. After Chile passed into public scrutiny, both the frequency and scope of meetings expanded. There were 13 meetings between March 1973 and December 1974, and these included Congressional newcomers to the subject such as the Senate Foreign Relations Subcommittee on Multinational Corporations and the House Foreign Affairs Subcommittee on Inter-American Affairs.

THE CLIMATE CHANGES

If Congress did not much want to ask about covert action and the CIA did not much want to tell, Watergate and Chile, coming on the heels of the war in Vietnam, changed all that. Congress's disinclination to ask was the first to change. In 1974 it passed the Hughes–Ryan act, the operative paragraph of which reads:[13]

> No funds appropriated under the authority of this or any other Act may be expended by or on behalf of the [CIA] for operations in foreign countries, other than activities intended solely for obtaining necessary intelligence, unless and until the President finds that each such operation is important to the national security of the United States and reports, in a timely fashion, a description and scope of such operation to the appropriate committees of Congress . . . .

'Finds' was turned into the noun of art 'finding' – a written document bearing the President's signature. As so often, Congress sought to change the pattern of Executive action not by determining specific decisions but rather by changing the process by which decisions were made. Hughes–Ryan reflected the demise of plausible denial, which seemed in the mid-1970s to have confused procedures within the Executive – and deluded Congress – more than it protected anyone.

Hughes–Ryan required the President to put his name and his reputation on the line. It was meant to ensure that there would be no future wrangles such as those over assassinations: covert actions, wise or foolish, would reflect presidential decision; there would be no doubt that someone was in charge. It also tied the hands of members of Congress: they would find it harder to assert that they had been kept in the dark. Less often could they make speeches in professed ignorance of covert action. The balance in coping with the paradox has shifted toward accountability.

119

This shifting balance caught the DCI at the time, William Colby, in a dilemma. He had concluded that times had changed, and that the change required new attitudes on the part of the intelligence services. In his words:

> There had been a time when the joint hearing held by the Senate's intelligence subcommittees would have been deemed sufficient [to] . . . end the matter. Senators with the seniority and clout of McClellan and Stennis then could easily have squelched any demands for further action on the part of their junior colleagues. But this was no longer the case.[14]

Colby was more resigned to the change than fond of it: 'The lesson was clear. The old power structure of the Congress could no longer control their junior colleagues . . . CIA was going to have to fend for itself'. Yet in the end he regarded the changed Congressional role as appropriate, a view that put him at loggerheads with many in the Ford White House: '. . . I must say that, unlike many in the White House and, for that matter, within the intelligence community, I believed that the Congress was within its constitutional rights to undertake a long-overdue and thoroughgoing review of the Agency . . .'.

Colby's conflict with his political masters came to a head in September 1975. The Pike Committee – a House committee parallel to the Church Committee, chaired by Representative Otis Pike (D, NY) – was prepared to publish its report criticizing the CIA for its past intelligence failures. That the report was mostly stitched together from the CIA's own internal post-mortems was galling enough; worse, Colby believed, publication of excerpts from CIA documents could harm intelligence 'sources and methods'. Pike agreed to some deletions but not to all, the President cut off the Committee from any further classified documents until the matter was resolved, and the Committee, in turn, prepared to cite Colby for contempt of Congress.

Colby was feeling more and more isolated within the administration. While he had argued against disclosure in this instance, in his words, he 'did not believe that, in the long run, the Executive could hold to a position that blocked a Congressional committee from pursuing an investigation of intelligence'.[15] But the White House made no move to resolve the impasse, and Colby's position among the 'doves' was more and more uncomfortable.

In the end, the House itself resolved this issue. It voted to shelve the entire Pike report. Already the climate in Congress and the country was beginning to shift again; in the press, stories fretting about the harm being done to American intelligence were beginning to outnumber accounts of CIA excesses – a shift capped in December 1975 by the brutal murder of Richard Welch, the CIA Station Chief in Athens. In this atmosphere, House members were becoming more and more uneasy over the bad publicity the Pike Committee was earning them.

Yet Colby was still the odd man out within the administration. The final straw, he believes, came in September 1975 when the Church Committee held its first open hearing – on poisonous toxins that the CIA had at one time produced and which it had failed to destroy as stipulated by international treaty. The failure was bureacratic oversight, not malice, but Colby found himself 'with some wonderment describing the story about the poisons and dart gun before TV cameras'.[16] The day was a bad one for Colby. No senator could resist the chance to be photographed holding the dart gun and making appropriately severe remarks. For many in the Ford administration, it was the final piece of evidence that the Congressional investigations should have been strangled at birth – and that Colby's willingness to co-operate bore much of the blame.

Colby, however, continued to

> believe in the Congress' constitutional right to investigate the intelligence community; and I believed that, as head of that community, I was required by the Constitution to cooperate with the Congress. I also believed that any other approach just wouldn't work.[17]

At eight o'clock on the first Sunday in November, Colby was called to the White House. This time, unlike others, it was not for a special meeting on a crisis then breaking. This time, Colby was dismissed.

THE SHIFTING BARGAIN: TENDING THE 'GOVERNMENT'S' SECRETS

Whatever their results, the committees, and the Church Committee in particular, were an innovation in constitutional relations between the Executive and Congress.[18] Our own language mirrors the ambiguity about what constitutes 'the government', particularly in foreign affairs. High-school civics textbooks show the Congress as a co-equal branch of 'the government', yet often we use 'government' more narrowly to refer to a particular administration in power. At the heart of the Church Committee's wranglings with the Ford administration over access to classified documents lay the constitutional issue: were those secret documents, written and classified by the CIA or State, the property of the Executive only? Or were they the 'government's' documents, to which Congress should have access on terms decided by it and which could be declassified by its decision as well as that of the Executive?

We did not, in 1975–76, reach a clean resolution of this fundamental question. Probably, in the nature of our system, we could not have done. But we did move a long way toward the view that even in matters of clandestine operations, Congress has its own right to the 'government's' secret documents

– and bears the responsibility that goes with that right. In seeking to establish that position, the Church Committee was fanatic about leaks. So far as I am aware, not a single secret worth mention seeped out through the Committee and its staff.[19]

The Ford administration was a grudging partner in reshaping the bargain between the Executive and Congress. A few in the administration, Colby foremost among them, believed the reshaping was fundamentally correct; others, no doubt, simply felt the administration had no choice. The administration had something of a dual approach to the Church Committee. At one level, as a matter of principle, it was opposed to the investigation and its results. It held, thus, that publication of the interim report on assassinations was a mistake, one that would harm the reputation of the United States.

At another level, however, it was prepared to work with the Committee, particularly to protect intelligence sources and methods. In that regard, it and the Committee shared an interest; the Committee had no reason to want to endanger intelligence methods or agents' lives, quite the contrary. In the case of the assassination report, the issue boiled down to whether we would publish the names of some 33 CIA officers. The administration argued that publishing the names would tarnish reputations and might, in one or two instances, endanger the individuals in question. Colby even took the issue to district court.

In the end, the Committee and the administration reached a sensible compromise. The Committee agreed to delete the names of 20 of the officers. Neither the substance nor the credibility of the report required those names. The remaining names were left in. Most of those were senior officers whose names were already in the public domain. We felt, moreover, that as senior officials, it was fair to hold them publicly accountable for their actions. Like most compromises, this one pleased neither side fully, but it was one with which both could live.[20]

In the end, the Church Committee's principal recommendation was that it be made permanent. It hoped it would in time absorb all the existing oversight functions and so provide a single focal point for the Senate's consideration of the intelligence community. That hope was realized. Yet in the short run all the permanent new committee did was increase the number of Congressional overseers of intelligence from six committees to seven, or eight including the House Select Committee, albeit ones with more access to information.

Yet the institutional legacy of permanent select committees in each house of Congress has turned out to be an important one. The committees include members who sit simultaneously on the armed services, foreign affairs, judiciary and appropriations committees, giving those committees the opportunity to relinquish their oversight function without feeling they have been entirely cut out. Moreover, the committees established the principle of rotating memberships, to broaden their representation within the Congress, thus guarding against a recurrence of the buddy system in image or in fact. An earlier innovation in Congressional oversight, the Joint Atomic Energy Committee, was widely regarded as having become the captive of those agencies it oversaw.

The procedural legacy, that messy constitutional bargain between Executive and Congress, was at least as important as the institutional one. Congress secured its access to information about intelligence activities, including covert action, as a matter of right, not of Executive courtesy. (Whether Congress always likes knowing about covert action is another matter.) Secret documents became the property of 'the government', not just the Executive.

Making the President sign on the dotted line for major covert actions, and reinforcing that with Congressional access to secret documents would, it was hoped, induce administrations to think and think again before resorting to covert intervention. Prudent presidents might come to use the overseers as a source of seasoned counsel about the political risks of an operation, and so as a check on the CIA's can-do mentality or the temptations of White House staffers. The process would also make Congress share the responsibility at both 'take-off and landing', in one staffer's phrase, even if the operation failed and the landing was a hard one.

Campaigning in the wake of the Congressional investigations, President Carter promised further intelligence reform. In office, he shied away from legislative charters but did issue Executive Order No. 12036 in January 1978, covering the whole range of intelligence activities. It made the Carter NSC's Special Coordination Committee (SCC) the successor to the 40 Committee as Executive Branch reviewer of covert action. The formal membership paralleled that of prececessor committees, including the Secretaries of State and Defense, the DCI, the chairman of the Joint Chiefs of Staff, the director of the Office of Management and Budget, and the assistant to the President for national security affairs; the Attorney General, however, was a significant addition. In an attempt to deal with the fact that clandestine operations not labelled 'covert action' sometimes have political effects, the SCC was also charged with reviewing sensitive collection and counter-intelligence projects.

The Carter administration also tightened Executive Branch procedures for reviewing covert action in other ways. It sought, in its first two years at least, to embody an inclination against covert action in the process of review. Within the CIA, proposals were passed to a number of offices outside the Directorate of Operations – the comptroller, general and legislative counsels, and, continuing a practice begun during Colby's tenure, the Directorate of Intelligence, then called the National Foreign Assessment Center. The Agency's analysts would have some chance of knowing what its covert operators were up to.

Before the DCI signed off on any proposal, it was also reviewed two places outside the CIA – the State Department and a staff-level working group of the SCC, composed of representatives of all the agencies on the parent SCC. The working group was advisory, not decision-making. But many proposals never got beyond its review, while others were sent back to the CIA to be recast. As earlier – and later – much depended on the views of the individuals that reviewed proposals, but no longer were decisions about what merited SCC review, presidential finding or consultation with Congress purely the province of the CIA.

The Carter administration's dealings with Congress over covert action were easy. With the administration using the instrument sparingly, Carter's continuation of the Ford practice of submitting blanket findings – covering, for instance, a range of covert actions against terrorist targets in a single finding – was not much of an issue. Nor was the the fact that Carter's DCI, Stansfield Turner, rejected the notion of 'prior notification' – that is, notifying the Congress before operations are under way.[21]

The administration and Congress co-operated in passing the Intelligence Oversight Act of 1980, the most important law passed by Congress in the realm of covert action.[22] The Act did cut back the Executive's reporting requirements for covert action to the two intelligence committees. It also made clear that Congress wanted to be notified of all covert actions, not just those carried out by the CIA; secret Executive recourse to other agencies, in particular the military, was denied.

Congress also tiptoed toward prior notification of covert action; the 'timely fashion' of Hughes–Ryan which allowed notification after the fact (within 24 hours came to be the understanding) became 'fully and currently informed', including 'any significant anticipated intelligence activity', in the 1980 Act. Yet notifying Congress still was not a 'condition precedent to the initiation' of covert action. And the Act gave the President another escape hatch, for in emergencies he was permitted to limit prior notice to eight members: the chairmen and ranking minority members of the intelligence committees, the Speaker and minority leader of the House and the majority and minority leaders of the Senate – the 'Gang of Eight'.

THE INHERENT TENSION

Tension between the Executive and Congress over covert action, muted when the administration in power and the Congressional overseers shared the view that the instrument should be used sparingly, increased with the surge of covert actions in the 1980s. The Reagan administration came into office determined to make covert assistance to 'freedom fighters' around the world a key element of its global pressure on the Soviet Union. In setting out what came to be called the 'Reagan Doctrine', the President said third-world trouble-spots 'are the consequence of an ideology imposed from without, dividing nations and creating regimes that are . . . at war with their own people . . . And in each case, Marxism-Leninism's war becomes war with their neighbors'.[23]

Reagan's Executive Order No. 12333 slightly expanded the definition of covert action, termed 'special activities', over the Carter order. And, strikingly in light of what came later, it gave the CIA full responsibility for those activities except in time of war or by specific presidential instruction.[24]

The administration reshaped its internal review processes to manage the increase in covert actions. In place of the SCC, it created the National Security Planning Group (NSPG). That group included the Vice President, the Secretaries of State and Defense, the DCI and the National Security Advisor, but, for reasons of secrecy, the other SCC members were dropped. In their place, three presidential advisors were added; the White House chief of staff, his deputy and the President's counselor. The President himself was a member of the Group. The intent was to make the process more responsive to the President's desire for more frequent resort to covert action. The risk was that sources of expert advice – the Attorney General or Joint Chiefs of Staff, for instance – especially advice that might be cautionary, were lost.[25]

By 1985 the administration had created a group to backstop the NSPG, somewhat in parallel to the SCC working group in the Carter administration. Like its predecessor, it was composed of the deputies of the NSPG members. Formally nameless, it was dubbed the '208 Committee' after the room where it met in the Old Executive Office Building in the White House complex.

With the new administration, attitudes changed more than procedures. One Congressional staffer referred to men like Oliver North as 'field grades', people eager for action, long on energy but short on political acumen. William Miller, the staff director of both the Church Committee and the first permanent Senate Intelligence Committee, observed that the CIA and its sister agencies were led in the late 1970s by people who had been through the experience of investigation and reform. They were 'so immersed in the constitutional questions that they could recite chapter and verse. Questions of law and balance occurred naturally to them'. By contrast, the Reagan leadership was dominated by 'advocates, people who were always trying to get around the roadblocks, who were looking for a way to get it done'.[26]

Nicaragua, and the first Reagan finding for aid to the Contras, was the first focal point of tension between Executive and Congress. The clash of interests was almost built into the process, for the administration, like the Ford and Carter administrations before it, preferred broad, general findings that would give the CIA room to adapt to changing circumstances, while, by contrast, Congress was wary of signing a blank check, particularly so since the administration wanted to do more by way of covert action than at least the House committee was prepared to countenance. Carter's DCI, Turner, summarized the conflict:

> Under a broad finding, an operation can be expanded considerably; with a narrow one, the CIA has to go back to the President to obtain a revised finding if there is any change of scope. The Congress is wary of broad findings; they can easily be abused. The CIA is afraid of narrow findings; they can be a nuisance.[27]

McGeorge Bundy, who ran the 303 Committee for the Kennedy and Johnson administrations, commented on the difficulty reviewers outside the CIA confront, a comment that Congressional overseers of the Contra operation would appreciate: '. . . I think it has happened that an operation is presented in one way to a committee and executed in a way that is different from what the committee thought it had considered'.[28]

Whether an operation that changed in midstream compelled the president to issue a new finding was a related point of tension. Hughes–Ryan required presidential findings for covert actions 'important to the national security' but could not explain how the 'important' was to be distinguished from the 'routine' in this special realm of covert action. Later provisions required every covert action to be covered by a finding, but whether an operational change required a new finding was a matter of judgement: did the change increase the risks of exposure or the harm if disclosed; did it represent a marked shift in the nature of the operation; or did it substantially increase costs?

All these questions required Congressional overseers to get deeply into the details of ongoing operations, hard for them and uncomfortable for covert operators in the Executive Branch. Critical details could fall between the cracks even with the best of wills on both sides. And needless to say wills were not always the best. The CIA's mining of Nicaraguan harbors is a case in point. The operation clearly was, at a minimum, risky since it threatened not only Nicaraguan vessels but also international shipping, including that of American allies. It also represented a new phase in the covert war, albeit a phase suggested by the original CIA proposal.

The president approved the recommendation in the winter, probably in December 1983.[29] The Sandinistas announced on 3 January that the Contras were laying mines in Nicaraguan harbors, and, catching up quickly on their lines, the rebel leaders announced on the 8th that they would do so.

On 31 January the DCI, William Casey, met the House committee, a persistent critic of covert action in Nicaragua, and mentioned the mining, though the meeting was primarily about releasing further funds for the overall

Contra project. Several members of the Senate committee and its staff may also have been briefed. The Senate, however, was pushing toward its February recess, and the administration twice asked for a delay so that Secretary of State Shultz could attend. As a result, a full briefing of the Senate committee was delayed, and many, perhaps most members remained unaware of the operation, especially of the direct CIA role in it. So did the staff director.

Casey first met the full committee on 8 March, for over an hour, but this meeting, too, dealt primarily with authorizing the release of funds, over which the Intelligence Committee was fighting a jurisdictional battle with Appropriations. Only one sentence dealt with the mining, and it, like the rest of the briefing, was delivered in Casey's inimitable mumble.[30] Many on the Committee did not learn of the mining until a month later, almost by accident on the floor of the Senate.

Casey honored the letter of the law with his brief reference, but the episode angered even Senator Barry Goldwater, the Committee chairman, a man not known for his opposition to covert action. He had not understood the reference. When he learned about the operation, once the Committee staff received a full briefing on 2 April, he was furious. His letter to Casey, leaked to the press, was notable for its unsenatorial expression as well as for its displeasure: 'It gets down to one, little, simple phrase: I am pissed off!'[31]

It may be that Committee members, like Goldwater, were not paying attention. The episode also demonstrates another peril of oversight: if the two houses share a distrust of the Executive, no matter which party is in power, they are jealous of each other as well and so the two committees do not automatically share information. However, as Turner concluded, Casey's performance, if it squared with the letter of the law, was 'hardly the intent . . . The CIA did go through the motions of informing, but it wasn't speaking very loudly'.[32]

POLITICAL STAKES AND NATIONAL INTERESTS

Most of the time, getting members of Congress to pay attention to covert action was not and is not a problem. They have little political reason to become involved, much less to take responsibility for particular actions, but the mystique of clandestine operations remains a powerful tug on their attentions. Again and again during the work of the Church Committee, I was struck by the prospect of Committee members listening, in secret session, to long disquisitions about codebreaking or satellite reconnaissance while their political aides fretted, their constituents waited and other hearings dealing with business that was less romantic but more relevant to their political stakes went on without them. At the beginning of the 100th Congress in 1987, 60 members of the House had signed up for four openings on the Intelligence Committee.

Still, even for members of the intelligence committees, the assignment is one among many, whatever its fascination. Even their staffs are hard-pressed to keep up with the details of 40-odd covert actions. As one staffer close to the process put it:

> How can you know which detail will jump up and bite you? Things move fast. How long did the mining take from beginning to end? A few weeks. Even the manual [for the Contras, one that had appeared to countenance assassination as a tool of the resistance] took only three months from printing to distribution[33]

And oversight is something of an unnatural act. Members have little political reason to become involved in it, much reason not to. Sometimes, they feel they know more than they want. As Senator Daniel Inouye, the first chairman once the permanent Senate Intelligence Committee was created, observed, in words not much different from Senator Saltonstall's a generation earlier: 'How would you like to know a very, very high official of a certain government was on our payroll?'[34]

Moreover, once they are briefed and understand an operation, committee members are in an awkward political position. They know about the covert action but cannot easily stop it if they disapprove. By custom, the CIA informs the White House of any dissent from the committees, and the lack of strong dissent is sure to be taken by the administration as tacit approval of the operation. Thus, the act of being briefed is more than receiving information; it is giving, or withholding assent, even if the committees do not vote on a particular action once it is briefed to them.

The committees have more responsibility than authority. The operation may already be under way or will be by the time the briefing is over. If the administration is determined to proceed, it can fund the operation for a year from the Contingency Reserve.[35] Only in the next budget cycle, do the committees have the opportunity to pass on the project as a line item in the budget.

The committees' power is the power to persuade. Presidents cannot lightly ignore their views, especially if those views are held by senior committee members reaching across party lines. The CIA needs to deal with the committees for its budget and for a range of intelligence issues; the President needs good relations with senior members for other business beyond intelligence. The committees have sought in several ways to enhance their power to persuade. Lest the President miss the point, committee members can write to or even visit him. On a number of occasions the Senate committee has taken a formal vote to underscore its opposition to a particular proposal; more than once, apparently, its vote has induced a president to rescind approval of the operation.[36] As with Nicaragua, the committees can press the administration to refine its finding to make the operation more accountable.

If an administration is still determined to proceed in the face of opposition from the committees, Congress has several other options, all of them messy and public. Members or their staffs can simply leak the operation to the press, which has happened on rare occasions. Or the committees can take their case to the full house meeting in secret session. That, however, is likely to disclose the operation simply because too many people will then know of it. It also makes a travesty of the oversight process that was meant to build accountability by centralizing authority in Congress.

In extreme cases, however, when passions are high on both sides and when the sense of frustration in Congress is deep, Congress has resorted to public legislation barring 'covert' action. It did so in the 1970s with the Clark–Tunney Amendment on Angola and in the 1980s with the Boland Amendment dealing with Nicaragua. In both cases, Congress said, in effect, that it did not trust the administration, or its designated overseers of covert action, or both.

More than a decade ago, in designing new oversight arrangements to cope with the paradox of secret operations, the attempt was to strike a delicate balance: Congress would have the power to persuade by having the ability to know; single points of oversight, constructed to be representative of the entire house, would enhance accountability by permitting a real sharing of information even about these most secret of governmental operations. At the same time, Congress would not have the right of prior approval; it would not have to vote up or down on every significant covert action. That did not then seem either wise or necessary, nor did it seem what either the Executive or Congress desired.

Most of the time the process seems to have worked as it was intended. The congressional overseers have been informed of covert action and recorded their views; sometimes those views have prevailed. In others, they have said, in the words of one staff member, 'Hey, do you know how risky that is?'[37] Hearing an affirmative response, they have let the program go ahead despite their doubts. Most of the time, in either case, the process has remained secret. The Reagan administration wanted to make use of covert action much more frequently than its predecessor, and the oversight committees, reflecting the mood of Congress and probably of the American people as well, assented to that expansion.

Sometimes, however, the Congressional overseers have been thrust into an unenviable position: either keep silent about an operation despite their misgivings or take actions that are almost certain to reveal that operation. In the one case, the power to persuade becomes instead the opportunity to be used by the Executive. In the other, the oversight process breaks down and, for better or worse, the option of covertness is foreclosed.

For instance, in first limiting, then cutting off, then resuming aid to the Contras, the Congress confronted an administration determined to continue to find ways to help them, an administration arguing that the United States had a commitment to the Contras. Congress was thus bound to pay attention to the spirit of the law, the administration to the letter. Congress was driven toward broad bans: was any administration official barred from doing anything to find other sources of such support? How could Congress enforce such a ban, much less do so privately?

There can be no full resolution to these dilemmas, for they are rooted in the paradox of secret operations in a democracy. It still does not seem appropriate to make Congress approve every covert action in advance. There is a constitutional issue about whether that is 'a legislative function', in former DCI Colby's words. More immediately, getting the intelligence committees to authorize and the Congress to appropriate specific budgets could take months. A partial remedy would be to require the intelligence committees to approve any withdrawal from the CIA Contingency Reserve. That would be uncomfortable for the committees in that it would put them more directly on the line in the eyes of the Congressional colleagues, but it would at least spare them the discomfort of having to choose between silent opposition to an operation and public exposure of it.

LESSONS AND THEIR LIMITS

At first sight, none of these delicate dilemmas in relations between Executive and Congress seems to apply to the Iran arms sales half of the Iran–Contra affair. The January 1986 finding for the operation was explicit: do not tell Congress. The Congressional overseers did not find out about the Iran operation until the following autumn – not 'fully and currently informed' by anyone's definition. Later on, it was the President himself who was not told, when the Iran and Contra operations crossed.

In another sense, however, the system 'worked'. In deciding to sell arms to Iran, the President pursued a line of policy which was opposed by both his Secretaries of State and Defense, about which he was afraid to inform the Congressional intelligence committees, and which was liable to be revealed by Iranian factions as and when it suited them. It is hard to imagine any system providing more warning signals. When the opposition of most of the government's senior foreign policy officials means they have to be cut out of the policy, it is likely that the policy, and not they, are wrong. The President thus proceeded at his peril.

Neither law nor process can override the effects of attitude and personality. Had relations between Casey and the committees been better, the Reagan administration might have leveled with them about the of Iranian arms sales. That would not necessarily have resulted in wiser policy, for it is conceivable that Congress would have been seduced down the path from geostrategic interests to releasing hostages just as the President was. But the subsequent debate would then have been about the wisdom of the policy, not about whether Congress was deceived.

Reagan and Casey did not always want to avail themselves of Congressional advice with regard to covert action, or they did not like what they heard. More colorfully, a Republican staffer described the attitude of one recent CIA director of Congressional Affairs, a career Clandestine Service officer: he behaved as if 'Washington was a foreign country and he was the station chief in hostile terrain, mounting operations against the Congress'.[38]

About overt 'covert' actions like Nicaragua, the main conclusion is straightforward: when covert operations are large and when both they and the larger foreign policies of which they are a part are fiercely contended by American political leaders, those covert operations cannot remain secret. In those cases, it is not that oversight has broken down, but rather that in a democratic society no tidy, secret process can be sustained.

With regard to the diversion of money for the Contras, the lesson is not that the NSC staff should be eliminated or the National Security Advisor made subject to Senate confirmation. Presidents will always have need of a source of private advice and a means of brokering the actions of the many foreign policy agencies of government. Moreover, if presidents are determined to get something done, they will be able to find someone, somewhere in the White House, to do it. So, too, if the United States continues to have a clandestine service, presidents will be tempted to resort to covert action as a middle resort, not a last.

Rather, the lesson is a caution for presidents and those who advise them: don't do it. Two decades ago, it would have been unthinkable for an administration to run a covert operation from the White House; then, the reason was that presidents wanted to stay at arms' length from such things, even if they could not in a pinch plausibly deny them. Now, if covert actions are to be undertaken, they should be done by the agency of government constructed to do them – the Central Intelligence Agency. It has both the expertise and the accountability.

Moreover, now as two decades ago, if the President's closest advisors become the operators, the President loses them as source of detached judgment on the operations. The President's own circle become advocates, like Allen Dulles in the Bay of Pigs, not protectors of the President's stakes (even if he does not quite realize his need for protection). So it was with National Security Advisors McFarlane and Poindexter; once committed, they had reason to overlook the warning signals thrown up by the process. Excluding Congress also excluded one more 'political scrub' one more source of advice about what the range of American people would find acceptable. And the chances increased that someone like Lieutenant-Colonel Oliver North, misguided, would interpret the President's interest after his own fashion, misinterpreting 'plausible denial' much as CIA officers had during the attempts to kill Castro a quarter of a century earlier.

The fact that these lesson seem to have to be reinforced every dozen years with a fresh scandal is worrying. So, too, is the aspect of the Iran–Contra affair to which the Congressional investigation gave too little attention: the apparent intention of Casey, North and their associates to create a CIA-outside-the-CIA and so escape the constitutional limits they felt were hampering their attempt to respond to the Soviet threat. In that perspective, there was no 'diversion' of profits from Iran to Nicaragua, only fungible proceeds from different 'profit centers'.

Yet the United States could not wish away the potential for secret operations if it chose; nor, Iran–Contra notwithstanding, is there evidence that the American people wish it. Presidents and those who work for them will be left with lessons that run against their convenience. The paradox of secret operations in an open society will remain.

NOTES

1. This chapter draws on Chapter 7 of my *Covert Action: The Limits of Intervention in the Postwar World* (New York, 1987).
2. *Alleged Assassination Plots Involving Foreign Leaders: Interim Report of the Senate Select Committee to Study ... Intelligence Activities*, 94 Cong., 1 sess. (20 November 1975), p.149.
3. Ibid., p.108ff.
4. Ibid., p.99ff.
5. Ibid., p.95.
6. Oral History No. 86, taped by Hughes Cates, 22 February 1977, Richard B. Russell Library, University of Georgia, Athens, cited in Loch Johnson, 'Covert Action and American Foreign Policy: Decision Paths for the "Quiet Option"', paper presented to the American Political Science Association Annual Meeting, Washington, DC, 1986, p.4.
7. Anne Karalekas, 'History of the Central Intelligence Agency', in *Supplementary Detailed Staff Reports on Foreign and Military Intelligence*, book 4 of *Final Report of the Senate Select Committee to Study ... Intelligence Activities*, 94 Cong., 2 sess. (23 April 1976), p.54 (hereafter cited as 'CIA History').
8. Ibid., p.55.
9. *Covert Action in Chile, 1963–1973, Staff Report to the Senate Select Committee to Study ... Intelligence Activities*, 94 Cong., 1 sess. (18 December 1975), p.42.
10. Ibid., p.41.
11. 'CIA History', p.72.

12. The numbers in this and the following paragraph are from *Covert Action in Chile*, p.49.
13. Officially, section 622 of the Foreign Assistance Act of 1974.
14. William Colby and Peter Forbath, *Honorable Men: My Life in the CIA* (New York, 1978), pp.402–4.
15. Colby, p.436.
16. Ibid., p.440.
17. Ibid., p.444.
18. For an intriguing account of the Senate Select Committee, see Loch Johnson, *A Season of Inquiry: The Senate Intelligence Investigation* (Lexington, KY, 1985).
19. The same could not be said of the Pike Committee, whose report found its way to the journalist Daniel Schorr after release had been voted down by the House. The Church Committee, however, was more often the victim of leaks than the perpetrator. See Johnson, pp.206–7.
20. For instance, Colby regards the outcome as 'not unreasonable'. See p.429.
21. See his *Secrecy and Democracy: The CIA in Transition* (Boston, 1985), p.170.
22. Officially, Section 413 of the Intelligence Oversight Act of 1980.
23. Speech to the United Nations, 25 October 1985, as quoted in *The Washington Post*.
24. The Order was printed in the *New York Times*, 5 December 1981.
26. Interview, 16 January 1986.
28. Quoted in the *Washington Star*, 12 November 1975.
29. See reports in the *New York Times*, 12, 16, and 17 April 1984. See also the account in *Report of the Senate Select Committee on Intelligence, 1 Jan. 1983–31 Dec. 1984*, 98 Cong., 2 sess. (1984), p. 4ff.
    Select Committee on Intelligence, *Report*, cited above, pp.4ff.
30. Interviews with intelligence committee staff members, January 1987.
31. The letter was dated 9 April; see *The Washington Post*, 11 April 1984.
32. Turner, p.168.
33. Interview, 9 January 1986.
34. As quoted in the *New York Times*, 7 July 1986.
35. Interview with the CIA officials, August 1986 and January 1987.
36. One reported instance was an operation in Suriname in early 1983. See the *New York Times* 15 June 1983.
37. Interview, 9 January 1987.
38. Interview, 18 January 1987.

7

Controlling the Security Threat: Foreign Counter-intelligence

MARION T. DOSS, JR.

Since President Ford first officially defined 'foreign counter-intelligence' (FCI) in 1976, that term and 'counter-intelligence' (CI) often have been used synonymously within the bureaucracy. Except where otherwise noted, this chapter follows that practice as it explores the nature of FCI, the agencies authorized to conduct FCI activities, and the problems presented by FCI in the American democratic context. The chapter relates how FCI is organized and controlled to protect against both threats to national security and individual rights, because national security and individual rights are interdependent.

WHAT IS FCI?

There are perhaps as many views on what constitute the basic CI functions as there are commentators. Some include domestic intelligence. Others include security functions such as vetting individuals and locking safes. Still others include law enforcement, double agent operations, and deception. Allen Dulles, Director of Central Intelligence (DCI) from 1954 to 1962, described CI as information derived from counter-espionage (CE) operations that transcend security measures and attempt to penetrate hostile intelligence services. According to Dulles, CE is 'directly concerned with uncovering secret aggression, subversion and sabotage'.[1] On the other hand, Sherman Kent viewed CI as essentially a defensive security function[2] and Harry Howe Ransom viewed it as a police function.[3] Unlike Dulles, neither Kent nor Ransom emphasized the relationship between CI and intelligence.[4] Jeffrey Richelson described what he considers the four basic functions of traditional CI as the penetration of hostile intelligence services; the recruitment of

134

agents and defectors; research and collection on opposition (both hostile and supposedly friendly) intelligence services; and the disruption and neutralization of hostile intelligence activity.[5] Newton Miler, a former Central Intelligence Agency (CIA) CI officer under James Angelton, takes a more expansive view, finding some eleven basic functions that must be performed by any centralized CI organization.[6]

There have been numerous official and unofficial efforts to define the terms CI and FCI over the years.[7] For the most part, these initiatives were prompted by the desire to either expand or limit the scope of an organization's authority to conduct CI activities. Until the intelligence scandals of the 1970s there was no universally accepted national definition of CI. Then on 18 February 1976, Executive Order 11905 provided one and, at the same time, further confused the situation by defining differently FCI ('activities conducted to protect the [US and US] citizens from foreign espionage, sabotage, subversion, assassination or terrorism') in section 2 and CI ('information concerning the protection of foreign intelligence or of national security information and its collection from detection or disclosure') in section 5, because one could read the adjective 'foreign' into the section 5 definition.[8] From this time to the present, the terms CI and FCI have been used interchangeably. The term FCI, later abandoned by executive orders 12036 and 12333, had in the meantime become institutionalized in the Attorney General's Foreign Counter-intelligence Investigation Guidelines (FCIG) and the reorganization of FCI within the Federal Bureau of Investigation (FBI) and the Department of Defense (DOD), and indirectly by statute. The current official definition of CI is provided by Executive Order 12333 which declares:

> [CI] means information gathered and activities conducted to protect against espionage, other intelligence activities, sabotage, or assassinations conducted for or on behalf of foreign powers, organizations or persons, or international terrorist activities, but not including personnel, physical, document or communications security programs.

(Notice that nothing in this definition limits CI to activities conducted abroad or to the activities of foreigners.)

THE FCI COMMUNITY

In the United States CI developed as an 'aspect of intelligence' by historical accident. Otherwise, it might be considered a function of security, or law enforcement, or even an independent discipline, related to, but not part of, the foregoing. In Canada for example, where CI is called 'security intelligence', it developed as an 'aspect of law enforcement' also by chance. In 1982, Canada removed CI from the Royal Canadian Mounted Police (RCMP) Security Service to a new civilian Canadian Security Intelligence Service (CSIS). This reorganization was the government's way of resolving a nasty security scandal, 'the Canadian Watergate', which resulted from allegations that the Mounties used illegal or improper practices to counter Quebec separatists. Canada has only one CI (security intelligence) agency and no foreign intelligence agency. In Britain two domestic security intelligence organizations, the Special Branch of Scotland Yard (law enforcement) and the Security Service (MI5), each perform different CI functions, and even the Secret Intelligence Service (MI6) (foreign intelligence), like the CIA, has a CI section. However, because national contexts (including the constitutional framework and laws) differ, there is no reason to assume that the Canadian, British, or any other Western democracy's arrangement is best suited for the United States.[9]

The membership and general authorities of the current FCI community are contained in the National Security Act as amended and Executive Order 12333.[10]

Because the National Security Act expressly prohibits the CIA from exercising 'any police, subpena, law-enforcement powers, or internal security functions',[11] the FBI is the leading CI organization within the United States, the CIA abroad. Therefore, CI activities in the United States must be co-ordinated with the FBI, those abroad with the CIA. The DCI, as head of the CIA and co-ordinator of the intelligence community (IC) under the President and the National Security Council, formulates policies concerning the conduct of CI activities with foreign governments and co-ordinates CI relationships between the IC and the intelligence or security services of foreign governments.

As the nation's senior law enforcement official, the Attorney General heads the Department of Justice (DOJ), controls the FBI, and receives reports of unlawful activity from the Intelligence Oversight Board (IOB). Separate divisions of the FBI, the primary federal criminal investigative agency, are responsible for both domestic intelligence and FCI. The Attorney General has issued separate investigation guidelines to control each function.[12]

The Secretary of Defense is authorized to conduct military-related FCI activities. The FCI components of the three military departments are authorized to engage in FCI activities under the direction, management and oversight of the Office of the Secretary of Defense (OSD). The military conducts FCI activities in co-ordination with either the FBI or CIA, depending upon geographic location. Army CI functions are performed by the Army Intelligence and Security Command (INSCOM), which combines a wide variety of security and FCI activities, but not criminal investigations (which are conducted by the US Army Criminal Investigations Command (USACIDC). The Naval Investigative Service (NIS), formerly under Naval Intelligence but now part of the Naval Security and Investigative Command (NAVSECINVCOM), is the primary investigative and CI agency within the Department of the Navy (DON), which includes both the Navy and Marine Corps (USMC). NIS conducts felony investigations and criminal intelligence operations and has exclusive jurisdiction in CI matters within the DON. The Air Force Office of Special Investigations (AFOSI) is a vertical, centrally directed, world-wide organization which provides criminal, FCI, internal security, and special investigative services for all Air Force activities. AFOSI reports to the inspector general, not to intelligence.

Two defense agencies also perform limited FCI functions. The Defense Intelligence Agency (DIA) Directorate For Security and CI (OS) produces CI and counter-terrorism analyses and provides CI staff support and liaison for OSD, the Office of the Joint Chiefs of Staff (JCS), JCS subordinate agencies, and the Defense Attaché System, and manages various security programs. DIA is largely concerned with protecting DIA personnel and classified information from foreign intelligence collection efforts. DIA exchanges information with the Secret Service and provides CI support in technology transfer related matters. The National Security Agency (NSA), created in 1952, collects, processes and disseminates signals intelligence information for FCI use.

Neither State, Treasury nor Energy was given any express CI responsibility by Executive Order 12333. State's Bureau of Diplomatic Security has a CI unit which performs preliminary inquiries and co-ordinates CI matters affecting State's personnel security program with the FBI or CIA as appropriate. The Secret Service, under Treasury, has a limited counter-surveillance function in connection with its protective service mission to report contacts with certain foreign nationals to the responsible FCI agency. Energy's Director of Safeguards and Security represents that department in national operational security matters including FCI. Although the Coast Guard (USGC) is by statute at all times a 'military service and a part of the armed forces',[13] Executive Order 12333 does not include it or Transportation in either the intelligence or FCI communities. USCG Intelligence (CGI), like any other agency's security manager, normally conducts preliminary CI investigations before referring them to the FBI. If the FBI declines jurisdiction, CGI resumes the investigation. Transportation considers the Coast Guard's security programs and port safety program are FCI related. While not mentioned in Executive Order 12333, the Postal Inspection Service's Mail Cover Program is authorized by the Postal Reorganization Act of 1970.

UNDERSTANDING FCI: QUESTIONS AND CONTEXT

As a vital subsystem of the national security system, FCI presents a fundamental dilemma, maintenance of national security while preserving individual rights, and the related problems of ensuring responsiveness to elected officials, ending misuse for partisan political advanage, preventing illegal or improper activities, providing adequate authority and resources, and minimizing turf struggles.

All democracies face essentially the same problem: how best to protect the nation against threats to its security, and even its existence, without abridging those fundamental liberties that give the nation its *raison d'être*. Stansfield Turner has noted that while CI is vital to protect America, 'no area of intelligence activity [is] more likely to abuse the rights of our citizens'.[14] To prevent abuses and illegalities, CI has been decentralized, redefined, chartered and subjected to systematic control. For example, to get the CIA's CI organization under control during the 1970s, it was decentralized and remained so until recentralized in 1988. Other reformers have tried to 'purify' CI to correct perceived abuses. To better protect individual rights, Secretary of Defense Melvin Laird issued a 1971 directive redefining CI within DOD to exclude domestic intelligence and endeavored to associate CI activities more generally with law enforcement. This particular initiative, implemented by the Defense Investigative Review Council (DIRC) (1971–79), was opposed by some intelligence professionals. Successive intelligence charters, Executive Orders 11905 and 12036, each represented movement in the general direction of more narrowly defining CI.

George Cole has said '[p]erhaps the most important question confronting American Society is how to control crime while preserving the due process and the elements of freedom and justice that quintessentially define a democracy'.[15] The national security dilemma is analagous. Herbert Packer's polar-opposite 'crime control' and 'due process' models[16] certainly have FCI analogies. The permissible scope of CI activities in any given situation will vary along a continuum between the 'national security' and 'individual liberties' models of the American system of FCI. Just which FCI activities may lawfully be conducted and the organizational relationships of FCI agencies is a question controlled by the contemporary American political context.

The problems facing law-makers and policy-makers responsible for FCI are legion. Both groups must ensure that the needs of both national security and individual liberty are met, make the FCI community more responsive to the priorities of policy-makers, avoid the temptation to use FCI for partisan political ends, either prevent or eradicate illegalities and improprieties committed in the name of national security, and provide adequate authority and resources for FCI needs.

The proper role of FCI is to serve and be responsive to the policy needs and priorities of elected and appointed officials. It must provide these officials with accurate and timely information for the decision-making process. In this role FCI serves a vital staff function. It is improper for FCI officials to substitute their priorities for those of the responsible officials. Despite occasional differences of opinion and bureaucratic turf battles, the NSC staff/committee system provides adequate mechanisms for the co-ordination and control of the FCIC within the executive branch. (Although FCI was not the major issue in the Iran–Contra matter, the Tower Commission recommended no substantive changes be made in either the structure or operation of the NSC system.)

As discussed below, the lesson of the 1960s and 1970s is that Congressional scrutiny is necessary to ensure administration officials do not misuse the FCI community for political purposes by spying on or harassing those whose views and activities are opposed to administration policies.

Both executive and legislative scrutiny and controls are necessary to prevent and detect illegalities or improprieties committed by officials from within the FCI community. The discretion of FCI officials must be circumscribed by law and policy. Their views, no matter how well intended, cannot be permitted to subvert the national consensus.

Recognizing a manifest need for legitimate FCI activities, those charged with the responsibility of conducting them must be empowered to do the job. Acceptable practices must be delimited by clear laws, unambiguous guidelines, and appropriations for adequate staffing and needed other expenditures.

Turf questions transcend mere jurisdictional competition between decentralized CI agencies. Turf involves the very nature of CI and where it should be relegated in the national scheme. There are at least two divergent views on the relationship between law enforcement and FCI. Under the leadership of Roy Godson, the Consortium for the Study of Intelligence conducted a series of colloquia to examine intelligence requirements for the 1980s. The April 1980 Colloquium on CI examined the nature of CI and the nature of the FCI threat to permit CI agencies the greatest scope of permissible activity commensurate with constitutional and statutory law. Some contributors advocated the complete separation of FCI from law enforcement and criminal investigations in order to permit the intelligence community to conduct CI investigations unhampered by the need to establish probable cause. Arnold Beichman and Roy Godson felt CI was adversely affected by its identification with criminal proceedings, the 'chilling effect' of constitutional rights, the failure to distinguish between CI and FCI, and potential civil liability issues.[17] Colloquia participants Angelo Codevilla, Kenneth de Graffenreid, and Roy Godson were also members of the Reagan CIA transition team which advocated the need to improve and expand CI efforts.[18]

A different conclusion regarding the relationship between law enforcement and FCI was expressed in a 1986 Senate study conducted to discover how to combat espionage more effectively. The Senate Select Committee on Intelligence (SSCI) found a need for greater CI and security awareness, earlier FBI and DOJ involvement in cases of suspected espionage, and more attention and better access to information concerning persons with sensitive information. The SSCI recommended the government not tolerate violations of the espionage laws, which should be enforced regardless of the nation involved.[19]

In order to understand the nature of the dilemma and associated problems and judge the merits of the different views, one must examine the FCI threat, the historical evolution of the FCI system, the controls available, and the conditions for effective control.

The perpetual problem in a democratic society is to decide just how much power to give the government to accomplish a given purpose. But before one can decide which CI activities are necessary, it is necessary to identify the threat(s). Only then can some consensus be reached concerning the role of FCI, which functions are necessary, what resources must be allocated, and what protections against the misuse of authority will be institutionalized.

To discover the nature of the CI threat it is necessary to identify its source(s), the activities involved, and both its immediacy and magnitude. By definition, the foreign intelligence threat is directed from abroad by a 'foreign power', which very broadly may be a government, a component thereof, a faction, an entity, a terrorist group, or a foreign-based political organization.[20] Moreover, even though the threat may be directed from abroad, the actual espionage or other proscribed activity may be conducted in the United States or by Americans.

According to Executive Order 12333, the activities threatened could include any combination of spying or espionage, sabotage, assassination or terrorism conducted on behalf of a foreign power. All of these activities constitute federal crimes defined and punished under title 18, *United States Code*.

Although 'subversion' is no longer included in the definition of CI, those Americans who are the illegal agents of foreign powers may be guilty of treason, sedition, or certain subversive activities described in Chapter 115 of title 18. Far too many Americans have sold out to foreign powers for a variety of reasons. As a result of the policy decision to bring more prosecutions for violations of the espionage laws, the public was progressively stunned during the years 1983, 1984 and 1985 to discover the actual extent of espionage activity and how much of it was conducted by Americans. Three noteworthy 1984 cases respectively involved a CIA mole, the scion of a prominent Boston family, and an FBI special agent.[21]

Karl Koecher was a classic penetration agent (mole). Koecher, who became a naturalized American, was actually a Czech spy working for the Soviets. Koecher infiltrated the CIA and, as a contract employee (translator) from 1973 to 1977, had access to extremely sensitive information. Koecher and his wife Hana were arrested in 1984, and exchanged for Natan Sharansky in 1986.

Samuel Loring Morison, a nephew of the distinguished naval historian Samuel Eliot Morison, was arrested in 1984 while working as a Navy civilian intelligence analyst. Convicted in 1985 and sentenced to two years in prison, Morison claimed he only gave classified satellite photos to a British publication to alert Americans to the increased Soviet naval threat. Free on bond pending appeal, Morison's conviction was upheld by the Fourth US Circuit Court of Appeals in 1988.

Richard Miller, the only FBI agent ever charged with espionage, was arrested in 1984 and convicted in 1986. Miller, who worked in FCI, apparently was motivated by sexual lust for a comely Soviet, dissatisfaction with his mundane existence, and greed. Miller was convicted in 1986 and sentenced to two life terms plus 50 years.

In 1985 alone, some eleven Americans were arrested for spying against the United States. During 'The Year of the Spy', their stories and those of others arrested earlier on espionage charges permeated the media. Two of the Americans arrested in 1985 had spied for Israel, one each for the People's Republic of China and Ghana, and the remaining seven for the Soviet Union.

Jay Pollard, a civilian CI analyst working for the Naval Investigative Service, was arrested along with his wife Anne for passing defense secrets to Israel. The Pollards needed money to support a lifestyle which included drug abuse and they considered Israel a US ally. In 1987 Pollard was sentenced to life while his wife received a five-year term. The Pollard case illustrates that there is no such thing as a 'friendly' foreign intelligence service.

Larry Chin, a retired CIA analyst, spied for Communist China during

141

the 30 years he was with that agency from 1952 until 1981 and beyond. Arrested in November 1985, Chin committed suicide rather than face prosecution.

Sharon Scrange, a CIA clerk stationed in Ghana, became romantically involved with Michael Soussoudis, a Ghanaian intelligence agent. Scrange supplied her lover with intelligence secrets including the identities of CIA agents in Ghana. Because she co-operated in securing his arrest and conviction, Scrange was permitted to plea bargain a five-year sentence.

Edward Howard, after receiving intensive training for a tour of duty as a clandestine agent handler in Moscow, failed a routine polygraph examination and was dismissed by the CIA after an investigation revealed severe problems including drug and alcohol abuse, violent behavior, and deception. In revenge, Howard sold out to the Soviets by providing them with secret information including the identities of American intelligence personnel and agents. Several were arrested, and at least one Soviet source disappeared and is presumed dead. Identified as a traitor along with Ronald Pelton by Soviet defector Vitaly Yurchenko, Howard fled to the Soviet Union to avoid arrest.

Ronald Pelton, also identified by Yurchenko, was a National Security Agency communications specialist who sold a wide range of extremely sensitive intelligence information to the Soviets during the last five of his 14 years with that agency. Dissatisfied with job and lifestyle, Pelton sought out the Soviets to trade secrets for the cash he wanted to extricate himself from debt and buy his fantasies. Pelton was convicted and sentenced to life in prison.

The Walker family spies included John ('Jaws' or 'John Walker, Red'), Arthur and Michael Walker and John's friend Jerry Whitworth. John, then a Navy warrant officer, initiated the enterprise in 1968 by selling classified materials, including 'crypto' (used to encode and decode communications) to the Soviets. John recruited the others to provide expanded access. John pleaded guilty and testified against Jerry Whitworth to secure a 25-year sentence for his son Michael. Arthur and John each received life sentences in separate trials. Jerry Whitworth got 365 years with no parole for at least 60 years.

Randy Jeffries, hired as a courier for a contractor providing stenographic services to Congress shortly after his release from drug rehabilitation, attempted to sell sensitive classified documents to the Soviets but found himself dealing with an undercover FBI agent instead. A small fish who caused no actual damage, Jeffries pleaded guilty and received three to nine years out of a possible 10 on the charge.

Two general views of the immediacy and magnitude of the threat can be identified. According to one view (apparently shared by James Angleton and William Casey among others), we live in a continually hostile and dangerous world. The threat is always immediate and dire. Beset on all sides, we are constantly at war fighting for our very survival. Only the form of warfare changes. Therefore, FCI agencies, among others, must have the widest possible latitude of action at all times to investigate potential threats. The other view holds that the threat is relative to the circumstances and situation of the moment. During war the threat is greater than it is during peace. Some foes might want to destroy our form of government while nominal friends and even allies might only want to secure an advantage against some third power, perhaps another friend or ally. According to this view the nature of the permissible response can vary with the nature of the threat.

Because FCI is necessarily a secretive undertaking, decisions and activities, including threat assessment, must be conducted under appropriate security. For example, when analysis of the Walker case revealed the numbers of foreign intelligence officers and collectors in the United States far exceeded the CI assets the United States could deploy against them, the threat was studied within the National Security Council (NSC) system by the Interagency Group on CI (IG/CI) and staffed through the Senior Interagency Group on Intelligence (SIG/I) to the National Security Planning Group (NSPG). Agreeing with the IG/CI recommendations as endorsed by the SIG/I and NSPG and with the NSPG recommendation to polygraph all individuals with access to certain special access program classified information, President Reagan issued National Security Decision Directive (NSDD) 196, which also created a task force for implementation.

There was no national-consensus problem in this particular case, but in other instances where a less obvious threat is posed by a liberation movement or a third world entity, the threat perceived by the US government may be unclear and differ from that perceived by some within the government or by the public. If a significant number of Americans disagree with the official assessment, the government must either secure public support or act in secret, which is increasingly difficult to do in this age of leaks and whistleblowers. Of course most Americans perceive threats based on their common culture, individual and group differences, and information from mostly public sources. The government can affect public opinion by releasing or withholding information. In the latter case discovery by other means could backfire and destroy a policy. Therefore, the President cannot afford to ignore public opinion, even when he believes he is acting in the national interest.

Historically certain functions, considered CI-related, were first formally undertaken by Navy, War and Justice, which assigned them respectively to the Office of Naval Intelligence (ONI), the Military Information Division (MID), and the Bureau of Investigation.[22]

The shift from a neutral to pro-Allied posture in 1915 brought about a dramatic increase in CI activity, which almost from the outset had incorporated domestic intelligence. In 1916, with impetus from Assistant Secretary Franklin Roosevelt, ONI became the first federal intelligence agency authorized to have undercover agents. These ONI agents were used to collect domestic intelligence as CI became the major ONI activity during the war.[23] The Army and the Bureau were not far behind. In 1917, Army undercover agents got involved in civilian law enforcement by investigating and even arresting civilians until Secretary of War Baker put an end to the practice.[24] During the war, ONI and MID investigated espionage, sabotage, disloyalty, fraud and graft. The Bureau became America's primary spy-catcher, investigating violations of espionage, sabotage and sedition laws, and collecting domestic intelligence on both those who sympathized with the Central Powers and radicals.[25]

After the war and until 1924, the Bureau increasingly concentrated on anti-radical matters. In that year, Attorney General Harlan Stone limited investigations to actual violations of law and promoted J. Edgar Hoover to acting director of the Bureau.[26] This hiatus in controversial CI activity let Hoover concentrate on crimefighting and public relations to rebuild the Bureau, formally renamed the Federal Bureau of Investigation (FBI) in 1935. By this time, fear of war in Europe had ignited American interest in Fascist and Communist subversion. By a secret 1936 directive, President Roosevelt put the FBI back in the business of investigating subversive activities. As the world situation continued to deteriorate during 1938, Congress gave the FBI funds to conduct espionage investigations. On 26 June 1939, President Roosevelt allocated intelligence responsibilities and directed all federal officials to refer all matters involving espionage, counter-espionage or sabotage to only the FBI, MID or ONI, which would co-ordinate their activities. Two months later, President Roosevelt requested all civilian law enforcement officers to turn over any information they might obtain concerning CI matters to the FBI.[27] As a result, the first in a continuing series of jurisdictional delimitation agreements was worked out in 1940 by the FBI, MID, and ONI.

Army and Navy CI capabilities, trimmed between wars, were rebuilt and came of age during the Second World War, performing a wide range of security and CI activities. The post-war intelligence community dates from the National Security Act of 1947 and the 1949 amendments, which together created the NSC, the NSC Staff, the CIA, the IC Staff and DOD, with three subordinate military departments, Army, Navy and Air Force. The NSC became the highest executive branch entity formulating and co-ordinating policy providing oversight to national CI. Over the years, NSC functions and responsibilities have been carried out by an assortment of committees or groups and their subdivisions. The precise organization and functions of the NSC and its components have depended in large measure on the individual President and his national security advisor.

Hoover's success over the years in incorporating 'subversive activities' into the CI mission and protecting FBI activities from outside interference, permitted the FBI and other CI agencies to practice domestic political CI on an unprecedented scale during the social and political unrest of the 1960s.[28]

Until a rash of disclosures in the early 1970s, CI had not concerned most Americans. However, the individual rights explosion of the due process revolution, social evolution during the 1960s and early 1970s, and the Watergate episode created a new context in which law enforcement and intelligence activities were subjected to more critical scrutiny. Concern over data banks, military surveillance of civilians (publicly revealed in 1970), questionable FBI practices (revealed in documents taken in 1971 from the Media, Pennsylvania FBI office), and the 'resignation' of James Angleton[29] (following the December 1974 revelation that the CIA had also 'spied' on anti-war protesters) progressively fed a growing scandal which could not be ended by merely acknowledging past excesses (the 1975 Rockefeller Commission *Report*) and demonstrating present control through increased oversight and restrictions. 'Domestic intelligence' was quickly written out of the definition of CI by President Ford in his 1976 Executive Order (EO) 11905, and Attorney General Levi quickly implemented EO 11905 by issuing the first comprehensive FCI investigations guidelines (FCIG).

The major legislative response was Senate Resolution 21[30] which established the Church Committee to investigate federal intelligence activities. The committee was highly critical of the adverse impact of domestic intelligence activity on the rights of Americans and found a number of abuses including illegalities, intrusive investigative techniques, and the misuse of information for political purposes. The committee wanted a statutory framework to codify prohibitions and controls on domestic security activities, which it would put under the Attorney General to prevent interference with criminal investigations and FCI. The committee also recommended limiting domestic security investigations by the criminal 'probable cause' standard, enhanced espionage laws, and intensified congressional oversight.[31] While

Congress did enact the Foreign Intelligence Surveillance Act (FISA) of 1978 in reaction to the committee's final report, the envisioned legislative charter was not achieved due to political problems.

Attempts to control intelligence during the Carter administration included issuance of a new, more restrictive Executive Order 12036 (which narrowed the definition of CI) and the appointment of Admiral Stansfield Turner as DCI to reform the CIA. Despite his best efforts, Admiral Turner reported that as late as 1979 Senator Sam Nunn had told him 'You know, we really have no [CI]'.[32] Glenn Hastedt has described CI during this period as 'a no man's land'.[33] Intelligence surprises such as the fall of the Shah, the Soviet invasion of Afghanistan, and the taking of American hostages in Tehran caused a strong reaction to the anti-intelligence excesses of the 1970s. In 1981, President Reagan set a new, more positive tone and directed special attention to CI because he viewed the revitalization of America's intelligence system, along with rebuilding national defense, as vital to national security.[34] While there is some suggestion President Reagan wanted a new CI organization with broad powers and a central records system, the initiative was opposed in both Congress and the administration.[35]

President Reagan intended to enhance national security while protecting individual rights and freedoms. Executive Order 12333 recognized the need for CI to support the decision-making and policy formulation processes. Despite initial gains, the President's efforts were damaged by new scandals involving the role of the NSC Staff and the DCI in the Iran–Contra episode and allegations that the FBI had resumed political spying with its probe of the Committee in Solidarity with the People of El Salvador (CISPES).

CONTROL AND OVERSIGHT OF FCI

A number of controls are available to ensure that CI policy is co-ordinated to serve the national interest and implemented in conformity with law. The executive branch formulates and co-ordinates CI policy through executive order, the NSC/IC system, FCI guidelines (FCIG), and departmental directives.

Starting with President Ford in 1976, each president has issued an executive order designed to balance the government's need for intelligence with the privacy and civil liberties of Americans. President Ford issued Executive Order 11905, to organize and control the intelligence community. Executive Order 11905 defined 'intelligence' as meaning both foreign intelligence and FCI. In 1978, President Carter replaced Executive Order 11905 with Executive Order 12036, which emphasized restrictions on intelligence activities as it attempted to clarify the responsibilities for

146

and limitations on intelligence and CI collection. Executive Order 12036 redefined CI, both expanding and limiting it by including international terrorist activities and deleting all personnel, physical, document and communications security programs. The term 'intelligence' included both foreign intelligence and CI (in lieu of FCI). 'Foreign Intelligence' excluded CI except for information on international terrorist activities. While generally adopting President Carter's definitions of CI and foreign intelligence in Executive Order 12333, President Reagan took a much more positive approach by placing emphasis on authorizations (goals, directions and duties) rather than on restrictions.

Execitive Order 11905 provided for the control and direction of intelligence organizations under the President, the NSC, the Committee on Foreign Intelligence (CFI), the Operations Advisory Group (Operation Group) and the DCI. Executive Order 12036 replaced the CFI and Operations Group with the NSC Policy Review Committee (PRC) and NSC Special Coordination Committee (SCC). The SCC developed CI policy, resolved inter-agency differences, acted as approval authority for certain CI activities, developed and monitored compliance with central CI records guidelines, and submitted an annual CI threat assessment to the President. Executive Order 12036 also created the National Foreign Intelligence Board (NFIB) to advise the DCI and a National Intelligence Tasking Center (NITC) to co-ordinate collection under the DCI. Executive Order 12333 did not specify the same organizational detail as its predecessors, but authorized the NSC to establish such committees as necessary. Likewise, the DCI was authorized to establish such boards, councils or groups as required. Under President Reagan, the NSC managed and co-ordinated the national security decision-making process. Inter-agency co-ordination is effected under the Assistant to the President for National Security Affairs (National Security Advisor) through the SIG/IG system.[36]

FCIG have existed since 1976 when first issued to implement Executive Order 11905. New FCIG were issued in 1980 and 1983 respectively to implement Executive Orders 12036 and 12333. FCIG provide the FBI with authority and guidance to conduct FI collection activities, FCI investigations, international terrorism investigations, espionage investigations and certain types of support activity for the IC and foreign governments.[37]

Each executive branch entity implements policy through a directives system. For example the FBI incorporates the FCIG into a more detailed *Foreign Counterintelligence Manual* which is directive in nature. By departmental directive, the Deputy Under Secretary of Defense for Policy (DUSD (P)) has overall responsibility for CI matters in DOD. DUSD (P) is advised and assisted by the Defense CI Board (DCIB). The Chairman of the DCIB is the Director for CI and Security Policy, and its Executive Secretary is the Director of CI and Investigative Programs. Both are staff assistants in the Office of the DUSD (P). Membership of the DCIB includes the Assistant General Counsel (International), the Assistant to the Secretary of Defense (Intelligence Oversight), and one representative from each of the military departments' CI components, DIA and NSA. DUSD (P) is program manager for the DOD FCI program.[38] There are numerous other DOD directives, instructions, and regulations on other aspects of CI. Each DOD component in turn implements the DOD directives as they pertain to that component.

Congress controls FCI through legislation, appropriations, and oversight. Congress created the current framework for national security through the National Security Act. Attempts to enact a comprehensive National Intelligence Act in 1980 failed. While Congress has yet to enact a comprehensive intelligence act, it incrementally has amended national security law on an ad hoc basis. The Foreign Intelligence Surveillance Act (FISA) of 1978 authorized (under tight rules and congressional oversight) electronic surveillance for FI purposes. The Classified Information Procedures Act of 1980 established special procedures for criminal cases involving classified information. The identities of FCI covert agents are protected by the Intelligence Identities Protection Act (IIPA) of 1982.[39] Some contend statutory charters are required so the rules cannot be changed by executive fiat.

All three co-ordinate branches of government exercise some oversight of FCI activities. The administration does it through command and control, the Intelligence Oversight Board (IOB), and an independent system of inspectors general. Congress does it through the power to legislate and appropriate funds, its committee system and the General Accounting Office (GAO). The judiciary does it through the courts.

Under Executive Order 11905, the President, the NSC, the Committee on Foreign Intelligence (CFI), the Operations Advisory Group (Operation Group) and the DCI were aided in oversight of the FCI community by a system of agency inspectors general and general counsels and the IOB reporting to the Attorney General, who in turn reported to the President. Under President Carter, oversight was again the responsibility of the IOB, an improved system of IC inspectors general and general counsels, the Attorney General and Congress. The DCI was made responsible to keep the respective select committees informed regarding intelligence and CI matters. President Reagan's IOB is governed by Executive Order 12334. Executive Order 12333 requires senior officials of the IC to keep the IOB and DCI informed, instruct employees to co-operate fully with the IOB, and allow inspectors general and general counsels access to all necessary information.

148

Until 1980, a plethora of congressional committees were involved in intelligence oversight. In that year, Congress reduced the number to two, the SSCI and the House Permanent Select Committee on Intelligence (HPSCI), and streamlined congressional oversight procedures.[40] In 1985, Congress increased operational control over intelligence agencies by limiting their ability to obligate or expend appropriated funds.[41]

The judicial branch exercises control and oversight of intelligence by ensuring compliance with the criminal law, the criminal procedural law, and national security law. In addition to trying cases and hearing appeals, the courts are called upon to issue warrants and court orders authorizing officials to take various actions. For instance, to obtain authorization to conduct electronic surveillance two alternative routes are available.[42] Under the criminal law, the Attorney General or his specially designated assistant attorney general may authorize application to a federal judge of competent jurisdiction for an interception order. Under FISA, the President through the Attorney General may, under stringent certification and reporting requirements, authorize without a court order limited electronic surveillance to acquire foreign intelligence. The Attorney General must transmit his certification under seal to one of seven designated foreign intelligence surveillance courts (FISCs) where it will remain under seal unless necessary to ascertain the legality of the surveillance or to support an application for a court order to conduct the surveillance. The FBI used the FISC option in the Walker case.

To create the conditions for the effective control of FCI, President Ford wrote domestic intelligence out of the definition of CI in 1976, and President Carter eliminated security programs in 1978. President Reagan retained both these modifications in his 1981 executive order, but wisely did not take the additional step of expressly deleting law enforcement from the definition.

In a nation of laws, law enforcement cannot escape being an aspect of CI because there are criminal statutes to protect the nation against the very conduct (foreign directed assassination, espionage, sabotage, subversion or terrorism) toward which CI activities are directed. On the other hand, merely placing CI organizationally under law enforcement would not guarantee freedom from illegal or improper investigations. The Church Committee found the FBI just as capable of untoward practices (Hoover's private files) and abusing the legal rights of Americans (CI Programs (COINTELPRO) targeting various domestic groups) as the CIA.[43] Wherever FCI is placed organizationally, CI personnel must be trained and supervised to obey the law. Keeping CI under law enforcement (DOJ/FBI) inside the United States facilitates this management problem and, it is hoped, ensures more frequent and more successful resort to prosecution than placing it in an agency with different primary concerns. Attention to legal requirements during the earliest stage of an investigation is essential if the fruits of that investigation will some day be needed to prosecute. Bringing in trained law enforcement professionals from the beginning of any CI investigation facilitates the collection and preservation of evidence for later use in a court of law. Therefore, by combining CI and law enforcement under common control, the nation's vital interests and individual rights are best accommodated.

It is really immaterial whether CI is considered an aspect of intelligence, law enforcement or security, or whether it is something else and they are aspects of it. While each is distinct, all are integrally related and must be organized and conducted within the context of American society and laws. Removing security programs from CI has not separated the two as aspects of each other. By its very title, the 1986 SSCI *Report* acknowledges this relationship. Despite the Carter and Reagan executive orders, security and CI functions have been combined under common command by the Army (INSCOM), Navy (NAVSECINVCOM), DIA (OS), and elsewhere. While functionally separated *within* the FBI, domestic intelligence (Criminal Division) and FCI (Intelligence Division) can be co-ordinated by a common superior when warranted. Any attempt to separate law enforcement from CI would create problems of accommodation and co-ordination.

CONCLUSION

The need for national consensus is apparent. CI is a profession that works best in secret out of public view. The FCI community is well organized and staffed by patriotic, dedicated Americans, faithfully serving their country. Occasionally, an individual seeking spies and traitors can become obsessed with his role and perception of what is best for America. When this happens he sees enemies all around and balances for himself the national security against the individual rights of others. While there is no comparison of their motives, the nation can be harmed as effectively by those who subvert its democratic processes as by those who sell it to a foreign power for whatever reason. Two men, Hoover and Angleton, because of long tenure in a linchpin position between CI and the outside, came to exercise unhealthy power and to abuse it. The former DIRC motto, '*Quis custodiet ipsos custodes?*' ('Who will watch the guardians?') remains ever relevant.

When consensus does not exist, the FCI community is more narrowly circumscribed. For this reason, FCI agencies cannot afford to do more than is reasonably necessary to counter bona fide threats to the nation. The FCI community must operate within the constraints of law.

Congress, for their part, must demonstrate constraint as well as effective oversight. The degree of control exercised over FCI will vary with the threat and can be resolved through the political process, except in extreme emergency conditions. This does not mean that every citizen or even every senator and congressman needs to know every detail of every FCI activity. Too many watchdogs and too may controllers can inhibit legitimate activity and cause unnecessary leaks of properly classified information. Watchdogs need to remain limited only to those necessary to assure accountability. While they occur all too frequently, leaks of classified information by anyone merely to win a policy point are anathema.

To prevent the individual from substituting his world view for the national consensus, the FCI community must continue to operate within a framework of laws, policies and rules that control abuses of power. Only to the extent that there is consensus on what those laws, policies and rules should be, and on the nature of the perceived threat, can Americans of all political persuasions support the FCI community. Unless this broad consensus exists, the FCI community can be manipulated from within, or by the administration or Congress for political purposes. In these circumstances, it becomes a threat to the rights of citizens and a potential apparatus of oppression. To safeguard against conspiratorial intrigues, power must be shared (or fragmented) and oversight conducted. No matter how good in theory the organizational and oversight structures, eternal vigilance must be maintained. Organizational form is not the paramount consideration. The key is good people, empowered to do their jobs, and held accountable for their performances.

NOTES

1. Allen Dulles, *The Craft of Intelligence* (New York, 1963), p.121.
2. Sherman Kent, *Strategic Intelligence: For American World Policy* (Princeton, 1951), pp.209–10.
3. Harry Howe Ransom, *The Intelligence Establishment* (Cambridge, MA, 1971), p.14.
4. Arthur A. Zuehlke, Jr., 'What Is Counterintelligence?', in Roy Godson (ed.), *Intelligence Requirements for the 1980's: Counterintelligence* (Washington, DC, 1985), p.14. (Hereafter *Counterintelligence.*)
5. Jeffrey T. Richelson, *The U.S. Intelligence Community* (Cambridge, MA, 1985), p.220.
6. Norman Miler, 'Counterintelligence At The Crossroads', in Roy Godson (ed.), *Intelligence Requirements for the 1980's: Elements Of Intelligence* (Washington, DC 1983), pp.53–4.
7. In response to a Freedom of Information Act request, the Army reported 'Army records indicate the term "counterintelligence" has been in existence at least since 1944 or possibly earlier'. That year Army *Technical Manual (TM) 20–205* very broadly defined CI as 'measures intended to destroy the effectiveness of the enemy's intelligence work'. Between 1953 and 1978, the Army recorded some 98 proposals to modify the definition of CI.
8. Executive Order 11905 (President Ford) may be found in the *Weekly Compilation of Presidential Documents*, Vol. 12, pp.234–43. Executive Order 12036 (President Carter) may be found in Vol. 14, pp.194–216. Executive Orders 12333 and 12334 (President Reagan) may be found in Vol. 17, pp.1336–48 and 1348–9. No further citations will be made to these documents in these notes.

POLICY AREAS

9. For further discussion of the organization of Canadian security intelligence see: Gerard F. Rutan, 'The Canadian Security Intelligence Service: Squaring the Demands of National Security with Canadian Democracy', *Conflict Quarterly* (Fall 1985) pp.17–30.; Geoffrey R. Weller, 'Restructuring the Royal Canadian Mounted Police: The Creation of a Civilian Security and Intelligence Agency', paper prepared for the annual meetings of the Western Political Science Association, San Diego, 5–27 March 1982; Geoffrey R. Weller, 'Legislative Oversight of Intelligence Services in Canada and the United States', paper prepared for the Annual Meeting of the American Political Science Association, New Orleans, 29 August–1 September 1985, pp.4–12.; and Peter H. Russell, 'The Proposed Charter For A Civilian Intelligence Agency: An Appraisal', *Canadian Public Policy*, IX, 3 (1983), pp.326–37. The British arrangement is addressed in Peter Wright, *Spy Catcher* (New York, 1987), pp.31–3.

10. *The National Security Act of 1947. Statutes at Large*, 61, 496 (1947). Codified at 50 U.S.C. sec. 401 *et seq.*; *Central Intelligence Agency Act of 1949. Statutes at Large*, 63, 208 (1949). Codified at 50 U.S.C. sec. 403a et seq.; and *National Security Act Amendments of 1949. Statutes at Large*, 63, 579 (1949). The following discussion of the current FCI community is based upon title 50, Executive Order 12333, and responses to Freedom of Information Act requests by the respective agencies.

11. 50 U.S.C. sec. 403(d)(3) (1982).

12. US Department of Justice, 'The Attorney General's Guidelines on General Crimes, Racketeering Enterprise and Domestic Security/Terrorism Investigations', 7 March 1983, and 'Attorney General Guidelines For FBI Foreign Intelligence Collection and Foreign Counterintelligence Investigations', 18 April 1983.

13. 14 U.S.C. sec. 1 (1982).

14. Stansfield Turner, *Secrecy and Democracy: The CIA in Transition* (New York, 1985), p.74.

15. George Cole, *The American System of Criminal Justice*, 4th ed. (Monterey, CA, 1986), pp.8–9.

16. Herbert L. Packer, 'Two Models of the Criminal Process', in George F. Cole (ed.), *Criminal Justice: Law and Politics*, 4th ed. (Monterey, CA, 1984), pp.15–29. Reprinted from Herbert L. Packer, *The Limits of the Criminal Sanction* (Stanford, 1968).

17. Arnold Beichman and Roy Godson, 'Legal Constraints And Incentives', in Godson (ed.), *Counterintelligence*, pp.281–302.

18. John Ranelagh, *The Agency: The Rise and Decline of the CIA* (New York, 1987), pp.659–71.

19. US Congress, Senate, *Meeting the Espionage Challenge: A Review of United States Counterintelligence and Security Programs: Report of the Senate Select Comm. on Intelligence, S.Report 99–522, 99th Cong., 2d Sess.* (Washington, DC, 1986), pp.6, 78, 82. As the title of the report suggests, the committee links CI and security programs in its response to the espionage challenge.

20. 50 U.S.C. section 1801 (1982).

21. The vignettes below were drawn from various issues of *The Washington Post* and *Newsweek* over the period since 1984. For additional details on the Walker case, including a damage assessment, see John Barron, *Breaking The Ring* (Boston, 1987).

22. A brief overview of the evolution and organization of the federal intelligence function from 1776 to 1975 is provided by US Congress, Senate, *Supplementary Reports on Intelligence Activities, Book VI. Final Report of the Select Committee To Study Governmental Operations with Respect to Intelligence Activities, S. Rept. 94–755, 94th Cong., 2d Sess.*, 1976. (Hereafter *Senate Book VI.*)

23. Wyman Packard, 'The History of ONI', *Naval Intelligence Professionals Quarterly*, IV, 1 (Winter 1988), pp.6–11, reprinted from the second of the four special 1982 issues of the ONI *Newsletter* commemorating the 100th birthday of ONI.

24. *Senate Book VI*, pp.77–9.

25. Ibid., pp.94–8. From this burgeoning of CI and domestic intelligence during the First World War until Executive Order 11905 effectively separated them in 1976, the two disciplines were combined.

152

FOREIGN COUNTER-INTELLIGENCE

26. Richard Gid Powers, *Secrecy and Power: The Life of J. Edgar Hoover* (New York, 1987), pp.146–7.
27. Ibid., pp.228–34; *Senate Book VI*, pp.133–6.
28. Athan Theoharis, *Spying on Americans: Political Surveillance from Hoover to the Huston Plan* (Philadelphia, 1978), pp.65–93, 133–55; Kenneth O'Reilly and Athan G. Theoharis, 'The FBI, the Congress, and McCarthyism' in Athan G. Theoharis (ed.), *Beyond the Hiss Case: The FBI, Congress, and the Cold War* (Philadelphia, 1982), pp.372–95; and Melvyn Dubofsky and Athan Theoharis, *Imperial Democracy: The United States since 1945* (Englewood Cliffs, NJ, 1983), pp.24–8, 49–56, 62–70, 140, 153–5, 162–7, 203–10.
29. During the 1960s, James Angleton's preoccupation with Soviet penetration of the CIA led him on a great mole hunt which progressively took him into a 'wilderness of mirrors'. His extra-legal activities resulting from this obsession contributed to his downfall and the temporary decentralization of CI within CIA. David C. Martin, *Wilderness of Mirrors* (New York, 1980), pp.64, 188–212. To gain additional perspective on the mole syndrome, see the autobiography of a frustrated senior British intelligence officer, Peter Wright, *Spy Catcher* (New York, 1987).
30. US Congress, Senate, *Resolution: To establish a select committee of the Senate to conduct an investigation and study with respect to intelligence activities carried out on behalf of the Federal Government*, S. Res. 21, 94th Cong., 1st sess., 1975.
31. US Congress, Senate, *Intelligence Activities And The Rights Of Americans, Book II. Final Report of the Select Committee To Study Governmental Operations with Respect to Intelligence Activities*, S. Rept. 94–755, 94th Cong., 2d Sess., 1976, pp.137–288, 296–339. (Hereafter *Senate Book II*.)
32. Turner, p.160.
33. Glenn Hastedt with Gordon Hoxie, 'The Intelligence Community and American Foreign Policy: The Reagan and Carter Administrations', in R. Gordon Hoxie (ed.), *The Presidency And National Security Policy* (New York, 1984), p.70.
34. US President (Ronald Reagan), Statement, 'United States Intelligence Activities', *Public Papers of the Presidents* (Washington, DC, 1981), p.1126.
35. Hastedt, p.71, and Ranelagh, pp.669–71.
36. Robert C. McFarlane with Richard Saunders and Thomas C. Shull, 'The National Security Council: Organization for Policy Making', in Hoxie (ed.), op. cit., pp.261–73.
37. US Department of Justice, Office of Intelligence Policy and Review, Memorandum for the Attorney General, 'Re: Attorney General Guidelines for FBI Foreign Intelligence Collection and *Foreign Counterintelligence Investigations*', 10 March 1983, and US Department of Justice, 'Attorney General Guidelines For FBI Foreign Intelligence Collection and Foreign Counterintelligence Investigations', 18 April 1983.
38. US, Department of Defense, DOD Directive 5240.2, 'DOD Counterintelligence', 6 June 1983.
39. *Foreign Intelligence Surveillance Act. Statutes at Large*, 92, 1783 (1978). Codified at 50 U.S.C. sec. 1801 *et seq.*; *The Classified Information Procedures Act. Statutes at Large*, 94, 2025 (1980). Codified at 18 U.S.C. Appendix; and *Intelligence Identities Protection Act. Statutes at Large*, 96, 122 (1982). Codified at 50 U.S.C. sec. 421 *et seq.*
40. *Intelligence Authorization Act for Fiscal Year 1981. Statutes at Large*, 94, Title IV, sec. 407(b), 1981 (1982). Codified at 50 U.S.C. sec. 413.
41. *Intelligence Authorization Act for Fiscal Year 1986. Statutes at Large*, 99, Title IV, sec. 401(a), 1004 (1985). Codified at 50 U.S.C. sec. 414.
42. 18 U.S.C. sec. 2510 *et seq.* (1982) and 50 U.S.C. sec. 1801 *et seq.* (1982).
43. *Senate Book II*.

153

PART THREE
A COMPARATIVE EXAMPLE

8

Restructuring Control in Canada: The McDonald Commission of Inquiry and its Legacy

STUART FARSON

The 1970s were a period of high drama and much trauma for Canada's security and intelligence community. In October 1970 separatist sentiments finally erupted in Quebec. Members of the Front de Libération du Québec (FLQ) kidnapped the British Trade Commissioner and murdered the province's Labour Minister. The Federal Government responded in force by proclaiming the War Measures Act. The decade ended with the Security Service demoralized and in disarray and with Canada undertaking the most extensive public inquiry into security and intelligence matters in its history.

This chapter concerns that inquiry and the dramatic changes that have resulted since its completion in 1981. It concentrates on the innovations that have been made to the control processes that govern security and intelligence agencies; tries to clarify such shorthand terms as accountability and responsible government; and offers some observations on Canadian experience by identifying concerns that still exist.

Three main arguments are presented here. First, the Canadian security and intelligence system is different from other democratic countries in that it is defensively oriented. It focuses on threats. There is no foreign intelligence service with either a HUMINT or a covert action capacity. Secondly, control is perceived as having two equally important and interlocking components. Obviously, threats to a state's security have to be brought under control. Here the purpose of control is primarily administrative. It ensures that the bureaucratic apparatus protects the state effectively and efficiently. But there is also a need to ensure that the security and intelligence apparatus is itself

157

properly controlled by the political executive. Here the purpose of control is to ensure that those entrusted with authority comply with their mandate. And finally, the reform of control structures is held to be a matter of occupation and perspective. Countering the threat to security implies different things to different people. For defence analysts the main threat is external. For civil rights lawyers the state itself probably constitutes the primary threat. Equally significant, perspectives within individual disciplines vary considerably. For example, criminologists, who view security and intelligence activities as policing functions, can see the problem from the polarities of police reform. There the extremes are represented by orthodox and revisionist schools. One sees organizations evolving as they should in an inevitable fashion. They respond to events and gradually become more effective and efficient. They act with the consent and in the interests of the community. They are perceived as an essential element of the democratic state. To revisionists law is merely a weapon. It legitimates the use of force by the state. In this sense reform helps to justify the continuation of a particular form of social order by legitimating the state's use of particular forms of coercive and intrusive policing tactics.

BACKGROUND TO THE ESTABLISHMENT OF THE COMMISSION

Invoking the War Measures Act put civil liberties on hold. Armed soldiers guarded the streets. Some 465 people were rounded up and detained without access to a lawyer. In the end only a small minority were charged and brought to trial. Those who complained about such sweeping provisions were called 'bleeding hearts' by the Prime Minister. While the decision to invoke the Act still remains clouded in secrecy, it is now clear that it was a gross over-reaction on the part of the Trudeau government. The Security Service of the Royal Canadian Mounted Police (RCMP) had warned the government about the FLQ threat, but they had been unable to identify the degree to which the various cells were co-ordinating their actions. This lack of knowledge was crucial in determining the government's reaction. At some point following the October crisis the government gave the Security Service notice that it needed to be better informed about Quebec separatists. In response the Service requested more explicit guidance on its functions. In 1975 a new mandate was provided which specifically permitted officers to counter and deter.

The Service apparently took these capacities to heart. At his trial for bombing a Montreal businessman's home a former RCMP officer acknowledged that he had done much worse while working for the Security Service and mentioned a break-in at the offices of the Agence de presse libre du Québec (APLQ). Initially, the RCMP were able to convince the Solicitor General that these were isolated incidents. When two former officers of the Force confirmed that such events were commonplace, the government faced a crisis of major proportions.

Three critically important issues needed to be resolved. The problem of how to restore public trust in a national symbol topped the list. Quite clearly the Security Service's activities had tarnished the whole organization, not just a part of it. The second was how to encourage simultaneously sets of interests which had diametrically opposed objectives. And the third was the unenviable task of indicating that this was being done.

In July 1977 the government created an independent public inquiry under Justice David McDonald. The mandate of the Royal Commission was to determine the prevalence of RCMP Security Service activities that were neither authorized nor provided for by law and to make recommendations concerning policies and procedures for protecting Canada's security.[1] In this way the government bought time to find appropriate solutions and garnered an opportunity to dispel the worst aspects of public disquiet.

CONCERNS OF THE MCDONALD COMMISSION

The Commissioner's initial investigations revealed that members of both the RCMP's Security Service and their Criminal Investigation Branch had made an extensive practice of conducting unlawful operations and that such officers had been supported by provincial and municipal police forces. They concluded that this problem could only be prevented by enacting legislation which brought the security and intelligence function under tighter political control and defined the limits of security and intelligence operations. On considering how political control should be applied the Commissioners recognized that police officers needed to act independently and to use discretionary powers. They considered that such independence and powers were inappropriate for security and intelligence personnel, and concluded that the Security Service should be severed from the RCMP and established as a separate civilian organization under the same minister.

A deeper analysis of the policies, procedures and functions of the Service led to the conclusion that the Security Service was defective in many respects and that a para-military policing organization constituted an inappropriate recruitment and training ground for security and intelligence personnel. These findings further supported their recommendations for separating functions along organizational lines.

The Commission's reports clearly indicate that the Commissioners believed that Canada's security and intelligence community was fragmented

159

and needed restructuring. While they identified the various elements of the community (units inside and outside the Security Service within the RCMP; the Security Planning and Research Group – now the Police and Security Branch – of the Solicitor General's Department; the Departments of External Affairs, National Defence, and Supply and Services; the Communications Security Establishment (CSE); the Canadian Employment and Immigration Commission; and the cabinet and interdepartmental committee system, the picture painted did not represent a well co-ordinated whole. Producers of intelligence out-balanced consumers. Organizations tended to have separate and individual functions. Decision-making lacked integration. The system favored foreign military intelligence-gathering at the expense of political and economic varieties. There were weaknesses in setting intelligence priorities and requirements, in co-ordination, and in conducting intelligence analysis. And in particular, the system lacked an important component.

The Commissioners were careful to make no recommendation about establishing a Canadian foreign intelligence agency. Nevertheless, they drew attention to Canada's failure to establish such an agency as a 'unique' omission among its close allies.[2] They saw it as a flaw in the system which would seriously limit the effectiveness of their proposal to establish an independent security intelligence agency.[3]

Specific Problems of Bureaucratic Efficacy

In developing a position on the state of bureaucratic efficiency and effectiveness within the Canadian security and intelligence community the Commissioners drew on the broader experience of three earlier inquiries into the state of organization and management within the federal government. In the early 1960s the Glassco Commission had reported on the organization and methods of operation of departments and agencies.[4] In so doing it had applied the principles of private enterprise to the public sector. Its theme had been 'let the managers manage'. It recommended a major transfer of power from central agencies to line departments. Two important shifts were established by this Commission. The Civil Service Commission began a deliberate program of delegating authority to departments for promotion, recruitment and selection; and the newly established Treasury Board, which had become responsible for expenditure management, was able to establish the premise that program efficacy should be judged through expenditures.

Even before the Glassco Commission's recommendations had been fully implemented, the Auditor General revealed that Parliament was in danger of losing control over the financial management of the state. The Lambert Commission which resulted, gave great prominence to the notions of accountability and control and specifically related their importance to the concepts of organizational effectiveness and efficiency. In particular, it recommended that:

> The cabinet and individual ministers should provide more leadership and direction to officials to ensure that they administer their operations with economy, efficiency and effectiveness, and should be more directly involved in holding them to account for carrying out their assigned tasks.[5]

The federal government established a further committee while the Lambert Commission was in progress. Under the chairmanship of Guy D'Avignon it argued that the current poor state of personnel management was the result of the failure of successive governments to instil a philosophy of management. Among the problems it identified were: 'excessive and inflexible regulations; slavish adherence to universally applied regulations in the name of merit at the expense of efficiency and effectiveness', and 'no accountability for effective personnel management'.[6]

With these general concerns in mind the McDonald Commission started its analysis with the Mackenzie Commission's Report of 1969. This had examined the effectiveness of the RCMP Security Service and related policy-making and co-ordination processes and had found them all lacking. It recognized a 'clear distinction between the operational work of the security service and that of a police force' and had recommended that a 'non-police' agency be established to perform the security functions.[7] With regard to policy-making and co-ordination it had found effectiveness 'more apparent than real' and had recommended that a formalized security secretariat be formed in the Privy Council Office with

> adequate status, resources and staff to formulate security policy, and more importantly, with effective authority to supervise the implementation of government security policies and regulations and to ensure their consistent application.[8]

The McDonald Commission observed that successive RCMP Commissioners avoided Prime Minister Trudeau's 1969 directive to establish a Security Service that was 'increasingly separate in structure and civilian in nature'. Even when the Service had a civilian Director General, he had been able to implement only minor changes in the management system.[9] The Commissioners also noted the Bureau of Management Consulting's 1973 Report which had recommended that the Service be given managerial control over both its operations and the administration of its resources. This recommendation had been based on the premise that the Security Service was 'intrinsically different' from a police force and the fact that the Director General did not have the delegated authority to manage effectively that part of the Service's mandate which required him to control or monitor its policies and programs'.[10] Among other BMC recommendations were:

> adopting the principle of 'centralization of policy and program control and decentralization of execution', revamping the planning process along 'management by objectives' lines, flattening the organizational pyramid by reducing the number of supervisory levels, improving training programmes, and upgrading selection criteria for entry into the Service.[11]

The Commissioners also noted that even after the Service had been given National Division status the new RCMP Commissioner instigated changes which further integrated the Service with the Force. These included the approval of all major operations of the Security Service by the Force's senior executive committee and the establishment of an operation audit unit to give the Commissioner yet another 'window' on the Service.[12]

The Commission was inevitably drawn to the position that the Security Service needed radical reform. Surveys conducted among all levels of Security Service personnel supported this view and led them to conclude that:

> This level of employee dissatisfaction, especially among civilian members, would be an unhealthy situation in any organization, but in a security service which is especially vulnerable to 'leaks' and – even more serious – penetration attempts by hostile foreign agencies, it is an intolerable and dangerous situation.[12]

Solutions to the Problems

In identifying what sort of solutions to recommend the Commission confronted two sets of problems, each with different implications. The basic principles of responsible government – accountability, political control, rule of law – were inoperative. Ministers had been unwilling or unable to control the Security Service. It had been acting independently, largely with full discretion and with little monitoring. As a result, it had been able to do things that were unlawful or not prescribed by law. And, the public had lost trust in the institution. The other set of problems suggested that while the Service was currently vulnerable, implications for the future were more serious. Keeping the Service under the administrative control of the police jeopardized the state's capacity to protect itself against future threats. Existing personnel and management policies concerning methods of recruitment and promotion, administrative structures, and internal regulations, made inefficiency and ineffectiveness inevitable.

The McDonald Commission saw separation as a critical recommendation on which others had to rest. Without this change, the level of independence and the discretionary powers normally enjoyed by federal police officers would remain and make proper political control over the security intelligence function impossible. Likewise, they considered that the Security Service could never be truly effective or efficient as currently constructed. Thus separation coupled with a new system of control and review came to be seen as the critical elements in resolving issues of *both* efficacy and propriety. Separation was the only means by which real structural change was possible. Only in this way could the Security Service obtain real operational and administrative autonomy. Without it the Service would have no chance of attracting the best people or of ensuring that administrative systems created an environment where people acted properly and lawfully. The system of accountability and control was the process chosen to make the Service truly effective. Through it political control would be both exercised and seen to be achieved. On it resided hope for avoiding abuse of the democratic system. Through its conduit criteria for effectiveness and efficiency would be introduced.

The Commission had two fundamental answers to the threats faced by the democratic state. One involved the separation of activities provided by the security and intelligence community along organizational lines. The other concerned the belief that the elements of the security and intelligence community should be brought under firm political control and direction and made fully accountable to Parliament. This system of control was not to be allowed to operate without a concomitant system of independent review and oversight.

Separating the Continuum of Activities

When the McDonald Commission recommended separation as the means for addressing both the issues of propriety and efficacy, they had more in mind than simply carving off the Security Service from the RCMP. Their plan had two specific purposes. On the one hand, they intended that the three key functions of the security and intelligence community – law enforcement, counter-intelligence and intelligence gathering activities – should be permanently separated from each other. While the separation of the Security Service from the RCMP had much to do with a desire for greater efficiency and effectiveness, the broader separation of functions was motivated by other concerns. Fear of an intelligence monolith was a major consideration. Likewise, the possibility of a future secret foreign intelligence

163

agency, closely tied to policing or internal security work, which would have to break the laws of foreign states on occasions, was considered undesirable because of the contagion effect it might have on domestic agencies. On the other hand, the Commissioners saw a need for separating the policy producing, policy co-ordinating, analysis, and operational elements of the community. Here the motivation was largely grounded on demands for greater efficiency and effectiveness.

In concluding that serious restructuring was needed, the Commissioners were touching on hallowed ground. An overt attempt to change the management and personnel systems of the entire Force was probably an impossible political task given the partisan and regional nature of public support for the RCMP. There was nothing new about the idea of separation. As early as 1955 an internal RCMP report had recommended the separation of the civilian Internal Security Branch from the Special Branch. And in 1969 the Mackenzie Commission had advocated complete separation of the Service from the Force. Even Prime Minister Trudeau's compromise instruction that the Service remain within the Force but become 'increasingly separate in structure and civilian in nature' had been ignored.

It is important to understand the impact that being within the RCMP structure had on civilian members of the Security Service. A former Solicitor General of Canada has compared the RCMP to a religious order. Only those with peace officer status and 'ordained' through the initiation process in Regina, ever become true 'members' of the Force. This attitude was reinforced by an extensive and well-defined set of rules governing personal conduct which allowed the Commissioner to arrest and detain such members for disobeying lawful orders or for being involved in *any activity* which was not in the best interests of the Force.[13] These factors, coupled with such inducements as pension schemes, molded loyalty to the organization rather than to the profession and made RCMP officers quite different from personnel in all other areas of government. Senior bureaucrats have, in fact, testified about the difficulty the organization has in dealing with and accepting outsiders. The second-class status allotted to civilian employees made it a particularly hard place for them to work and resulted in a high staff turnover. This had a significant impact on research and analysis, areas normally associated with civilians.

Working within the broad framework of the RCMP also created problems for the Security Service as a whole. Until 1976 when the Security Service obtained National Division status within the Force, divisional units of the Security Service had to report through the divisional RCMP commanders. Thus, the divisions rather than Security Service headquarters exercised control over the operational administrative resources – human, physical and financial – of Security Service field units.

The Commission's recommendations regarding separation can be grouped into five general categories. The first concerned finding the right people for the right job. Here they envisaged two specific elements of policy as being likely to increase efficacy. These were finding the senior management for the Agency and recruiting a wider variety of people to provide all the necessary functions. The selection of the Director was considered to be critical. While the Commissioners did not believe that it was essential for the person to have had intelligence experience, they considered it important that the individual have management and administrative skills and be able to exhibit high capacity and probity. They also thought it vital that the Director should show sound, unbiased judgement in political matters, possess a good grasp of international affairs and how government functions, and strongly value liberal democratic principles.[14] They also believed that the leadership should collectively exhibit a broad expertise if it was to prove to be an effective decision-making body. As a result, they recommended a team approach to senior management where the collective mind would have had government department and agency experience (particularly of those kinds relevant to security and intelligence work), extensive exposure to investigate practice, legal training, and would possess an extensive knowledge of modern management techniques and theories.[15] The Commission was highly critical of the pool of talent made available through the RCMP recruitment process as it tended not to be university-educated and to have limited knowledge in a number of essential areas. Of particular importance was the lack of knowledge of international affairs, legal and policy analysis, and management skills.[16] Not only did the Commission recommend attracting university graduates from a wide variety of disciplines and work backgrounds but it also advocated selection on the basis of certain common characteristics:

> discretion; emotional stability; maturity; tolerance; the capacity to work in an organization about which little is said publicly; no exploitable character weaknesses; a keen sense of, and support for, what the security intelligence agency is ultimately securing (i.e. democratic processes, structures and values); and political acumen. Perhaps patience should be added to this list as well.[17]

The second category concerned how the organization could establish an appropriate style for the functions it had to provide. Recommendations in this category were important in developing an appropriate ethos for the organization. Here the Commission extended their notion of a team approach to management to the organization as a whole. They thought that it would encourage participation in decision-making and would provide the difference in perspective needed to produce high-quality decisions and would reduce the likelihood of poorly considered policies and operations.[18] To support the notion of a team approach they recommended reducing the number of seniority layers and pay bands in the organization. They also saw a need for developing training courses on small group decision-making techniques, eliminating environments which were based on job levels (such as different eating and social facilities)[19] and for having only one category of employee.[20] The Commission also considered that an administrative style based on a reliance on obedience was quite inappropriate for a security and intelligence organization. In this regard they concluded that:

> To function effectively within a security intelligence agency often requires getting things done by working with other people with whom no superior/subordinate relationship exists. In sum, a leadership style based on giving orders must give way to a team approach where the emphasis is on shared decision-making, and where control by superiors is largely replaced by self-control and self-direction, based on a common understanding of shared goals. This is not to argue that giving orders is never appropriate, only that there are often more effective means of getting things done.[21]

A further aspect of setting an appropriate style for the organization is to be seen in the Commission's attitude towards trade unions and employee associations. The Commissioners were opposed to the unionization on grounds that union/management negotiations might allow valuable information to fall into the wrong hands. Nevertheless, they recommended an alternative approach which would compensate for this restriction. This had three essential components. One was the recommendation that the new Agency should encourage the formation of an employee association. This would have the right to represent the employees in discussions with the Agency's management over working conditions and salaries and would provide a forum by which employees could influence important aspects of agency decision-making. The second was the formation of the managerial style discussed above which would stress individual participation. The final component was the recommendation that salaries and benefits of employees should be tied to those of the Public Service of Canada by a predetermined formula.[22]

The third category concerned ways in which the talents within the organization could be nurtured. One aspect concerned the training facilities. Despite the fact that three new courses had been added while the Inquiry was in progress, the Commissioners believed that further significant changes were necessary. In the introductory course for analysts and investigators, for example, they believed that 'the emphasis should be on developing a much more sophisticated skill in dealing with legal, political and moral contexts of security intelligence work and mastering tradecraft techniques'.[23] They also considered that measures should be taken to combat the tendency towards insularity. To this end they recommended a variety of external courses. The Commissioners also noted that while troubled employees could incur significant costs for any organization, the potential damage for security and intelligence agencies could be much more substantial because they constituted a prime target for those wanting to penetrate the agency. To meet this eventuality they recommended the use of specialist counselors.[24] Another avenue examined by the Commission was the likely career paths of security and intelligence personnel. Here they found the generalist career model adopted in police forces quite inappropriate. It acted against the continuity which helped build in-depth expertise and it often placed people in jobs they did not enjoy. Also, it required more frequent movement of families about the country than most personnel were willing to accept. In its place the Commission recommended greater specialization for individuals supported by an improved capacity on the part of the Agency to plan careers.[25] To help effect this they recommended fewer bureaucratic levels within the organization and wider pay bands. This, they considered, was likely to encourage greater stability.[26] They also recommended that a number of senior positions should be available – such as those for analysts – which did not incur heavy administrative responsibilities. This, they believed, would allow individuals to develop a higher degree of specialized knowledge.

The fourth category that the McDonald Commission considered concerned methods of assessment. The Commissioners believed that there were serious flaws in the existing system of auditing the security function. In its stead they recommended a three-pronged approach. The first was the belief that the major responsibility for conducting operational audits should lie outside, and be independent of, the organization. The Commission did not believe that this body should be responsible for assessing the effectiveness of the security organization. Rather, they saw its function as monitoring operations to ensure that they were lawful, morally acceptable, and within the statutory mandate.[27] The second was the establishment of a small investigative unit to handle complaints. The third concerned a managerial audit. The Commission considered the benefits of the existing system did not match up to the costs and that because senior management's involvement in the process was normally limited to a review of the final report, few of the really important issues ever got resolved. The Commission was not entirely helpful in suggesting ways in which the new agency might identify areas in which it was either ineffective or inefficient. They left matters open, simply suggesting that the Service should experiment with various methods. Nevertheless, while they did not suggest methods to evaluate effectiveness and efficiency, they did indicate characteristics that selected methods should have. These included the use of outsiders to act as catalysts for change and the committed involvement of senior management to the process.[28] The Commission also believed that Parliament had too little opportunity to evaluate and to scrutinize the security and intelligence function. To effect an important change in this regard the Commission recommended the establishment of a small joint committee of both Houses of Parliament. This committee, they noted, 'should be as much concerned with effectiveness of the security intelligence organization as with the legality or propriety of its operations'.[29] They also thought that it should, like the Security Commission in Britain, be responsible for examining breaches of security.

The final category concerned matters which were immediately outside the CSIS but which bore directly on the new Service. Critically important was the Commission's recommendation to place the CSIS under the direction of the Solicitor General of Canada. This was premised on the need for co-operation between the RCMP and the CSIS and on the belief that this was best achieved by having one minister responsible for developing it.[31]

Perhaps because the Commissioners believed that the establishment of a foreign intelligence agency was beyond their terms of reference, they expressly avoided making recommendations on this issue. Nevertheless, they suggested that the matter should be further evaluated. In the event that such an organization was considered necessary they thought that it should be established by statute and kept quite separate from other entities. In particular they thought it should not be asked to conduct paramilitary operations or be given the authority to destabilize foreign governments.[32]

The Commissioners made a number of important recommendations concerning the integrations of security and intelligence information with the decision-making and co-ordination processes of government. Significantly, they did not follow the Mackenzie Commission in recommending an enlarged secretariat for the Privy Council Office as they saw the PCO providing a co-ordinating function, not an operational role. Instead, they concentrated their attention on the committee system.

The Cabinet Committee seemed to be defective in three ways. First, it met neither regularly nor frequently. It seemed only to be called into action at times of crisis. Secondly, it appeared to respond more to policy initiatives of lower committees than to instigate policy itself. And thirdly, there were no individual ministers responsible for specific aspects of policy. To make the cabinet a full participant in the policy-making and co-ordination process, particularly in the area of setting priorities,[33] the Commission recommended that the committee should be enlarged to include consumers of intelligence as well as producers and that there should be two lead ministers responsible for security and intelligence policy. One would be responsible for all matters relating to both foreign and domestic security intelligence. The other would be responsible for all security measures, such as protecting buildings and VIPs, and security clearances.

The Commission also noted defects at the interdepartmental level. Of particular importance was the poor linkage between the deputy ministers on the Interdepartmental Committee on Security and Intelligence (ICSI) and their representatives on the junior Security Advisory Committee (SAC) and Intelligence Advisory Committee (IAC). To effect an improvement in security policy and co-ordination the Commission recommended that SAC should not be left to make policy initiatives and that ICSI set SAC clear mandates and deadlines for its work projects.

In the intelligence field the Commission saw two problem areas. One concerned the need to establish a more effective method of identifying intelligence requirements for Cabinet. The other was related to both the need to improve the analysis of intelligence that had been collected and the method by which this intelligence was to be used by consuming departments. To improve matters the Commission recommended the transfer of the intelligence assessment and dissemination functions in SAC to IAC. Were such a change to be made they considered it inappropriate for IAC to be dominated by one ministry. Consequently, they recommended that IAC be chaired by the Assistant Secretary to the Cabinet (Security and Intelligence), not, as previously, by the Deputy Under-Secretary for External Affairs. The Commission also recommended that the economic departments (Finance, Treasury Board, Industry, Trade and Commerce and Energy, Mines and Resources) should receive better representation on the IAC. In line with this recommendation the Commissioners noted that the central assessment of intelligence needs and intelligence products had tended to focus on military and political affairs. They considered this emphasis to be too narrow and suggested that it should be expanded to include economic interests.[34]

The Commission also saw a need to improve the preparation of longer-term strategic estimates. To rectify the situation the Commission proposed the formation of a new organization to be called the Bureau of Intelligence Assessments (BIA). This was to be modeled on Australia's Office of National Assessment.[35] In a somewhat contradictory fashion they recommended that the BIA should be located in the PCO. Again they stressed the need to keep it separate from the Security Intelligence Secretariat and that it should be an assessment not a collecting agency.[36]

169

LEGISLATIVE CONCERNS

For some people the statutory reforms which brought the security intelligence function under firm political control are the major contribution of the McDonald Commission. For others the Canadian Security Intelligence Act epitomizes the legalization of activities that had hitherto been illegal. These positions need further examination.

Better Political Control

There is justification to support the premise that the new legislation represents a step forward. The McDonald Commission recognized, implicitly at least, that the concepts of accountability, control, independence and discretion were inter-related concepts and that they were all aspects of political control. Further, they realized that different organizations required differing degrees of each to operate effectively. For example, Canadian police officers required quite a different balance from personnel in security and intelligence fields. Those involved in local law and order maintenance needed a level of independence from political authority in order to be seen to administer the law fairly and a degree of individual discretion at the street level if they were to avoid overloading the criminal justice system. Such needs are not shared by security and intelligence personnel.

The methods by which political control was established over the security intelligence function is worthy of detailed analysis because it represents a significant achievement of the Canadian approach to the problem. The CSIS Act, passed in 1984, delegated authority, introduced counterbalancing controlling powers, made specific key individuals accountable, dealt with the subject of political authority, and established a comprehensive oversight and review system for the Canadian Security Intelligence Service.[37] The Act's principal actors were the Cabinet, the responsible minister (that is, the Solicitor General of Canada), the Director of the Security Service, the Deputy Solicitor General, the Inspector General of the Service, the Review Committee and selected judges of the Federal Court.

Responsibilities A primary purpose in establishing a security service that was separate from the RCMP was to make the Federal government fully responsible for the functions that the Service provided. The identification of responsibilities (i.e. duties) and the process of making individual political actors responsible for those duties was an essential first step in establishing political control. Unlike all Canadian police legislation the Act specifically laid out the duties that the service was to perform. Under Section 12 the

CSIS was given the power to collect, analyse and retain information and intelligence that relates to threats to the security of Canada and to report and advise the Federal government on such matters. It was not given the authority to deter or counter threats. The Service was further limited to conducting investigations that were 'strictly necessary' Where intrusive investigations were required there had to be 'reasonable grounds to believe that a threat to the security of Canada existed' before a warrant would be issued.

The Act specifically identified the people in the government and the bureaucracy who would ultimately be responsible for the actions performed by the Service. The cabinet was given the capacity to appoint the Director (S 4.(12)) and the Inspector General (S. 30.(1)). While the Director was given responsibility for the 'control and management of the service' his role was made subject to the direction of the Solicitor General of Canada, the minister responsible for the Service (S. 6.(1)). Of particular significance was the fact that the minister was given two principal advisers on security and intelligence matters: the Director of the Service and the Deputy Solicitor General. Under the old system the minister's deputy had no right to attend meetings, let alone the authority to contradict the head of the Security Service where there was disagreement.

The ultimate responsibility for permitting the Service to operate in areas that contravened individual rights and freedoms was removed from the political domain and placed under judicial control. No clandestine searches of property could be conducted, no seizure of goods made, and no communication intercepted without a warrant signed by a specially designated Federal Court judge (S. 21.(3).

Prosecution of security offences and offences against internationally protected persons was not left with the provinces but given to the federal government (S. 57). For this reason the Attorney General of Canada was expressly given the right to exercise a fiat over provincial attorneys general on security offenses (S. 59.(2)).

Controls While individual responsibilities were dispensed, a wide variety of controls were placed over the Service and the principal actors involved. This system of controls was countervailing in design. The Prime Minister has been empowered to appoint the Review Committee but its composition cannot be of his own choosing. He must seek the approval of the other parties in the House of Commons (S.34.(1)). Likewise, the Director has the responsibility for the control and management of the Agency, but the cabinet can limit his actions by establishing regulations that curtail his powers and control the conduct of his employees (S.8.(4)). They may also dismiss him for cause (S.4.(2)).

Besides giving directions to the Director, the Solicitor General can affect the functioning of the Service in more subtle ways. He can determine where the Agency has offices (S.3.(3)), what arrangements the Agency makes with federal and provincial government departments (S.17.(1), (2)(ii)), as well as those with foreign governments and international organizations (S17.(1)(b)). The minister must also approve all warrant applications before they are presented to the Federal Court (S.21.(1)).

The Deputy Solicitor General can constrain the Service by forcing its Director to consult with him on the general operational policies. Furthermore, he can ensure that all warrant requests and renewals go through him before being passed to the minister for approval (S.7.(1)(a) and (2)).

Certain federal and provincial cabinet ministers are obliged to exercise certain controls. The Secretary of State for External Affairs must approve all arrangement with foreign states and international organizations (S.17.(1)(b)). He or the Minister of National Defence must request in writing the Service's help in obtaining information on intelligence relating to the capabilities, intentions or activities of foreign states or nationals (S.16.(1)(3)(a)). And provincial ministers responsible for policing must approve arrangements made by the Service with police in their jurisdictions (S.17.(1)(a)(ii)).

The Security Intelligence Review Committee (SIRC) has a critically important controlling power because of its access to information. The Solicitor General must provide it with all ministerial directives (S.6.(2)). It has access to 'any information under the control of the Service or of the Inspector General' (S.19.(2)(a)) with the important exception of cabinet documents (S.39.(3)) which may be withheld. It may also instruct the Inspector General to conduct a review of specific activities and to report on them (S.40.(a)).

The Inspector General, whose role was not recommended by the McDonald Commission, has an obligation to 'monitor the compliance by the Service with its operational policies' (S30.(2)(a)). Insofar as the Inspector General reports to the Deputy Solicitor General his role is an important factor in helping the Deputy to perform his countervailing function. The exact purpose of the Inspector General's monitoring is unclear as his reports are not made public. One interpretation is that he simply identifies whether the Service is complying with its operational policies in a legal sense. A broader interpretation would have him analyse whether the Service is also performing its function effectively and efficiently.

Finally, certain formal procedures have a controlling influence. Oaths of office, allegiance and secrecy (S.10, S.32, and S.37) are designed to ensure that the Director, the employees of the Service, the Inspector General,

172

and the Review Committee all behave in an appropriate manner. The requirement that all warrant applications be in writing and list all previous occasions on which application has been made to the Federal Court has been specifically geared to control the practice of 'judge-shopping' (s.21.(2)(h)).

Protections   Abuse of the democratic system has been controlled by providing those who might be investigated by the CSIS with specific protections. Besides the control, accountability, review and oversight processes, citizens and permanent residents are protected in five ways. First, the Act limits the Service to dealing with threats to the security of Canada (S.2.). Here the Service is limited to collecting, analysing and retaining information and intelligence. No authority has been delegated for deterring or countering actions. The Act also defines such threats in explicit terms. In particular, investigations of lawful advocacy, protests and dissent are limited to occasions when they are carried on in conjunction with the threats defined in the Act. Another protection is identified in Section 16.(2). This specifically excludes the new agency from assisting the Minister of National Defence or the Secretary of State for External Affairs within Canada in collecting 'information or intelligence relating to capabilities, intentions or activities' of Canadian citizens, permanent residents and Canadian corporations in relation to 'the defence of Canada or the conduct of the international affairs of Canada'. Lastly, and of considerable importance, employees of the new Service have not been given the powers of peace officers. Consequently, citizens, permanent residents and visitors alike cannot be taken into custody, detained or forced to answer questions by members of the Service. Only peace officers have such powers.[38]

The Government of Canada has also been protected by the Act. At issue here is the possibility that the Director might abuse his power by exploiting knowledge gained during his tenure. To reduce the possibility of political blackmail the Act restricts the directorship to a maximum of ten years in aggregate (S.4.(4)).

Modes and Types of Accountability   The McDonald Commission and the drafters of the legislation were under no illusions about the functions of accountability. They saw them as being to ensure that political control was exercised and to illustrate that such control was being exercised. The system of accountability introduced by the CSIS Act is complex in both form and variety. Three premises underpin it. The first is that responsible ministers and Parliament should be protected against unlawful or ineffective acts taking place without their knowledge. To avoid this eventuality, back-up systems for receiving information about CSIS activities have been provided. The second, is the belief that independent political actors need to be involved

173

to instil public confidence. And finally, the system must be truly interlocking to ensure that the Service is kept firmly under elected political supervision and runs effectively and efficiently.

The responsible minister, the Solicitor General of Canada, receives reports from three different sources. The Director and the Deputy Solicitor General, as co-equal advisers, may be called upon at any time. At least once a year the Director must submit a formal report to both the minister and the Inspector General about the operational activities of the Service (S.33.(1)). The Inspector General must review the operational activities of the Service and supply the Solicitor General, through his deputy, with a certificate which indicates that the Service's activities have been in line with ministerial policy directives (S.30). This must state the degree to which he is satisfied with the Director's reports to the minister, and identify all incidents where acts not authorized by law have occurred or where directions have been contravened. It must also draw attention to all occasions where unnecessary or unreasonable powers have been exercised (S.33.(2)).

The Solicitor General must also receive an annual report from the SIRC within three months of the end of each fiscal year. This should provide a general review of how the Service performed its duties and functions and analyse the Director's report and the Inspector General's certificate (S.38). Besides these annual reports the SIRC has the option of providing the minister with *ad hoc* reports on special subjects or on any matter that relates to the performance of the Committee's duties (S.54). In order to ensure that these reflect the full picture, SIRC has been given the right to receive from the Inspector General, the Director, and employees 'such information, reports and explanations as the Committee deems necessary' (S.39.(2)(a)) and copies of all written agreements made between the Service and any department of government – federal or provincial – or any police force, or any foreign government (S.17). The SIRC is also required to hear and investigate complaints which fall under its jurisdiction. Where security clearances are denied the SIRC is obliged to advise the complainant of the reasons for denial and to send statements to the Director and the deputy head concerned (S.46 and S.47). The Committee is also obliged to submit a report to the minister on the completion of any investigation into complaints conducted under the Canadian Human Rights Act (S.73), the Citizenship Act (actually to cabinet) (S.75) or the Immigration Act (also to cabinet) (S.80).

The Solicitor General, in turn, is obliged by law to submit reports to the Attorney General, the Review Committee, and to Parliament. In instances where the minister becomes aware of an unlawful act on the part of the Service he must submit a copy of any report that he receives along with 'any comments he considers appropriate' to the leading law officer of the Crown, the Attorney General of Canada. At the same time, he must forward a duplicate copy of all materials sent to the Attorney General to the SIRC (S.20). The minister is also under an obligation to provide an account of his actions to the SIRC. The final accounting process to Parliament is also a responsibility of the minister. He must answer questions relating to that part of the Estimates which deal specifically with the Service. In addition, the Solicitor General is responsible for tabling SIRC's annual report in each House of Parliament within a very limited timeframe (S.58). Parliament itself is also charged with providing an account. The final accounting process to the public is shared by Parliament and the Review Committee insofar as SIRC's annual reports become public documents on being tabled in Parliament. Under Section 69.(1) a committee of the Commons or of both Houses of Parliament must be struck to undertake a comprehensive review of the provisions *and operation* of the Act after five years of its coming into force. The report of this review must then be tabled along with any changes to the Act that the committee recommends (S.69.(2)).

Independence The legislation ensures that specific bodies and individuals can provide their functions independently. However, the degree of independence allotted to each actor varies substantially. For example, the Director's independence is very limited. Because his appointment is 'during pleasure', he may be dismissed at any time for just cause. He must not only accept directions from the minister and consult with his deputy but follow the regulations established by the cabinet. Only regarding internal administration does he have the exclusive authority to appoint employees and (with the exception of those attached or seconded to the Service) to set the terms and conditions of their employment (S.8).

By contrast, Federal Court judges designated by the Chief Justice to oversee warrant applications are appointed during 'good behaviour'. Consequently, their actions are largely unrestricted. Subject only to judicial review such judges may act with total independence in deciding whether an application for a warrant falls within the limits of the Act.

Similarly, SIRC enjoys a high level of independence. The Act explicitly establishes a method for its members to act — and be seen to act — independently of political control. Only people who have exercised a position of public trust can become members. The criterion here is that they be Privy Councillors. In addition, such persons may not currently be involved in federal politics: that is to say, they must not be either Members of Parliament or Senators. In addition, selection of the Committee must be made only after the Prime Minister has consulted with the Leader of the

Opposition and leaders of all other parties with more than twelve members in the Commons (S.34.(1). Once appointed members hold office during 'good behaviour' not 'pleasure' and have tenure for a period of five years which is only renewable for one further term (S.34.(1) and (2)).

Discretionary Powers   The Act delegates an extensive list of discretionary powers to the political actors involved. Most often the discretionary aspect of these powers is illusory. What the Act imparts, it frequently limits and makes conditional upon someone else's control. The discretionary powers given to the Service represent a case in point. Besides its primary functions of collecting, analysing, and retaining information and intelligence, and reporting to and advising the government, the Service may provide security assessments (S.13.(1)), make arrangements with provincial governments and police forces (S.13.(3)), and help *within Canada* the Minister of Defence or Secretary of State for External Affairs to collect information on a foreign state or its citizens (S.16.(1)(2) and (b)). In all matters the ultimate control is in the hands of federal or provincial ministers. This does not mean, however, that the Service has no real discretion. In deciding what targets to investigate and whether to employ surveillance the Director and his staff have considerable leeway. But in each instance the discretion is structured and reviewable.

Only Federal Court judges and members of SIRC can exercise their duties without extensive controls. The discretion of the Federal Court to issue warrants is only restricted by the Act itself. Of equal importance is SIRC's license to determine 'the procedure to be followed in the performance of any of its duties or functions' (S.39.(1)) and to conduct reviews where it believes it inappropriate for the Inspector General to act (S.40.(b)).

Legalization of Activities

Arguments which support the conclusion that the CSIS Act is enabling and merely justifies previously illegal activities through the use of the legal apparatus seldom give due consideration to either the countervailing nature of the controlling powers in the legislation or to the way in which independent action and discretionary powers are harnessed. Nevertheless, such arguments earn credibility when the functions of the security and intelligence community as a whole are considered. While the CSIS Act may make it harder for the Service to conduct certain types of investigations, the threshold standard for intrusive investigations is now lower than for ordinary criminal code offences. And while CSIS may be generally better controlled, there is no legislation which covers the activities of other members of the security and intelligence community which have the *capacity* to place surveillance over, and conduct an investigations of, particular groups and individuals.

What is more, the RCMP have been given the ambiguous duty of being primarily responsible for 'performing the duties assigned to a peace officer' in relation to security offences (S.61.(2)). It is to be stressed that in no one place or Act are the specific duties of peace officers in Canada clearly set out. Nor are their powers specifically proclaimed. In addition, the Director and employees of the Service have been given 'the same protection under the law as peace officers' (S.20.(1)). The full implications of this provision are far from clear and will remain so until Section 20, or something akin to it, is tested at law.

CONCERNS OF OMISSION AND COMMISSION

Omission

The Commission approached the discussion of threats in two particular ways. Discussions of such tangible threats to the security of Canada as espionage, sabotage, subversion, and terrorism were conducted in vague terms. Solutions were provided by implication. By contrast, less tangible threats posed by state agents to Canadian democracy, though not quantified, were discussed at some length quite explicitly. Here solutions served both to provide answers to immediate problems and to act vicariously in providing solutions to threats of the first order.

Tangible Threats   The Commissioners believed that the 'security of Canada' was synonymous with 'national security' and that these terms incorporated both preventative and proactive obligations on the part of government. There was a need to protect the country from external overt and clandestine attacks and a need to preserve and maintain the democratic processes of government.[39]

Their examination of the RCMP Security Service revealed that it organized its work around three categories of threats: the activities of foreign intelligence agencies; political terrorism; and the subversion of democratic institutions. These three categories are now reflected in the definition of threats in Section 2 of the new legislation.

They noted the growing number of foreign intelligence agencies that were operating in Canada and that they were being used to obtain intelligence and to influence policy. They failed to indicate, however, which agencies should be considered the most important for reasons of budget, size, sophistication, etc. Nor did they mention the types of institutions or policies at greatest risk.

They also drew attention to the dramatic increase in international terrorism since the 1960s. Despite the fact that there had been few Canadian incidents, they concluded that the threat to Canada had increased. Again, no analysis was provided of the capacity, extensiveness and origins of such terrorists. Nor was a detailed analysis provided of likely targets.

By contrast, the Commissioners considered that no subversive organization, of either the right or the left, had posed a serious threat since the Second World War. They noted, however, the presence of 'a few small groups, some with considerable support', which were committed to the destruction of Canadian democracy.[40] Again no organizations were identified. Neither was what was meant by 'small'. Nor was any assessment made of how such groups were supported or how they might destroy Canadian democracy.

Threats by State Agents In the terms of reference of the Inquiry the Commissioners' attention was also drawn to the threats to the democratic order. Specifically, they were asked to analyse the activities that were used by the RCMP to protect the security of Canada that were not 'authorized or provided for by law'.[41] When it came to analysing this threat, the Commissioners did not find it necessary to establish by empirical research what were perceived as the essential elements of the democratic order. Nor did they attempt to identify what individual citizens generally perceived as constituting the national interest. Likewise, they conducted no analysis which would determine the extent and order of rights that were considered fundamental or which rights were considered to be threatened. Rather, the Commissioners believed they were justified in asserting that it was the democratic order, as currently prescribed, with its concomitant notion of rights and freedoms, that needed to be protected.[42]

It is appropriate to ask how serious these omissions are and what sort of implications they have for future security and intelligence policy-making. Two sorts of arguments are used to defend the omissions. It is regularly argued that explicit data about the actions of foreign intelligence agencies, terrorist cells and subversive groups should not be made public. Support for this position is based on two interdependent notions. One is the belief that such data will inform targeted organizations about what is known about them. The other is that such knowledge will detract from the ability to combat them. Arguments used to defend not doing quantitative research to determine the extent and nature of threats to civil liberties are largely based on cost. The adequacy of both sorts of arguments may be questioned from a number of perspectives. In the first case the argument overlooks the content of the information released. There is an implicit assumption that it is currently secret. There is, however, quite frequently sufficient information in the public domain to make the threat from foreign intelligence agencies, terrorist organizations and subversives quite explicit. Where there is not a comparative analysis the experiences of other democratic states may be used to draw analogous conclusions. The argument also dodges the issue of the information's nature. Again there is an implicit assumption. This time it is that the information is necessarily harmful. It need not be. Information can be dispensed in such a way as to represent the matter constructively. Most important of all, the argument overlooks the dangers of not informing the public. Security and intelligence organizations, like police forces, require public trust to work effectively. And both can be particularly vulnerable to public pressures for reform. Certainly, the CSIS is more vulnerable to such pressures than the Security Service ever was under the protective mantle of the RCMP. An essential element in maintaining trust lies in convincing the public that the powers entrusted to security and intelligence agencies are really necessary. The most effective way of doing this, perhaps the only way, is to identify what is being threatened and exactly how great the risk is. Only by knowing this can one distinguish between objectives that are quintessential and those that are merely desirable; only by determining the priority of specific objectives can one define the levels of effectiveness and efficiency that specific policy objectives demand; and only by defining what levels of efficacy are required can one decide on the necessary means.

In the second case the argument dispenses with other possible objectives than the obvious. While it successfully rationalizes using less reliable data on which to assess threat thresholds than are perhaps desirable, it overlooks the essential ingredient of obtaining a benchmark in the public's trust in organizations involved in security and intelligence operations. Monitoring the public's perception of which rights are being threatened in qualitative and quantitative terms could be a useful indicator in this regard.

Commission

Concerns also arise from the context in which the Commission carried out its work and from the terms of reference provided to the Commission by the Liberal government.

The Canadian Context   The McDonald Commission was not the first inquiry to place the security and intelligence community under official scrutiny. It had become a major topic of public discussion on at least four occasions since the Second World War. In the first two instances it was Soviet and Eastern Bloc intelligence activities that created attention. In 1970 domestic terrorism was the issue. Royal commissioners were established in each instance.[43]

The orientation of the McDonald and Keable[44] Commissions were dramatically different. This difference may be explained by the quantitative and qualitative nature of the threats that were perceived at the time. While earlier inquiries focused on Eastern Bloc espionage, foreign instigated subversion, and separatism, the primary threat for these commissions was the damage that security and intelligence personnel were doing to the democratic system of government in Canada and to civil liberties.[45]

Frame of Reference   In many respects the McDonald Commission was more restricted by its terms of reference than its predecessors. For example, the Mackenzie Commission received a very broad mandate to explore Canada's security methods and procedures and to evaluate their effectiveness. It was not required to restrict its investigations to a particular organization and it certainly could have examined intelligence capacity as part of its analysis of the effectiveness of the system. But the Commissioners chose to interpret their mandate narrowly. The McDonald Commission's terms of reference were more specific and restricted its focus to the RCMP. Nevertheless, the Commissioners interpreted it liberally and provided a broad range of analyses and conclusions. But the terms of reference and the context in which the Commission started its work have had a specific influence on the way security and intelligence functions have been examined. They have concentrated attention on certain threats at the expense of others. In the future this orientation may create an imbalance in how threats are perceived and resolved. By focusing on specific functions along the organizational continuum it may inadvertently draw attention away from other functions that need to be organized differently, or better funded, or brought under firmer political control.

CONCERNS RELATING TO IMPLEMENTATION

The establishment of CSIS by statute was a positive step. In separating the Security Service from the RCMP it provided an opportunity to restructure an essential component of Canada's security and intelligence community into a more effective and efficient form. The new organization now has the ability to recruit independently and to develop training systems which will fit its future requirements more closely. This operational freedom should lead to an improvement in the caliber of those who are recruited and in the analytical capacity of the Service. Separation should also allow CSIS to develop new administrative practices which will instigate the spread of a more positive ethos throughout the Service. This should make the system of accountability and control more vital. These factors, together with the removal of the old hierarchical structure and the division in the way members of the old Service were socialized *should* make CSIS a better place to work.

The mere fact that separation has been achieved does not mean that organizational concerns no longer apply. Many of the factors which made the old Service ineffective and inefficient are still present. The SIRC noted that 95 per cent of the RCMP Security Service employees opted to join the new organization.[46] The chairman of the Committee has gone on record as being concerned about the amount of 'old wine' that has been induced into 'the new bottle'.[47] These figures indicate that there is little likelihood of 'civilianization' having the impact that the McDonald Commission envisaged. It is for this reason that Section 69 of the Act must be viewed with serious concern. This section details how and when a comprehensive review of the provisions and operations of the Act are to be reported upon by a parliamentary committee. Insofar as this committee did not examine management and administration and the effectiveness and morale of the Service until late 1989 vital information about the organizational culture may have been too late in coming. By that time the new Service may well have developed the character and habits of a service more similar to that of the old RCMP Security Service than to the one envisaged by the McDonald Commission.

Nor does the reconstitution of the Service do anything to alleviate concerns about the other members of the intelligence and security community. In this regard Richard French has suggested that it is useful to think of the community as a whole providing a continuum of activities. He argues that if we do this, we are more likely to note that certain features vary in intensity (e.g. degree of judicial oversight of operations, technological intensity of operations, emphasis on apprehension and criminal justice as opposed to prevention and national security, role of politics and ideology in the mission of the organization, etc.) from one element of the community to another.[48] Historical studies have clearly indicated the difficulty outsiders experience in discerning which security and intelligence agency is doing what and where, and which has what power and responsibility where. Shearing *et al.* are therefore right to be skeptical about the trust that can be placed in organizational charts.[49]

Canadians have cause to worry about the avoidance of legislative controls by the transfer of responsibilities from CSIS to other organizations. The CSE represents a case in point. Given the cost of similar organizations in Britain and the United States and the capacities they have, the refusal of successive governments to place it under legislative control is particularly serious. It makes the whole discussion of wiretap warrants moot, to say nothing about banks of personal files which are not governed by the same protections as those of CSIS. It may be recalled that a former Solicitor General 'stumbled upon' the CSE while in office. He is reported to have concluded that:

failure to bring the CSE under the same controls (as the CSIS) would make the Review Committee a 'toothless paper tiger' whose real function would be 'to lull the public' into believing civil liberties are being protected.[50]

Other agencies in the security and intelligence community have escaped the legislative net. In fact, no other agency employing peace officers, investigators or intelligence operatives has had any restrictions placed on their security and intelligence functions since the completion of the McDonald Commission's work. This is particularly worrying in the case of the police. It is to be recalled that regular police units of federal, provincial and municipal forces, not just members of the Security Service, had been involved in a variety of serious crimes (arson, breaking and entering, kidnapping, illegal mail opening, etc.). It is of no matter that this police deviance stemmed from noble intentions. Nor is it of consequence that the 'bad apple' (the Security Service) has been removed. Police structures remain largely intact. The RCMP have retained much of the responsibility for internal security, particularly in the areas of counter-terrorism and the investigation of national security crimes. Their activities are not subject to review by SIRC. In particular, it is to be noted that they have not been proscribed from 'deterring' or 'countering', practices that are common in conventional police work. Another cause for concern pertains to matters of jurisdiction. Already we have seen the RCMP refuse CSIS access to their computer banks. Their argument has been based on the premise that CSIS members are not eligible for access to Canadian Police Intelligence Data (CPIC) because they are not peace officers. Given that the FBI had immediate access to CPIC data, that discussion were in process at the time to integrate CPIC data with its American equivalent NCIP so that more US police forces could obtain CPIC data,[51] and that such non-police (but *not* non-policing) organizations as the Toronto Stock Exchange and Ontario Hydro had access, the argument is more revealing about what it says about the relationship between CSIS and police forces than anything else. Also of concern is the fact that the McDonald Commission did little to resolve the issue of whether the police have the right to break the law. At the release of the Commission's final reports the government provided a package containing two legal opinions.[52] These posited that many of the so-called illegal RCMP activities had been legal. The legality of these acts is still a matter of political concern as may be demonstrated by the debate initiated by the more recent publication of the McLeod Report.[53] This debate hinges on the distinctions between 'not authorized or provided for by law' and 'prohibited by law'.[54] The fact that the Act gives the Director and CSIS employees protections, as if they were peace officers, when the powers of peace officers are nowhere clearly defined, only adds further ambiguity to the issue.

Besides relationships between CSIS and the police, there is no indication how CSIS should relate to the Police and Security Branch of the Solicitor General's Department, the Security and Intelligence Secretariat of the Privy Council Office or the various existing security and intelligence committees. It may be recalled that the McDonald Commission noted that there were difficulties in establishing 'the appropriate division of responsibilities between the Secretariat in the Privy Council Office and the Solicitor General'.[55]

The McDonald Commission also considered the possibility of an 'offensive' external service in a very peripheral manner. In this regard they were against the new Service doing both jobs. Nevertheless, it appears that the new agency will operate abroad in a limited manner. In states where they obtain the consent of the government concerned they will be allowed to conduct surveillance of individuals and to liaise with 'friendly' intelligence services.[56] This may represent the thin edge of the wedge and may lead to the development of an external service in an unplanned manner. And it may prevent an examination of whether an 'offensive' external service is necessary.

Related to foreign intelligence-gathering is the Commission's recommendation to establish a new organization, on Australian lines, to provide long-term intelligence assessments. On this matter there has been no public discourse or legislation to effect a Bureau of Intelligence Assessments.

There are two critical omissions in the Act. Both seriously limit the capacity of SIRC to do an effective job. It is important to recall that the McDonald Commission considered that a permanent Joint Parliamentary Committee should be established to evaluate whether security and intelligence operations were being conducted efficiently and effectively. The absence of such a committee makes it unclear whether the SIRC's mandate, or that of the Inspector General, includes the capacity to evaluate either the effectiveness and efficiency of CSIS or that of any other component organization in the security and intelligence community. This would leave *only* organizations within the bureaucracy and standing parliamentary committees. The former can not provide an independent opinion. The latter, if past experience is anything to go by, appear not to be up to the task.[57]

The other issue concerns the government's capacity to prevent cabinet documents coming into the hands of the review agents. The senior legal adviser to the Commission has since called this a temptation for future governments and ministers 'to engage in questionable policies that will

183

remain hidden from public scrutiny.'[58] It makes a mockery of political responsibility and removes protections that the Director and his staff should have. This situation may well lay them open to all sorts of false accusations. It is an unprincipled position and makes the political and legal position of employees untenable.

CONCLUSIONS

The McDonald Commission represents an important contribution to Canadian constitutional, administrative and organizational theory. Of prime importance is the complex, countervailing system of accountability and control that developed to bring about *both* full political control and organizational effectiveness. Legislators failed them on two important scores. They allowed cabinet documents to be withheld from the Review Committee and the Inspector General, and they failed to establish an on-going parliamentary committee to monitor the new Service's effectiveness and efficiency. It is unclear as yet whether these defects are as serious as some suspect.

The Commissioners are to be congratulated on confronting the essential problem of removing the security and intelligence functions from the realm of police administration. While investigating skills are of considerable importance, those of other disciplines are critical. Without separation, proper political control would have been impossible and the analytical capacity of the Service would have stagnated. Likewise, the emphasis placed by the Commissioners on developing an appropriate ethos for the organization is of particular importance. So too is the desire to change the organizational culture. These are essential ingredients in making the other contributions work.

In addition, the Commission has alerted casual observers of security and intelligence affairs to many of the subtle problems faced by organizations in this area. Giving some substance to the members of the community and an indication of the division of labour within its boundaries has added flesh to an otherwise inhuman face. The subject of security and intelligence is now closer to hand and there is reason to hope that Canadians will be better able to determine the sorts of security and intelligence apparatus that the country should have.

But the Commission's legacy also includes pitfalls. The very fact that the Commission was set up to investigate RCMP wrongdoings may have cemented the way Canadians view security and intelligence matters for years to come. It may be responsible for developing a general perception that threats to Canadian democracy are more likely to come from the state's own agents than from those of foreign powers. This view, if it prevails, could be particularly dangerous. It may engender a feeling of safety to which there is no entitlement. The fact that a sophisticated system of accountability and control now exists may make Canadians believe that there is no need to fear further abuse of individual rights by the security and intelligence community. Likewise, the failure of the Commission to emphasize events before 1969 and its omission of any qualitative and quantitative dimensions to the external threats faced by Canada may encourage less vigilance than is required in this direction.[59] In this regard it is important to note that the Commission focused attention inward towards police practices and the CSIS. In an environment where the collective mindset is currently boxed within a criminal justice framework the purpose of intelligence-gathering needs also to be viewed in counterfactual terms,[60] or from the longer-term, broader historical context. Otherwise, it may be narrowed to identifying and countering threats. Viewed in protective, preventive terms there is a real danger in overlooking Canada's need for a foreign intelligence agency and a Bureau of Intelligence Assessments which could provide essential data on which to base long-term political, economic and foreign policy goals and military strategy. Also, it should be noted that focusing on the discrete practices of the police and the CSIS tends to divert attention away from 'embedded' policing functions and their potential threat to civil rights and liberties.[61]

While much has theoretically been done to instil a new, more appropriate ethos in CSIS, the vast majority of CSIS's employees learned their trade in the Security Service and picked up their traditions and habits in the RCMP. This raises severe doubts about whether there has been any real structural change within the Security Service, particularly regarding its organization culture. Not only does it make one doubt whether any of the useful recommendations made by the McDonald Commission for improving effectiveness and efficiency within the organization have been incorporated but it generates concerns about whether the new management can be any more successful in incorporating their ideas than past leaders. The early resignation of CSIS's first Director tends to confirm this view.

In the absence of a *permanent* parliamentary committee, a heavy burden of responsibility inevitably rests with the SIRC. It will be interesting to see whether it interprets its function as being simply a watchdog for CSIS or whether it takes on a broader mandate, one which overlooks the whole security and intelligence continuum of activities. If it is able to draw attention to threats to civil liberties regardless of agency and to provide regular assessments of the status and the needs of all the members of the security and intelligence community by identifying what powers and resources they really need, it will have served the state and its citizens well.

NOTES

1. See Canada, Commission of Inquiry Concerning Certain Activities of the Royal Canadian Mounted Police, *Reports* (Ottawa, Supply and Services, 1979–81). (Chairman Justice David C. McDonald) There were three reports in all. The Second consisted of two volumes; the others of one.
2. McDonald Commission, *Second Report*, Volume 1, p.629.
3. Ibid., p.632ff.
4. See Canada, Royal Commission on Government Organization, *Report*, 5 Volumes, (Ottawa, Queen's Printer, 1962) (Chairman: J Grant Glassco).
5. See Canada, Royal Commission on Financial Management and Accountability, *Report*, (Ottawa, Supply and Services: 1979) (Chairman: Allen T. Lambert), p.7.
6. Canada, Special Committee to Review Personnel Management and the Merit Principle in the Public Service, *Report* (Ottawa, Supply and Services. 1979) (Chairman: Guy R. D'Avignon), p.5.
7. Canada, Royal Commission on Security, *Report* (Ottawa: Supply and Services Canada, 1969) (Chairman: M.W. Mackenzie), p.21.
8. Ibid, pp.17–18.
9. McDonald Commission, *Second Report*, Volume 2, p.680.
10. Ibid., p.682.
11. Ibid.
12. Ibid., p.688.
13. Ibid., pp.689–90.
14. Ibid., p.690.
15. Ibid., p.704.
16. Ibid., pp.706–7.
17. Ibid., p.711.
18. Ibid., p.734.
19. Ibid., pp.734–5.
20. Ibid., p.714.
21. Ibid., pp.732–3.
22. Ibid., p.724.
23. Ibid., p.722.
24. Ibid., p.725.
25. Ibid., p.719.
26. Ibid., p.719.
27. Ibid., p.884.
28. Ibid., p.743.
29. Ibid., p.899.
31. Ibid., p.771.
32. Ibid., Second Report, Vol. 1, p.645.
33. Ibid., Second Report, Vol. 2, p.840.
34. Ibid., pp.852–3.
35. For details of the Australian enactment see: Australia, Office of National Assessments Act, No. 107 of 1977.
36. McDonald Commission, *Second Report*, Vol. 2, pp.854–5.
37. Canada, *The Canadian Security Intelligence Service Act*, 1984 (hereafter the CSIS Act). Notations marked in the text are to this Act.
38. It should be noted that the value of this measure is largely theoretical. The McDonald Commission identified that in practice Security Service personnel seldom used this power.
39. See McDonald Commission, *First Report*, p.15 and *Second Report*, Vol. 1, p.40.

40. McDonald Commission, *Second Report*, Vol. 1, p.40.
41. See ibid., Vol. 2: Appendix 'B', pp.1149–51 for the terms of reference.
42. It may be argued that the Commission did by holding open hearings and soliciting briefs attempt to do these things. The brief of the Commission's Research Director, dated October 1978, militates against this position. This document was prepared after the Inquiry had focused on the first part of the mandate (RCMP wrongdoings) but before parts (b) and (c) had been investigated. See particularly paragraph 11 of this document. It appears to establish the primary philosophical premise of the analysis before the major research was conducted.
43. See (i) Canada, Royal Commission of Inquiry Appointed to Investigate the Facts Relating to the Circumstances Surrounding the Communication by Public Officials and Other Persons in Positions of Trust of Secret and Confidential Information to Agents of a Foreign Power, *Reports* (Ottawa, 1946) (Chairman: Justice R. Taschereau and Justice R.L. Kellock) This related to the Gouzenko defection; (ii) Between 1966 and 1969 three commissions were established: Royal Commission on Complaints made by G.V. Spencer, *Report* (Ottawa, 1966) (Chairman: Justice D.C. Wells); Commission of Inquiry into Matters Relating to Gerda Munsinger, *Report* (Ottawa, 1966) (Chairman: Justice W.F. Spence); and Royal Commission on Security, *Report* (Ottawa, 1969) (Chairman: Mr M.W. Mackenzie). The first two concerned specific allegations of individual espionage. The third looked at this issue more broadly and how to protect against it. (iii) In 1977 a provincial inquiry was established to examine the October Crisis of 1970. Canada, Quebec, *Rapport sur les Evènements d'Octobre 1970* (Quebec, 1981) (Chairman: J.F. Duchaine).
44. This inquiry was established by the Quebec government. It also dealt with RCMP wrongdoing. See Canada, Quebec, *Rapport de la Commission d'Enquête sur des Opérations Policières en Territoire Quebécois* (Quebec, 1981) (Chairman: J.F. Keable).
45. One might also add that in so doing it also brought the whole system of law and order into disrepute, represented a major potential conflict between Quebec and Ottawa and brought the reputation of every liberal Minister who had held the Solicitor General's portfolio into disrepute.
46. See Canada, Security Intelligence Review Committee, *Annual Report, 1984–85*, p.19.
47. See *Globe and Mail*, 11 July 1985.
48. Richard French, 'A Framework for Security and Intelligence Management', unpublished paper, Faculty of Management, University of McGill, 1979, p.19.
49. Clifford D. Shearing, Susan Addario and Philip C. Stenning, 'Why Organizational Charts Cannot be Trusted: Rehabilitating Realism within Sociology', paper presented at the Conference on Qualitative Research and Ethnographic Interactionist Perspective, 15–17 May 1985, University of Waterloo, Canada.
50. The comments are those of Alan Lawrence, Solicitor General during Prime Minister Joe Clark's short-lived Progressive Conservative government. *The Globe and Mail*, 11 April 1984.
51. See *The Globe and Mail*, 17 October 1984.
52. One was provided by R.J.Wright Q.C.; the other by retired Justice Spence. For a discussion of this process see Michael Mandel, 'Discrediting the McDonald Commission', *The Canadian Forum*, LXI, 76 (March, 1982), pp.14–17.
53. See Canada, Federal/Provincial Committee of Criminal Justice Officials with Respect to the McDonald Commission, *Report* (Ottawa, 1983).
54. For a discussion of the complexities of this issue see the important contribution by Rosemary Cairns Way, 'The Law of Police Authority: The McDonald Commission and the McLeod Report', *The Dalhousie Law Journal*, Vol. 9, No 3 (December, 1985), pp.682–723.
55. See McDonald Commission, *Second Report*, Vol. 1, p.91.
56. See *The Globe and Mail*, 3 April 1984.
57. See John Ll. J. Edwards, 'The Canadian Security Intelligence Act: A Canadian Appraisal', *Oxford Journal of Socio-Legal Studies* (1984), typescript of submission, p.16.

187

58. Ibid., p.19.
59. While the Gouzenko affair is old news now, the events that took place provide us with a very poignant reminder. For some contemporary Soviet and Eastern bloc activity see, for example, Mirun Rezun, 'The Illicit Flow of Western Technology for Military Purposes', paper presented at the Learned Societies Conference, University of Montreal, 1985. See also *The Globe and Mail*, 24 January 1984, for details of the Soviet 'Red Book' and how Soviet personnel are specifically instructed 'to get around or exploit laws, regulations and trade practices in the Western host country'.
60. Suitable counterfactual cases would be: the sinking of the *Rainbow Warrior* in Vancouver, the massacre of Israeli athletes at the Olympic village in Montreal, the defection of a senior KGB Officer in Ottawa, the bugging of the new Canadian Embassy in Washington, manipulation of the Toronto Stock Exchange by foreign organizations.
61. The notion of 'embedded policing' has been broached by Clifford Shearing and Philip Stenning in 'Private Security: Implications for Social Control', *Social Problems*, Vol.30, No.5 (June, 1983), pp.493–506.

Notes on the Contributors

Marion T. Doss, Jr. is an assistant professor of political science at James Madison University. A graduate of the US Naval Academy, he gained experience in counter-intelligence and investigative activities with the Naval Investigative Service and the Office of the Secretary of Defense during his 22-year career as a naval aviator and intelligence officer. He holds a Master's degree in public administration from Harvard and juris doctor degree from the College of William and Mary. He has written several articles on counter-intelligence and legal issues in the administration of criminal justice.

Stuart Farson is currently acting as Director of Research for the Special Committee of the House of Commons (Canada) on the Review of the *Canadian Security Intelligence Service Act* and the *Security Offences Act*. He is a former Secretary-Treasurer of the Canadian Association for Security and Intelligence Studies and is co-editor of *Security and Intelligence: New Perspectives for the 1990s* (1991, forthcoming). He has written a number of articles on security and intelligence matters as well as on policing issues. He holds graduate degrees in both political science and history from the University of Toronto and the University of British Columbia respectively.

Glenn P. Hastedt is an associate professor of political science at James Madison University where he also serves as director of the international affairs major. He earned his PhD at Indiana University. His primary area research in the field of intelligence policy relate to problems of strategic surprise and intelligence failures, and controlling intelligence. In addition to having written several journal articles and essays in edited volumes on these topics he is the author of *American Foreign Policy: Past, Present, Future* (second edition, 1990) and co-author of *Dimensions of World Politics*.

Arthur S. Hulnick is a veteran of more than 32 years in the profession of intelligence. He joined the Central Intelligence Agency in 1965 after serving seven years in Air Force Intelligence. During his service in the CIA, Mr Hulnick worked as an analyst, served as a liaison officer, and as an editor of the *National Intelligence Daily*. He joined the Public Affairs

189

Office in 1983 and later became Chief of the Public Relations Unit and Coordinator for Academic Affairs. In 1989 Mr Hulnick began a two-year assignment as an Officer-in-Residence at Boston University, where he teaches both undergraduate and graduate-level courses in intelligence.

Loch K. Johnson received his PhD. from the University of California, Riverside, and is Regents Professor of Political Science at the University of Georgia. He has served as a staff member on the House Foreign Affairs Committee, assistant to the chair of the Senate Select Committee on Intelligence (the Church Committee), and staff director of the Subcommittee on Intelligence Oversight in the US House of Representatives. He is the author of *A Season of Inquiry* (1988), *America's Secret Power* (1989), and *America as a World Power* (1990).

Stafford T. Thomas is a professor of political science at California State University, Chico. He received his PhD. in 1975 from the University of Colorado (Boulder). His published works include a basic introductory text, *The U.S. Intelligence Community* (1983), and articles and chapters in journals and readers. His research attempts to apply various theories of politics to the study of intelligence as a political-governmental phenomenon.

Gregory F. Treverton is Senior Fellow at the Council of Foreign Relations in New York, with responsibility for European and politico-military issues. Educated at Princeton and Harvard, he has worked in the government on the staff of the first Senate Select Committee on Intelligence (the Church Committee) and as staff member for Western Europe on the National Security Council during the Carter administration. He was Director of Studies of the International Institute of Strategic Studies in London and was for six years a faculty member of the John F. Kennedy School of Government at Harvard. He is the author of *The 'Dollar Drain' and American Forces in Germany* (1978), *Nuclear Weapons in Europe* (1981), *Making the Alliance Work: The United States and Western Europe* (1985) and most recently, *Covert Action: The Limits of Intervention in the Postwar World* (1987).